About the author

Bill Carroll is a professor of sociology at the University of Victoria, where he directs the Social Justice Studies Programme. His research interests are in the areas of the political economy of corporate capitalism, social movements and social justice, and critical social theory and method. Among his recent books are *Remaking Media: The Struggle to Democratize Public Communication* (co-authored with Bob Hackett), *Challenges and Perils: Social Democracy in Neo-Liberal Times* and *Critical Strategies for Social Research*. He has won the Canadian Sociological Association's John Porter Prize twice, for his books on the structure of corporate power in Canada. He has held visiting fellowships and appointments at the University of Amsterdam, Griffith University, Kanazawa State University, the Netherlands Institute for Advanced Study in the Humanities and Social Sciences, and the Institute of Political Economy at Carleton University. He is a research associate with the Canadian Centre for Policy Alternatives, an associate editor of the journal *Socialist Studies*, and a member of Sociologists without Borders.

Praise for *The Making of a Transnational Capitalist Class*

'Building on Fennema's pathbreaking research on corporate networks in the 1980s, Carroll and his colleagues have produced an impressive array of evidence to suggest that a transnational capitalist class is in the making. This book is the most significant recent contribution on the transnational capitalist class.' *Leslie Sklair, emeritus professor of sociology, London School of Economics*

'*The Making of a Transnational Capitalist Class* is a state-of-the art analysis of the global political-economic power structure as it has developed into the current century. I know of no author in the field who has been able to combine a mastery of empirical method in analysing corporate and planning-group interlocks on a world scale, with an incisive political analysis of the forces occupying the most central locations in the networks that emerge from this analysis. Combining theoretical acumen with an unfailing commitment to social justice and fairness, Carroll brings to this enterprise decades of research experience, which has only gained in sophistication over the years. Not only do his findings represent the most up-to-date and detailed information on the global structures of power. The work equally includes, in a brilliant concluding chapter, an analysis of the social forces ranged against the intricate structures of corporate power and a realistic assessment of the balance of strength in each case. At a time when the capitalist world economy is in the throes of one of the deepest crises in its existence, a fine-grained mapping of the personalities, corporations, and private consultative bodies that actually were running the show to right before it came crashing down, this book is a bombshell that will help clear the way for a renovated global political economy.' *Kees van der Pijl, professor of international relations, University of Sussex*

'William Carroll provides a superb analysis of global corporate power and the complexities surrounding the issue of transnational capitalist class formation. Sensitive to the relations between the global, regional and national, the challenges posed by state capitalism, and the early impact of the global financial crisis, this will remain the definitive work on the subject for years to come.' *Professor Stephen McBride, Department of Political Science, McMaster University*

'With this exciting book Bill Carroll has written a landmark study on transnational class formation setting a new standard for years to come. The longitudinal approach, rigorous empirical research, and great theoretical sensitivity and nuance give the book a unique and exemplary quality. It raises numerous questions for further research and debate and makes a major contribution to critical social research.' *Henk Overbeek, professor of international relations, VU University*

'This is a truly excellent book. Carroll and his co-workers take the debates on global capitalism and the network society to a new level. Powerful research using techniques of social network analysis shows that corporate power holders have become increasingly cosmopolitan and are the key agents of regional and global financial hegemony within the world economic system. All those interested in this topic will find the book a fascinating and enjoyable read.' *John Scott, professor of sociology, University of Plymouth*

'This lucid, illuminating and much-needed analysis reveals the underlying structure of the global community of big business at the beginning of the twenty-first century. It provides valuable answers to important questions, including a measured analysis of the degree of unity and division among the most powerful corporations in the world and a vivid portrait of the role transnational policy groups in linking together the world's largest firms. *The Making of the Transnational Capitalist Class* provides the essential empirical base for the emerging field of global power structure research.' *Michael Schwartz, professor of sociology, Stony Brook University*

The making of a transnational capitalist class

Corporate power in the twenty-first century

William K. Carroll

with Colin Carson, Meindert Fennema,
Eelke Heemskerk and J. P. Sapinski

Zed Books
LONDON | NEW YORK

The making of a transnational capitalist class: Corporate power in the twenty-first century was first published in 2010 by Zed Books Ltd, 7 Cynthia Street, London N1 9JF, UK and Room 400, 175 Fifth Avenue, New York, NY 10010, USA

www.zedbooks.co.uk

Set in OurType Arnhem and Gill Sans Heavy by Ewan Smith, London
Index: ed.emery@thefreeuniversity.com
Cover designed by www.thisistransmission.com
Printed and bound in Great Britain by CPI Group (UK) Ltd, Croydon, CR0 4YY

Distributed in the USA exclusively by Palgrave Macmillan, a division of St Martin's Press, LLC, 175 Fifth Avenue, New York, NY 10010, USA

A catalogue record for this book is available from the British Library
Library of Congress Cataloging in Publication Data available

ISBN 978 1 84813 443 0 pb
ISBN 978 1 84813 442 3 hb
ISBN 978 1 84813 444 7 eb

Contents

Tables and figures

Acronyms

ALBA	Bolivarian Alternative for the Americas
ANOVA	analysis of variance
BRIC	Brazil, Russia, India, China
BT	British Telecom
CEO	chief executive officer
CFRIAB	International Advisory Board to the Council on Foreign Relations
CSR	Corporate Social Responsibility
EC	European Commission
EFR	European Financial Services Round Table
EJBRT	European Union–Japan Business Round Table
ERT	European Round Table of Industrialists
ESF	European Social Forum
FoEI	Friends of the Earth International
GATT	General Agreement on Tariffs and Trade
GDP	gross domestic product
IBSA	India, Brazil, South Africa
ICC	International Chamber of Commerce
IFG	International Forum on Globalization
IMF	International Monetary Fund
ITUC	International Trade Union Confederation
MAI	Multilateral Agreement on Investment
MPS	Mont Pèlerin Society
NACC	North American Competitiveness Council
SPP	Security and Prosperity Partnership
TABD	TransAtlantic Business Dialogue
TC	Trilateral Commission
TCC	transnational capitalist class
TNC	transnational corporation
TNI	Transnational Institute
TNI	Transnationality Index
UNCED	United Nations Conference on Environment and Development
UNCTAD	United Nations Conference on Trade and Development
UNEP	United Nations Environmental Programme
UNGC	United Nations Global Compact

WBCSD	World Business Council for Sustainable Development
WCF	World Chambers Federation
WEF	World Economic Forum
WSF	World Social Forum
WTO	World Trade Organization
WWFI	World Wildlife Fund International

Acknowledgements

Like all books, this volume is the product of efforts by many people. It has been gestating since I undertook my doctoral dissertation in the late 1970s, a project deftly facilitated at York University by my co-supervisors, John Fox and Michael Ornstein. To borrow from Gramsci, although the entry point for my studies of the social organization of corporate power was national – intensely focused upon debates on the character of Canada's capitalist class – the trajectory has always been international. The course I have followed has been partly a matter of choice but to some extent dictated by the ineluctable fact that, as Saskia Sassen (2007: 1) has put it, 'the global partly inhabits and partly arises out of the national'. A major task for this study is to probe how the national, regional and transnational intersect in constituting global corporate power.

I have Meindert Fennema to thank for encouraging me to pursue an international research agenda in the analysis of corporate elites, and in a sense for inspiring this book. Author of the first major study of transnational corporate interlocking, Meindert hosted my sabbatical in political science at the University of Amsterdam (1987–88). With Rob Mokken, he led the international theme group on globalization and social organization at the Netherlands Institute for Advanced Study in the Humanities and Social Sciences (NIAS), where he and I wrote the article that forms the basis of Chapter 1 in 2001. It was Meindert who suggested, during a visit to Victoria in the summer of 2008 mixing holidays with work, that the research I had been publishing in the form of articles deserved book-length treatment. Other colleagues have left traces of various kinds that have enhanced this text. Without pretending to include everyone, I must single out, with thanks, Greg Albo, Malcolm Alexander, Yildiz Atasoy, Roy Barnes, Val Burris, Chris Chase-Dunn, Bill Domhoff, Koji Morioka, Georgina Murray, Henk Overbeek, John Scott and Kees van der Pijl.

All my collaborators have, of course, made substantial contributions. For the record, Meindert Fennema and I jointly authored Chapter 1, which first appeared as 'Is there a transnational business community?', *International Sociology* (2002) 17: 393–419. In the other collaborations, I served as primary author, with important contributions by Colin Carson – Chapter 2, first published as 'The network of global corporations and policy groups: a structure for transnational capitalist class formation?', *Global Networks* (2003) 3(1): 29–57; Meindert Fennema and Eelke Heemskerk – Chapter 7, first published as 'Constituting corporate Europe: a study of elite social organization', *Antipode* (2010) 42(4);

and J. P. Sapinski – Chapter 8, first published as 'The global corporate elite and the transnational policy-planning network, 1996–2006: a structural analysis', *International Sociology* (2010) 25(4). Three additional chapters are reworked versions of articles for which I was the sole author. Chapter 3 first appeared as 'Global cities in the global corporate network', *Environment and Planning A* (2007) 39: 2297–323; Chapter 5 as 'Transnationalists and national networkers in the global corporate elite', *Global Networks* (2009) 9(2): 289–314; Chapter 9 as 'Hegemony and counter-hegemony in a global field', *Studies in Social Justice* (2007) 1(1): 36–66. Finally, the Introduction and Conclusion incorporate some material from my 'Tracking the transnational capitalist class: the view from on high', in Yildiz Atasoy (ed.), *Hegemonic Transitions, the State and Crisis in Neoliberal Capitalism* (London: Routledge, 2008, pp. 43–64). I am thankful to all the scholars mentioned above, but the usual disclaimer applies regarding my responsibility for any shortcomings in this book.

The data informing this study were assembled and analysed over a period of fifteen years, with the help of many dedicated research assistants: James Beaton, Seb Bonet, Jennifer Campbell, Colin Carson, Stephanie Constantine, Conor Douglas, Galena Dubeau, Jean Hansen, Ian Hussey, David Huxtable, Melissa Moroz, Mark Reed, Leslie Rewega, Theona Russow, J. P. Sapinski, Murray Shaw and Chelsea Tully. The research could not have proceeded without their help. Institutional support has been no less crucial. Bookending my year as fellow-in-residence at NIAS (2000–01), which really served to launch this project, two standard research grants from the Social Sciences and Humanities Research Council of Canada (awarded in 1995 and 2005) enabled the database to take shape.

Ken Barlow, commissioning editor at Zed Books, took an immediate interest in this book and I am very grateful for his support, from the prospectus I submitted in January 2009 to the final version submitted in March 2010. The comments of anonymous reviewers of the prospectus and draft manuscript were of great help to me, and have no doubt improved the final product. On the production side, Zoe Lu helped assemble the bibliography, Ewan Smith showed great patience and remarkable skill in setting the text and graphics – crucial for a book of this kind – and Ian Paten lent his keen eye to the task of copy editing.

As with other books I have written, my wife Anne Preyde and sons Myles and Wes have provided indispensable support, sometimes tangible and often imperceptible, amid the quotidian flow. Notwithstanding these vital local supports, I dedicate this work to those whose political activism points, extra-locally, towards global justice, and unavoidably contests the power of capital in human affairs.

William K. Carroll

June 2010

Introduction

'There's class warfare, all right, but it's my class, the rich class, that's making war, and we're winning.' Warren Buffett, chairman of Berkshire Hathaway, 2006 (quoted in Stein 2006)

In an era acknowledged by at least one prominent insider as one of class warfare from above, the question of a transnational capitalist class (TCC), commanding the heights of the global economy and shaping politics and culture, looms large. There can be little doubt that the complex array of practices constituting what Bryan (1995) has called recent globalization has created the objective conditions for such a class. In its most basic sense, the globalization of capital means the globalization of the capitalist mode of production, a process in which capitalist classes have always been directly active, but not necessarily as members of a transnational capitalist class. Indeed, Marx and Engels, writing in the middle of the nineteenth century, provided the classic description of the bourgeoisie's globalizing mission, without invoking the imagery of a transnational capitalist class: 'The need of a constantly expanding market for its products chases the bourgeoisie over the entire surface of the globe. It must nestle everywhere, settle everywhere, establish connexions everywhere' (1968 [1848]: 38). In this characterization, the objective need for self-expansion obliges the many capitals that compose the bourgeoisie to globalize, but there is no implication that national affinities, identities and forms of capitalist organization fall away in the process.

As the capitalist mode of production globalizes, as the circuitry of accumulation crosses national borders, the relations of production and the forces of production also globalize. Rising volumes of trade and foreign investment, the growing share of the world economy claimed by the largest transnational corporations (TNCs), the expansion of global transportation and communication flows and the formation of integrated global financial markets are all indicative of this process (Dicken 2003). Even so, the increasingly integrated character of global capitalism does not in itself dictate a specific form of capitalist class organization. This is so because capital is not a unified macro subject but is divided microeconomically into competing units which themselves are positioned within and across national boundaries in an international political system, rendering tendencies towards global capitalist unity always tenuous. Thus, the question of the transnational capitalist class cannot be reduced to the globalization of capitalism per se. Rather, it remains amenable to sociological investigation of how capitalists and their advisers are embedded in a panoply of socio-political relations. That panoply forms the object of this investigation.

The debate on the transnational capitalist class

The contingent relation between global accumulation and class formation has spurred a vigorous debate as to whether, by the close of the twentieth century, a transnational capitalist class was already a fait accompli, or perhaps still only a possibility continually contained by countervailing tendencies towards national capitalist organization. Canadian political economist Stephen Hymer was among the first to discern a nascent transnational capitalist class, in the 1970s. For Hymer,

> an international capitalist class is emerging whose interests lie in the world economy as a whole and a system of international private property which allows free movement of capital between countries. [...] [T]here is a strong tendency for the most powerful segments of the capitalist class increasingly to see their future in the further growth of the world market rather than its curtailment. (1979: 262)

It was not until recently, however, that scholars began to assert that a transnational capitalist class had actually formed out of the processes of globalization. Leslie Sklair (2001) presented the first in-depth investigation, based on interviews with leading CEOs of TNCs. He posited a weak version of the thesis, emphasizing transnational practices[1] such as (1) the foreign direct investments that fuel the industrialization of the semi-periphery and (2) the consolidation and diffusion of a culture-ideology of consumerism throughout both the global North and South. Sklair divided the transnational capitalist class into four fractions ('corporate executives, globalizing bureaucrats and politicians, globalizing professionals, and consumerist elites') that create and satiate desires for ever-growing quantities of commodities. Although he posited extensive communication among the four fractions, through interlocking directorates and other cross-memberships, Sklair did not map the transnational capitalist class's social organization. He did, however, aver that 'the concept of the transnational capitalist class implies that there is one central inner circle that makes system-wide decisions, and that it connects in a variety of ways with subsidiary members in communities, cities, countries, and supranational regions' (ibid.: 21).

Like Sklair's, William Robinson's prodigious writings on the ascendance of a transnational capitalist class rely primarily on aggregated statistical evidence, supplemented by citation of instances of transnational corporate mergers and quotation of corporate CEOs, rather than on sociological analysis of class organization. On the basis of the aggregated evidence, Robinson asserts that the transnational capitalist class is in the process of constructing a new globalist historic bloc whose policies and politics are conditioned by the logic of global

2

rather than national accumulation. Surrounding the owners and managers of major corporations, who form the core of the bloc, are the elites and the bureaucratic staffs of the supranational state agencies such as the World Bank, and the dominant political parties, media conglomerates, technocratic elites and state managers – both North and South (Robinson 2004: 75).

Compared to Sklair, Robinson offers a narrower definition of the TCC as 'the owners of transnational capital [...] the group that owns the leading worldwide means of production as embodied principally in the TNCs and private financial institutions' (ibid.: 47). In effect, his concept of the globalist bloc corresponds to Sklair's more expansive concept of the TCC. But Robinson advocates a stronger thesis of transnational capitalist class formation, claiming with Harris that the TCC 'is increasingly a class-in-itself and for-itself'; that it has 'become conscious of its transnationality and has been pursuing a class project of capitalist globalization, as reflected in a transnational state under its auspices' (Robinson and Harris 2000: 22–3).

Robinson's work is notable not only for its clarity of expression but for the spirited responses it evoked.[2] Analysts like Walden Bello sharply disagree with Robinson's prognosis. Pointing to the turn in 2002/03 to national imperialism by the George W. Bush administration – with the attendant disciplining of peripheral states – Bello argues that globalization has actually been going into reverse:

> What was seen, by many people on both the left and the right, as the wave of the future – that is, a functionally integrated global economy marked by massive flows of commodities, capital and labour across the borders of weakened nation states and presided over by a 'transnational capitalist class' – has retreated in a chain reaction of economic crises, growing inter-capitalist rivalries and wars. Only by a stretch of the imagination can the USA under the George W. Bush administration be said to be promoting a 'globalist agenda'. (Bello 2006: 1346)

Radhika Desai also questions the cumulative character of globalization but allows for the possibility of global governance superseding a declining US hegemony. She identifies 'globalization' with the conjuncture of the Clinton presidency, as 'the ideology under which, for a time, the rest of the world seemed quite happy to lend the USA more money than it ever had, and moreover, to lend it to US private industry' (2007: 451). For Desai, the period since 2000 has been marked on the one hand by a far more political and unstable debt relation between the USA and the rest of the world and on the other by US attempts to regain its declining hegemony through imperial aggression (cf. Pieterse 2004). The new US imperialism is unstable, however, based more in weakness than strength, and most likely to eventuate in the kind of collective international economic and political organization that Robinson places under the rubric of the transnational state and globalist bloc.

Beyond the question of whether the globalization that drives TCC formation is really a cumulative process, there is the issue of how the TCC is articulated to the still nationally defined spaces (i.e. territories) into which world capitalism is structured. For Robinson, the TCC is ascendant in an era of global deterritorialization. As he has put it more recently, '[...] spatial relations have been territorially-defined relations. But this territorialization is in no way immanent to social relations and may well be fading in significance as globalization advances' (2007: 14). Even the belligerent unilateralism of the G. W. Bush administration (2001–09) can be seen in this light. Although its military adventures pursued narrow corporate interests, 'the beneficiaries of US military action around the world are not US but transnational capitalist groups' (Robinson 2004: 139). Doug Stokes sees this formulation as putting the cart before the horse. In Stokes's view 'the US state acts to secure the generic global conditions for transnational capital accumulation less at the behest of a TCC, but rather because, in so doing, the US state is, by default, acting in the generic interests of its national capital because of its high level of internationalisation' (2005: 228).

For Kees van der Pijl, Robinson's claims about the TCC and the transnational state are both true and false. At a very abstract level of analysis, there may well be a convergence of interests which aligns capitalists from anywhere in the world with whatever project opens markets and investment opportunities. Yet,

> specific ruling classes have also built up, over decades or longer, specific transnational networks which offer them competitive advantages. Thus the US and the UK have used (in Iraq for instance) their military 'comparative advantage' to trump the Russian and French willingness to strike oil deals with the Saddam Hussein regime when it appeared that UN sanctions were unravelling. (Van der Pijl 2005: 276)

In Robinson's formulation 'a formal unity between concepts leads us astray' (ibid.: 275): terms like globalization, the transnational state and TCC 'remain *abstract* whereas they claim to denote concrete realities' (ibid.: 274). Jason Moore has also noted the abstract placelessness at the heart of Robinson's characterization of the late twentieth century as a new, global era in which stateless, mobile, transnational capital gains ascendancy. Moore points to new forms of territorialization and regionalization and suggests that capital's 'global' moment 'depends upon very particular *places*' (2002: 481) – in which case what appear, abstractly, as aspects of transnational capitalist class formation may actually be macro-regional processes, as in the rise of South and East Asia or the economic integration of Europe.

Saskia Sassen's (2001) close analysis of New York, London and Tokyo as 'global cities' – production sites for the information industries needed to run the globalized corporate economy – highlights one emergent form of territorialization. Her later discussion of the 'northern transatlantic economic system' as globalization's centre of gravity (Sassen 2002: 10) reminds us that globalization transforms but does not transcend territorial division. For Sassen (2007: 1), 'the global partly inhabits and partly arises out of the national', and in so doing troubles two core propositions in modern social science: 1) that the nation-state is the container of political and social processes and 2) that the national and the global are two mutually exclusive entities. Robinson's thesis of TCC formation may be seen as dispensing with the first of these but retaining elements of the second, as in the assertion that 'contradictory logics of national and global accumulation are expressed in distinct political projects' championed by national and transnational fractions of capital (Robinson 2004: 49). Rather than partly inhabiting and partly arising out of the national, the hegemony of Robinson's TCC issues from its 'capture' (in the 1980s and 1990s) of national states:

> Once they have been captured by transnational groups, national states internalize the authority structures of global capitalism; the global is incarnated in local structures and processes. The disciplinary power of global capitalism shifts the actual policymaking power within national states to the global capitalist bloc, which is represented by local groups tied to the global economy. (Ibid.: 50)

This formulation locates the prime *agency* for economic globalization within the transnational capitalist class, and begs for a systematic empirical analysis of that class's actual social organization. This book responds to that call, but it does so in a way that also addresses issues of the national and the regional that have been raised by authors such as Moore (2002), van der Pijl (2005), Sassen (2007) and Tabb (2009).

A global corporate community?

Such an analysis must grapple with the social form that has predominated among leading capitalist enterprises since the merger movements of the early twentieth century, namely the modern corporation. In nineteenth-century industrial capitalism, the owners of capital were also the proprietors of companies, but the corporate form creates the possibility for a disjuncture between ownership of capital and control of a firm. The total capital of a corporation is parcelled into tradable shares that give their owners the right to vote in the election of the directors of the company, with each share affording one vote. In such a system, it is the elected directors who hold authority over the firm, and it is the firm, not the shareholders, which owns its business assets (Scott 1997: 3).

Particularly in the United States, dispersal of corporate shares among many small investors (often reconcentrated within pension funds and other institutional investors) has over the years inspired fanciful pronouncements of a 'people's capitalism' (Johnston 1944), a 'decomposition of the capitalist class' (Dahrendorf 1959), an 'economic democracy' (Baum and Stiles 1965) and, most recently, an 'ownership society'.[3] In actuality, the historical implication of share dispersal was not the end of the capitalist class, but its reconstitution as 'an "organized minority" possessing substantial resources, both economic and cultural, to enable it to represent itself as a "natural" and effective ruling group' (Bottomore 1991: 37). Share dispersal concentrates real economic power in the hands of wealthy shareholders whose ownership of significant blocks of stock enables them to nominate the directors, and thus to control 'other people's money' (Brandeis 1913) – corporate assets owned by a multitude of small-scale passive investors (Perlo 1958). As the centre of sovereign authority, the board of directors comprises a 'constellation of interests', taking in major shareholders (including wealthy families and, increasingly, institutional investors) as well as top managers, whose interests are closely aligned with those of the firm, through bonus systems that give them substantial stakes in the corporation (Sweezy 1953; Scott 1997). The composition of corporate boards and the interlocking of boards to form elite networks give us a window on the top tier of the capitalist class.

Corporate elites, however, are not the same entities as capitalist classes. On the one hand, corporate elites include not only functioning capitalists (directors who are executives or major shareholders) but their *organic intellectuals* (Gramsci 1971;[4] Niosi 1978) – directors who are advisers to business owners and top management, and who often sit on multiple boards. The service of lawyers, consultants, academics, retired politicians and the like is integral to corporate business today. In the structure of economic power such advisers are subordinate to functioning capitalists, yet in the political and cultural fields they often lead the way in representing corporate interests or in mediating between those interests and others (Carroll 2004). On the other hand, corporate elites exclude the many capitalists who are not active on the boards of the largest firms. Yet, since the bourgeoisie 'has always been strongly hierarchical within itself', since 'there have always been factions of that class which govern the dominant heights of the economic system' (Amin 2008: 51), study of the corporate elite does shed light on the organization of the capitalist class, or at least its top tier or, viewed laterally, its 'leading edge'.

The hierarchical structure of corporate organization, and of the capitalist class, ensures the corporate elite's dominance in any advanced capitalist economy. Such an elite is simply 'an inter-organizational group of people who hold positions of dominance in business organizations' (Scott 2008: 37), irrespective of whether they maintain bonds of association or interaction. In assessing whether a corporate elite gives evidence of capitalist class formation, the latter criterion is critical. In a recent authoritative work on political elites, Higley and Burton (2006: 9) draw a distinction between *united* and *disunited* elites:

> Dense and interlocked networks of communication and influence, along with basic value agreements and a shared code of political behavior, characterize united elites. Conversely, the persons and factions forming disunited elites are clearly divided and separated from each other, they disagree fundamentally

about political norms and institutions, and they adhere to no single code of political behavior.

G. William Domhoff (2006 [1967; 1998]), following the path cut by C. Wright Mills in his classic *The Power Elite* (1956), has introduced the term 'corporate community' as a root metaphor for charting capitalist class formation at its higher reaches. Domhoff notes that large corporations share common values and goals, especially the profit motive, and are intricately interconnected through the overlapping memberships of business leaders, whether on corporate boards of directors or on policy-planning boards and other elite vehicles for building consensus. Drawn together through interlocking directorships, large corporations and corporate directors form a corporate community – a more or less cohesive elite with common goals and shared understandings on how to reach these goals (see also Heemskerk 2007). Of course, a corporate community, especially a transnational one spanning many national borders, differs from a traditional, locally embedded community on several counts. Like other emergent formations of late modernity, it is disembedded from any one locality; it gains its social cohesion through the 'facework' of interlocking corporate directors, which serves to re-embed them in a transnational network (see Giddens 1990: 79–80). Moreover, a corporate community is organized not at the grass roots, but at the top: it is an 'organized minority' within which capitals ostensibly in competition are unified around a common interest in securing or protecting the conditions for accumulation in a given zone, or globally; hence it implies a hegemonic project of some sort.

Forms of corporate power

Since 1905, when Otto Jeidels published the results of his research on the relationship of the German big banks to industry, an empirical literature on the overlapping elite affiliations of corporate directors has grown up in sociology and related fields. This literature is vast, and ranges from comparative investigations of national business systems (Stokman et al. 1985; Windolf 2002; MacLean et al. 2006) through a plethora of single-country studies (many of them focused on the USA; e.g. Mintz and Schwartz 1985; Davis and Mizruchi 1999; Barnes and Ritter 2001), to case studies of networks in particular cities (e.g. Ratcliff 1980). Space does not permit a thorough review of this literature (cf. Fennema and Schijf 1979; Mizruchi 1996; Scott 1997; Carroll and Sapinski 2011). Here, it is sufficient to locate interlocking directorates as practices within the larger organization of corporate power.

Put simply, interlocking directorates link the key centres of command within the corporate economy. In doing so, they may contribute to the exercise of economic as well as cultural-political power, through serving two analytically distinct functions. Corporate interlocks can serve *instrumental* purposes of capital control, coordination and allocation, contributing to the strategic exercise of economic power within the accumulation process. But they also serve as *expressive*, cultural relations, building solidarity among leading corporate directors and underwriting a certain class hegemony – a cultural-political power (Sonquist and Koenig 1975; Carroll 2004: 3–8).

Regarding the first of these, in the synthesis of organizational and political-economic theories offered by Scott (1997: 36) the corporate form of economic organization entails three kinds of economic power: strategic, operational and allocative. *Strategic* power occurs at the level of structural decision-making and concerns the determination of basic long-term goals and the adoption of initiatives to realize those goals. *Operational* power involves the actual implementation of corporate strategy within head office and in subordinate offices, subsidiaries and plants. Finally, there is the *allocative* power wielded by financial institutions, whose collective control over the availability of capital 'gives them the power to determine the broad conditions under which other enterprises must decide their corporate strategies' (ibid.: 139).

As sovereign bodies of command, corporate boards are obviously loci of strategic power, but they also are typically interwoven with operational power via their executive directors, and they may be articulated with allocative power, as in interlocks between banks and industrial companies dependent on credit. Boards are thus key nodes in networks of economic power. Note, however, that relations of operational power are purely *intra*-organizational: they follow a chain of command from the CEO, typically a member of the board, down through the ranks and terminating on the shop floor. Interlocking directorates, as elite *inter*-organizational ties, are often 'traces' of strategic and allocative power across firms (Mokken and Stokman 1978) – as when a CEO sits on the board of a firm in which his/her company owns stock, or shares a joint venture; or when a banker sits on the board of an industrial client. Interlocks of this sort are undergirded by capital relations (Scott 2003: 159); they are manifestations of a certain 'coalescence' of capital across legally distinct firms.

Since Hilferding's seminal study *Finance Capital* (1981 [1910]), such coalescence has been recognized as an integral feature of corporate capital.

> By finance capital we mean the integration of the circuits of money capital, productive capital and commodity capital under the conditions of monopolization and internationalization of capital by means of a series of links and relationships between individual capitals. The integration of these circuits takes on a durable structural character which is expressed in a network of relations between individual capitals [...] (Overbeek 1980: 102)

Hilferding, writing in early twentieth-century Germany, emphasized the specific relations between large banks and industrial corporations, leading some interpreters to adopt a narrow sense of the concept which limits its applicability beyond the case of Germany, whose universal banks wielded both allocative and strategic power over industrial firms (cf. Niosi 1978; Lapavitsas 2009; Nowell 2009). More useful to researchers of corporate power structure, however, has been a generous conception of finance capital such as Overbeek's (above; cf. Hussein 1976; G. Thompson 1977; Richardson 1982; Carroll 2008a). In this perspective, the capital coalescence or integration characteristic of finance capital may take various forms, as in the 'financial groups' of aligned capitalists and corporations that cohere through inter-corporate ownership (Aglietta 1979: 252–3) and the 'hub-and-spokes' systems of financial hegemony that have placed financial institutions at the centre of national networks of capital allocation (Mintz and Schwartz 1985). Indeed, across the twentieth century, national differences in the legal frameworks for corporate governance gave rise to several distinct patterns of finance capital and corporate networking (Scott 1997: 103–203).

Yet beyond their significance as traces of economic power, interlocking directorates can also serve as *expressive*, cultural-political relations that build solidarity and trust among leading corporate directors, underwriting what Sonquist and Koenig (1975) call class hegemony. Indeed, interlocks carried by corporate advisers – lawyers, consultants, university presidents and the like, who hold no insider positions in corporations – serve no immediately instrumental function for any given firm. Rather, they contribute 'expressively' to the corporate elite's social integration and (often) to its reach into civil and political society.

As expressions of class hegemony, interlocking directorships link individual members of the corporate elite – capitalists and organic intellectuals alike – in ways that help cement general class cohesion (Brownlee 2005). If, as Marx (1967) held, the alienation inherent in intense inter-capitalist competition could goad capitalists to become 'hostile brothers' to each other, sharing directors across corporate boards pulls in the opposite direction. Interlocks serve as channels of communication among directors, facilitating a common worldview (Koenig and Gogel 1981) and allowing for the integration of potentially contradictory interests based on property ownership alone (Soref and Zeitlin 1987: 60).

The tendency for elite affiliations to reach beyond the corporate boardrooms, into civil and political society, is a particularly important aspect of class hegemony. As Useem (1984) found in his study of American and British corporate networks, directors who serve on multiple boards – members of the 'inner circle' – tend also to serve on government advisory bodies and on the boards of non-profit institutions and policy-planning organizations. Useem holds that the inner circle 'has become the leading edge of business political activity, a special leadership cadre' (ibid.: 115) whose hegemonic power was a formative element in the political shift to the right in the early 1980s (ibid.: 192–3). Useem's study and similar investigations (e.g. Maman 1997; Carroll and Shaw 2001; Domhoff 2006 [1967; 1998]) reveal the crucial role that elite policy groups and the like play as sites for the construction and dissemination of hegemonic projects.

9

There is no doubt that *within* each advanced capitalist country the directors of the largest corporations form corporate communities in which both the instrumentalities of economic power and the expression of class hegemony play out. The question for this study is whether the same claim might have purchase, increasingly, in a global field. A considerable literature has accumulated consisting of such speculations, sometimes backed up with anecdotal evidence (e.g. Kennedy 1998; van der Pijl 1998, 2006; Mazlish and Morss 2005; Rothkopf 2008); what is needed is a more systematic and comprehensive empirical investigation.

The concept of hegemony pulls us towards a closely related aspect of global corporate power: in what sense and to what extent can we discern, as an aspect of class formation, the emergence of a *transnational historic bloc* of social forces with the potential to secure a modicum of consent to global governance by corporate capital and its organic intellectuals? A rich vein of scholarship that begins with Kees van der Pijl's *The Making of an Atlantic Ruling Class* (1984), from which this book's title has been adapted,[5] has documented the intricate history of transnational historic bloc formation (cf. Cox 1987; Gill 1990; van der Pijl 1998; Rupert 2002; Robinson 2005). The hegemonic project pursued by this nascent globalist bloc has been one of transnational neoliberalism – the vision of a 'neoliberal market civilization' (Gill 1995a), organized around the free flow of capital and commodities and protected by institutions of global governance, such as the International Monetary Fund and the World Trade Organization (Soederberg 2006). Although the globalist bloc may have appeared triumphant in the early 1990s, in the ensuing decade or so that forms the centrepiece of this study its project began to unravel in a series of crises of capital accumulation and political legitimacy (Robinson 2004), inspiring a new politics of counter-hegemony (Carroll 2006; Santos 2006).

Networks of corporate power

Characteristically, Gramscian scholarship on class formation in global capitalism has employed narrative and case-study methods that illuminate how human agents, individual and collective, shaped and enabled by social structure, make history. In Chapter 9, we employ these methods in taking up the dialectic of hegemony and counter-hegemony in a global field. For the most part, however, this book offers a systematic, sociological enquiry into elite social organization, by means of social network analysis, the most rigorous technique in social science's methodological canon for mapping social relations (Scott and Carrington 2011).

Since the appearance of Manuel Castells's *The Rise of the Network Society* (1996), the 'network' metaphor has become prevalent in analyses of global capitalism. Although Castells has been criticized for depoliticizing globalization (Marcuse 2002), he did recognize the importance of elite cohesion in the power structure of global capital:

Articulation of the elites, segmentation and social disorganization of the masses seem to be the twin mechanisms of social domination in our societies [...] In short: elites are cosmopolitan, people are local. The space of power and wealth is projected throughout the world, while people's life and experience is rooted in places [...] (1996: 414)

Castells provided no explicit analysis of the actual networks through which elites are articulated into a shared global space. As Wellman (1988) has pointed out, however, the real strengths of a network approach reside less in evocative metaphor than in substantive method. By examining the actual relations that link persons and/or organizations into specific configurations of social structure, network analysis enables a cartography of social space that moves beyond the impressionistic and anecdotal. Maps, however, are static depictions. In tracing the networks of global corporate power, we lose narrative detail – the contingent flow of human agency through interconnected events – yet we gain a more systematic representation of the actual elite structures that both enable agency and channelize it, to some extent, along preconstituted pathways.

It is important at the outset to take note of the *duality* of these networks (Carroll 2004; Bearden and Mintz 1987; Carroll and Sapinski 2011): in corporate interlocking, not only *firms* but individual *directors* exert the agency that constitutes the network of overlapping affiliations. Such networks have a dual character: they are formations both of corporations whose boards interlock and of directors whose multiple affiliations create the interlocks, and we shall analyse them at both levels.

Our primary source of data is corporate annual reports, typically published shortly after the end of the fiscal year (often, though not always, on 31 December). For a given year, board data reflect memberships at the end of the year, and early in the following year. Besides board membership, we noted any other statuses that each director held with each company (e.g. chair or vice-chair of the board, president or other executive position). Long-standing national differences in corporate governance have meant that some corporations adhere to the Germanic two-board system, with a management board that is accountable to an independent supervisory board, while others follow the Anglo-American one-board system, which combines into one board top management and 'outside' directors (Clarke 2007). In accordance with established practice (Stokman et al. 1985; Windolf 2002), in the former cases we treated the two boards as a single entity.

Once the board data were in hand, an alphabetic sort of surnames and given names, for all the records of corporate affiliations, revealed multiple corporate affiliations of individuals in the database. At this point, ambiguous cases were cross-checked, to minimize false positives (records showing identical names that actually refer to different people) and false negatives (actual interlocks that go undetected; Carroll 1986).[6] The network of directors and their corporate affiliations was analysed using three software packages: GRADAP (Sprenger and Stokman 1989), UCINET (Borgatti et al. 2002) and NetDraw (Borgatti 2005).

This study evolved over several years, and as it did, our capacity to include in the analysis a range of the world's largest corporations expanded. Practical considerations limited the 1976–96 analysis in Chapter 1 to a comparatively restrictive set of 176 giant corporations. In the two follow-up investigations in Chapters 2 and 3, which focus exclusively on the network at 1996, we were able to expand the set of corporations to 350. In the third phase of research, which covers the decade beginning at year-end 1996 (Chapters 4–8), the analysis was extended to the world's 500 leading corporations, assessed at two-year intervals.

What follows

This book is divided into three parts. Part One examines the formation of the global corporate community in the closing decades of the twentieth century, to year-end 1996. Its chapters focus on the community's basic architecture (Chapter 1), the elite ties that in 1996 hooked corporate boards into hegemonic practices of transnational policy formation (Chapter 2), and the network's spatiality as in inter-urban configuration of corporate command (Chapter 3).

Part Two brings the analysis into the twenty-first century, through systematic comparisons of the global corporate network from year-end 1996 until 2006. Chapter 4 maps the network of corporate interlocks and explores the interplay of capital accumulation and corporate interlocking. Chapter 5 presents a parallel analysis at the level of individual directors that distinguishes directors embedded exclusively in national networks from those engaged in cross-border interlocking. Chapter 6 examines the relationship between corporate power and personal wealth, personified respectively in the global corporate elite and the world's billionaires.

In Part Three questions of regionalism and hegemony are revisited, with a focus on the state of play in the first decade of the twenty-first century. The consolidation of corporate Europe as a pivotal zone merits its own chapter (Chapter 7), as does the consolidation of a corporate-policy network that provides an expanding structural basis for transnational (and particularly North Atlantic) capitalists to act collectively (Chapter 8). Chapter 9 shifts to a more explicit analysis of hegemony than can be delivered through network analysis of corporate power's architecture, while opening up the crucial question of resistance to that power. To this end, we compare several organizations of global civil society that have helped shape or have emerged within the changing landscape of neoliberal globalization, either as purveyors of ruling perspectives or as anti-systemic popular forums and activist groups.

The conclusion offers an analytical synthesis of what we have learned, and some reflections on limits to TCC formation. Since the financial collapse of autumn 2008, these have become more visible, amplifying the basis for tensions among regional fractions of capital and stirring a hegemonic crisis of transnational neoliberalism. Against this backdrop, we briefly consider what lies ahead for the transnational capitalist class, and for the rest of us.

PART ONE

The formation of a transnational corporate community

1 | Is there a transnational corporate community?

At the end of the twentieth century, a wave of literature proclaimed a new phase in the internationalization of capitalism, under the rubric of globalization. This was said to include developments such as (1) increasing international competition, (2) the internationalization of production, now accompanied by increasing levels of international labour migration, (3) the global ecological effect of capitalist production, (4) new forms of international governance, and (5) the decline and disintegration of the nation-state (Therborn 2000). Some scholars, as we saw in this book's introduction, also proclaimed the formation of a transnational capitalist class as a feature of globalization (Sklair 2001).

In this chapter we investigate a more modest theoretical claim. We will see whether, in the last quarter of the century, a *transnational corporate community* developed. Beyond considering *whether* a transnational corporate community took shape in the closing decades of the twentieth century, this chapter considers *how* the global corporate network was reshaped by the changing strategies and structures of corporate governance, which have been associated with the rise of transnational capitalism (van Apeldoorn 1999).

Four bodies of literature serve to situate the analysis. We first consider whether there is actually an economic base, in the patterns of international trade and investment, for the formation of a transnational corporate community. We then take up Sklair's (2001) analysis of the transnational capitalist class, whose ethnographic detail complements our network-analytic approach and inspires our first hypothesis, but whose lack of attention to specific institutional forms of corporate governance leads us into the comparative literature on corporate governance practices. In this literature we find more sensitivity to national and regional specificities that adds nuance to our analysis and enables us to venture four further hypotheses about the shape and form of the global corporate network, interpreted as a marker for voice- and exit-based systems of governance. Finally, we revisit the major research in this field to date, Fennema's (1982) study of international networks of banks and industry, which provides the empirical basis for our analysis of the network in 1976.

Internationalization of ownership

As Hirst and Thompson (1996) have shown, 'globalization' has not been a smooth, continuous economic process. In the perspective of the twentieth century as a whole we see after 1913 a decline of exports and of foreign direct investments (expressed as a proportion of GDP) that is not reversed until well after the Second World War. Foreign investment within the Western world, however, increased spectacularly in the late twentieth century. By 1996 the inflow of foreign capital into the USA equalled the outflow of direct foreign investment (Burbach and Robinson 1999: 17). In Japan, on the other hand, there is still a relatively small amount of foreign investment: even in 1996 less than 1 per cent of GDP (Bairoch 2000: 209). Japan remains predominantly an exporter of capital. As is well known, with the increased volume of foreign investment has come a change in the pattern of internationalization. In 1970 nearly three-quarters of all foreign investment went to developed countries. By 1996 60 per cent of the foreign investment flows was between developed countries (Burbach and Robinson 1999: 18). Although the post-1970 trend is indeed towards more 'globalized' foreign investment, the developed countries still form the principal site of the capitalist world economy.

In the 1960s and 1970s we witnessed yet another form of internationalization of property and control relations. Following the example of Royal Dutch/Shell and Unilever, which had been established as binational firms at the beginning of the twentieth century, several companies tried to form binational corporations in the sixties and the seventies. But none of these new binational firms survived the eighties (Fennema and Schijf 1985: 256). Difficulties that dogged the most illustrious binational merger of the 1990s – Daimler-Chrysler – make a similar point.

It seems, therefore, that the wave of international mergers did not lead to stable transnational firms. Transnational ownership structures did not seem a viable option. This should warn us not to interpret transnational class formation as an irrepressible tendency. When it comes to day-to-day organizational cooperation, differences in national cultures and perceived national interests still carry a heavy weight. What we did see in the eighties, however, was a massive wave of international takeovers that increased the number of foreign subsidiaries.

We may conclude that the economies of capitalism's core have shown a sharp increase in exports after 1970 and in direct investment after 1985. The import and export flows became more balanced in the last three decades, as did the flows of direct foreign investments among the core countries. This warrants the term globalization to a certain extent, even though this can also be interpreted as a recovery from autarkic tendencies set in motion by two world wars and a Great Depression and reinforced by the Fordist–Keynesian pattern of accumulation and regulation prevalent in the 1950s and 1960s. But does the situation also warrant the term transnational capitalist class (Sklair 2001; Robinson 2004), Atlantic bourgeoisie (van der Pijl 1984) or transnational capitalism (van Apeldoorn 1999)?

A transnational capitalist class?

Scholars who speak of a transnational capitalist class or of transnational classes often focus on strategies and perspectives. Most pronounced in this sense is the work of van der Pijl (1984, 1998), Van Apeldoorn (2000), Gill (1990) and Sklair (2001). Sklair ends his important book *The Transnational Capitalist Class* with a long chapter on 'Global vision and the culture-ideology of consumerism'. There, he tries to demonstrate that corporate executives think globally and that the ideology of global capitalism is consumerism. He finds this aspect of globalization so important that he includes merchants and mass media in the transnational capitalist class, along with globalizing personnel, globalizing bureaucrats and politicians and TNC executives and their local affiliates. He makes the plausible claim that such groups operate from a global perspective, although it is not quite clear whether they have all disengaged from their national embeddedness. What Sklair does not show, however, is that these corporate leaders really form a transnational community that operates in such a way as to warrant the term transnational class in the structural sense. Sklair does not answer the illuminating question posed by Therborn in his introduction to the special issue of *International Sociology* on globalization: 'Is the world a system shaping the actors in it and directing their strivings, or is it an arena, where actors who were formed outside act and interact?' (Therborn 2000: 155).

Following Therborn, we should speak of a transnational capitalist class only if there are structural conditions that reproduce a transnational corporate community, independent of its national 'home' base, to such an extent that their collective 'transnational' identity shapes their behaviour more than the identities they carry with them as national citizens. To prove the existence of a transnational capitalist class is a far from easy task and we do not pretend to have a full answer to the question posed by Therborn. This chapter provides some of the pieces of evidence from which the full answer might eventually be deduced. Through a longitudinal analysis of the global network of directorship interlocks, we can gain a clearer sense of whether the closing decades of the twentieth century bore witness to the emergence of a transnational capitalist class in the sense not of strategic vision but of structural condition.

Interlocking directorates come about as a result of corporate or personal strategies, but once established they do much more than serve the interests of the sending or receiving corporations. They may have been established to exercise control over or to monitor another firm, to act in collusion, to create legitimacy or even for reasons of personal career advancement (Mizruchi 1996). But their structural effect goes far beyond that. The network of interlocking directors has a unifying or fragmenting impact of its own, a unity or fragmentation that is not intended by anybody in particular and cannot be disarticulated or ignored by any single player in the field. By mapping the global network of corporate interlocks we will investigate whether or not these interlocks link the world's largest firms in one connected component or whether the network falls apart in separate national components. In the latter case, there is no transnational corporate community even if most corporate executives can be shown to have a global vision and even if they would like to create a transnational corporate community. This brings us to our first hypothesis:

H₁: In the closing decades of the twentieth century, the world's largest firms created an increasing number of transnational corporate interlocks that formed a more inclusive, integrated transnational network.

Corporate governance in international perspective

Three trends seem to have characterized the development of the international business system in the 1970s. First, we saw a spectacular increase in the networks of interlocking directorates among firms from the North Atlantic world (to be discussed below). Second, there was the shift of labour-intensive production to global capitalism's semi-periphery (the New International Division of Labour), a tendency that could eventuate in a diffusion of the corporate network to 'newly industrializing' centres such as Seoul and São Paulo. Third was the globalization of the commodity and financial markets (illustrated by trade and portfolio investment data) and the move of banks into international consortia. Fennema and van der Pijl (1987) have argued that there was a shift of economic policy and corporate strategy towards rentier investment rather than productive investment. The logic of money capital seemed to replace the logic of productive capital. Such shifts can, however, also be interpreted as a move from what Nooteboom (1999) calls voice-based to exit-based strategies of corporate governance.

Corporate governance in a broad sense is commonly defined as 'the rules and norms that guide the internal relationships among various stakeholders in a business enterprise' (Doremus, Keller et al. 1998: 222). The question is whether the global corporate network has been reshaped along the lines of a particular local form of corporate governance that is becoming 'universal'. Here the issue is not whether the global network provides a stronger basis over time for *class* hegemony in the sense of a cohesive transnational corporate community, but whether a specific form of business organization is becoming hegemonic, i.e. normative, in the world economy. This issue directs our attention to the forms of corporate governance that have persisted at national or regional levels in the world economy, and to the compatibility of these forms with the patterns of internationalized accumulation and neoliberal state management that became predominant globally after the 1970s. Do we indeed find a diffusion of Anglo-American, exit-based corporate governance in the European Union and Japan? Or do we find corporate governance in European countries continuing to take a European form, while corporate governance in Japan follows a Japanese road to globalization? In other words, is path dependency working in the field of corporate governance or is international competition leading to an American-ization of corporate governance? Note that this question cannot be reduced to the problematic of transnational class formation. Americanization of corporate governance does not necessarily lead to a transnational corporate community (although this is what Sklair and other theorists of globalization implicitly as-sume), while path dependency in itself does not exclude the formation of a transnational corporate community. These are two different questions and they deserve to be analysed separately.

The comparative analysis of Doremus, Keller et al. (1998; cf. Clarke 2007) clarifies how differences in institutional frameworks and business culture have produced an exit-based pattern of corporate governance in the USA, but a voice-based pattern in Germany and Japan. In the USA, banks are traditionally weak because of legal restrictions that go back to the Glass Steagall Act in 1933 and which made the American business system strongly stock market oriented. The monitoring of business is relatively transparent so that the shareholders have an 'early warning system' that allows them to sell their shares in case of poor performance. Shareholders' use of their exit option leads to a lower value of the company's shares on the stock market and an increasing risk of a (hostile) takeover of the company (Nooteboom 1999).

In Germany things work differently. There, non-financial corporations have held large blocks of shares while the relationship between banks and industry has been traditionally very close. In this voice-based system, the banks monitor their industrial debtors and tend to intervene directly and discreetly if things go wrong. But the banks' reaction is in general not as swift as that of the stock market and the restructuring of the firm in trouble is not as rigorously pursued as is the case in the USA. German banks and financial institutions have been more patient owners and they quite often collaborate with German government to solve industrial crises. Such an institutional framework may be slower in reacting to bad management and sectoral crisis, but it is clearly a system that is gentler than the US system and can have a better view on long-term develop-ments. Doremus, Keller et al. (1998) have shown that the German institutional system has hardly moved in the direction of the Anglo-American stock market system. On the contrary, the industrial problems due to economic recession and in particular the reunification of Germany were solved by falling back on the old system of *finance capital* rather than by Americanizing corporate governance. The same goes for Japan, where the *keiretsu* system seemed to strengthen in the economic crisis that hit Japanese business in the 1990s:

> While there is no doubt that corporations from around the world are increas-ingly interested in tapping large pools of capital, no matter where they are located, core Japanese and German capital markets are not likely to be over-whelmed by American institutions. (Ibid.: 55)

In this study, we focus on the directors of large corporations and investigate only an aspect of corporate governance. Since we investigate interlocking directorships among corporate boards, however, we also take the concept of corporate governance farther than is conventionally done in the field of business administration. In a system of corporate governance that is stock market oriented and dominated by exit-based strategies there is no need for interlocking directorates to control or monitor corporations. Does this mean that interlocking directors become redundant? We will argue that their function shifts away from the instrumentalities of hierarchy and control, and towards a hegemonic role. Interlocking directorates become devices of consensus- and class formation. In an exit-based system they serve to spread information that is relevant to the corporate community, to hammer out notions of the general interest and to marginalize those firms that seem to 'free-ride' on the corporate community. Interlocking directorates create trust within the transnational business system and are therefore crucial in the formation of a corporate community that lacks state institutions.

In considering how a shift to exit-based corporate governance might register in the global network, we distinguish

1 *primary lines* – interlocks created when an officer of one corporation sits on the board of another firm – from
2 *secondary lines* – interlocks created when an outside director of one company serves as an outside director of a second company; and
3 *thin* (single-director) lines from
4 *thick* (multiple-director) lines.

Wherever a pair of corporations is linked by a primary or a thick tie there may well be a hierarchy of control in place, or at least a formalized coordination of business strategies. But in the case of single-director, non-officer interlocks, i.e. thin, secondary ties, no such interpretation can be reasonably drawn. Such ties are more vehicles for class formation and corporate community development. From an individual firm's perspective they can be considered 'weak ties', but such weak ties can be very efficient at relaying relevant information (Granovetter 1973). The move from voice-based to exit-based corporate governance, then, should be reflected in a shift away from primary and thick lines and towards secondary and thin lines. Yet the path dependencies of emergent practices upon established practices can also be expected to reproduce national and regional differences in these kinds of inter-corporate lines. This discussion allows us to formulate a second and a third hypothesis:

H$_2$: Since the triumph of neoliberalism in the 1980s made most corporations move in the direction of exit-based strategies, we expect the transnational network of corporate interlocks to contain in 1996 fewer primary and thick lines, but more secondary, thin lines as compared to 1976.

H₃: Since Anglo-American corporate strategies are traditionally more exit based while the continental European and Japanese corporate strategies are more voice based, we expect the network of interlocking directorates in continental Europe and Japan to contain more primary and thick lines.

From the theoretical framework that has been provided by Nooteboom and the authors who have written on capitalist class formation we can also formulate some thoughts on the persons that carry the network of corporate interlocks. In a voice based system, interlocking directors are more often than not representing specific owners or other stakeholding interests in the firm. In an exit-based system, the interlocking directors will more likely not be associated with specific interests. To build consensus in a system of conflicting aims and interests a non-aligned position will be more effective than a position that appears related to the interests of a specific firm. A director who has only outside positions can more easily formulate policy goals that go beyond the goals of a specific corporation or group of corporations. His or her proposals will be more easily acceptable for other parties that may have to overcome certain *parti pris* and give up some of their specific company goals for the sake of a common class interest. Hence, our fourth hypothesis:

H₄: Owing to the declining importance of voice-based corporate govern-ance and the increasing importance of exit-based strategies, we expect the transnational linkers (hereafter, 'transnationsalists') in the 1996 global network to be more often outside directors than in the 1976 network.

Evidence from earlier studies

The focus of this chapter is on the 1976–96 period. To situate our empirical material, however, we need to review the findings of the only other longitudinal study of this kind. Fennema (1982) studied the interlocking directorates in a panel of 176 large firms from twelve countries in 1970 and 1976, a watershed period in which many of the features ascribed to recent globalization took shape. Fennema included in his network analysis the advisory boards of several North American banks – which are not vehicles of corporate ownership and control but may facilitate business scan. He found one big component of North Atlantic firms and one small component of nearly all Japanese firms in the 1970 network. By 1976 the large component of Western firms had increased in size and now included two Japanese firms, which were, however, cut off from the Japanese network, which had disintegrated into four small components. In the North Atlantic the proportion of interlocks that cut across national borders – hereafter *transnational interlocks* – grew from one in four to one in three. Concomitantly, the total number of corporate lines increased by 16 per cent, along with most of the national densities. Internationalization and nationalization of the network went hand in hand.

23

The structure of the global network also changed somewhat between 1970 and 1976. German firms nearly tripled their transnational lines (from twenty-five to sixty-five) and Dutch, Swiss and French firms doubled their transnational lines (ibid.: 186, 187). All this suggests that capitalist class formation was accelerating in Europe. This did not coincide, as Scott (1997) has suggested, with a disarticulation of the national networks. Indeed, the densities of the national networks of interlocking directorates increased substantially between 1970 and 1976, except for Japan, the Netherlands and the United Kingdom. The same institutional embeddedness of ownership and control relations, which made the life expectations for binational firms so grim, may also explain why processes of transnationalization tend to strengthen rather than weaken national corporate networks. This leads us to our fifth hypothesis.

H_5: The transnationalization of the corporate network has *not* fragmented national corporate networks.

The datasets of 1976 and 1996

Because of the large number of mergers and takeovers that occurred after 1976 a panel study was not feasible; thus we opted for a study of two cross-sectional samples. Our 1976 data are taken from Fennema's (ibid.) study and include all the directors of a stratified sample of the 176 leading international corporations of 1976. We have collected data on corporate interlocks from 176 international corporations in 1996, selected so that the composition of the 1996 sample matches that of the 1976 sample. The 1976 dataset consisted of the largest 135 industrial corporations and the largest forty-one banks domiciled in eight countries or regions of the world economy (see Table 1.1). Such a stratified sample was necessary, particularly in 1976, to avoid the sample being dominated by the US-based firms. So US firms were intentionally under-represented, while the firms from other domiciles were intentionally over-represented. We constructed the 1996 sample to match exactly the 1976 numbers of industrial and financial companies in each domicile, so that in those respects the two cross-sections are equivalent.[1] But they differ substantially when we look at the size of the companies. While the smallest US company in the 1976 sample was *thirty* times as big as the smallest Japanese company, by 1996 the smallest Japanese company in the sample was slightly *bigger* than its US counterpart. Similar trends in Europe meant that, in step with the decline in American economic hegemony after the 1970s, by 1996 our stratified sampling yielded much more balanced representation of companies from the various domiciles.

Despite our exact matching of the sample by domicile, the two samples differ greatly in industrial composition, reflecting sectoral differences in the concentration and centralization of capital as well as the shifting importance of specific industries in the world economy. In 1976 the 135 industrial companies

TABLE 1.1 Strata in the 1976 and 1996 samples

Domicile	N of non-financials	N of financials	Total N in sample
USA	26	8	34
Japan	26	8	34
UK	22	4	26
Canada	7	4	11
EC (1976 members)	39	13	52
Rest of Europe	10	3	13
Australia/New Zealand	1	0	1
Semi-periphery	4	1	5
TOTAL	135	41	176

in the sample included 31 with principal activities in oil, 19 electronic and electro-technical firms, 17 automobile firms, 17 chemical firms, 13 iron and steel producers and 10 heavy machinery producers; another 10 produced food and tobacco.

In 1996 the picture had changed completely. Now the electronic industry included telecommunications and 27 of these firms were in the sample. The oil industry was in 1996 represented by 16 firms, barely half the number of the 1976 sample. Another spectacular change in the sample is seen in the iron and steel producers (declining from 13 to 3) and non-ferrous metals (from 7 to 1). But most intriguing is the appearance of 13 trading and 16 retail companies that were not represented at all in 1976. With the shift from 'old economy' to 'new economy', logistics and telecommunications have become more important in the world economy and commercial capital more concentrated, while the traditional industrial products have become far less important.

Changes in the global network of corporate interlocks

In this chapter and the ones that follow, a key distinction must be drawn between *national* and *transnational* interlocks. We can think of the global network as the combination of both sets of lines as they link together the largest corporations worldwide, with national interlocks *bonding* boards within countries and transnational interlocks *bridging* across national corporate communities (Burt 2005; Coleman 1988). In presenting our findings we move from:

1 the most abstract and general characterization of the global network in terms of its integration and efficiency, through
2 a more concrete analysis in which we distinguish between the national and transnational intercorporate lines, to
3 a concrete analysis of the transnational interlocks and corporations that

constitute the network's centre and of the individual directors who carry the transnational interlocks.

Our first results consider the extent to which the network has become more or less integrated over the two decades, irrespective of whether the change has its source in national or transnational developments. We may measure network integration by looking at two different indicators. The first and most primitive one is *degree*: the number of lines connecting a firm to other firms in the network. We can see in the first row of Table 1.2 that, among the entire sample of 176 firms, the mean degree falls slightly. According to this very crude measure, network integration slightly drops. The slight decline in network integration is, however, entirely due to the decline in primary and thick lines.[2] The mean degree of thin secondary lines has *increased substantially*. The network has become less integrated by primary and thick lines, but more integrated by thin, secondary lines.

TABLE 1.2 Mean degree by type of line for the global network

	1976	1996
All lines	4.18	4.03
Thin secondary lines	1.78	2.19
Thick secondary lines	0.51	0.35
Thin primary lines	1.13	0.98
Thick primary lines	0.76	0.51

Another aspect of network integration consists of its connectivity, i.e. the chance that two randomly selected firms are connected by a path. We will call this connectivity overall network integration. The connectivity of the network in 1976 was 42 per cent, while in 1996 it was 47 per cent. This increase in overall network integration is entirely due to the secondary lines in the network. Considering only primary lines, connectivity drops sharply, from 21 per cent to 8 per cent.

Another measure of communicative efficiency is the diameter of the network of connected firms: the length of the shortest path that connects the two firms most distant from each other. This measure of efficiency can be calculated, for obvious reasons, only for firms in a connected component (i.e. all mutually reachable). Despite the slight decrease in the number of interlocked pairs of firms, the diameter of the largest component decreased from eleven to eight, along with the increase in connectivity we observed earlier. The network has become *more efficient* in connecting corporations. The potential for community building has increased substantially. Again, it was precisely the secondary lines which produced the increase in efficiency. By 1996, the global network was

TABLE 1.3 Mean degree of interlocking for corporations domiciled in four regions, by type of line

	Secondary, thin	Secondary, thick	Primary, thin	Primary, thick
1976				
North America	2.51	0.49	1.04	0.87
Japan	0.06	0	0.82	0.12
UK	1.35	0.31	0.35	0
Continental	2.52	0.92	1.74	1.40
1996				
North America	2.78	0.36	0.91	0.36
Japan	0.65	0	1.03	0.24
UK	2.08	0.08	0.73	0.08
Continental	2.85	0.68	1.18	0.98

predominantly a network of secondary lines. These results lend support to H_2, which predicts that the network of corporate interlocks would in 1996 contain fewer primary and thick lines and more thin and secondary lines as compared to 1976. The network has become less a system of power and influence and more a communication system.

Further support for H_2 comes from an analysis of the connected components in the network, at increasing levels of line multiplicity. Considering all interlocks, the 1976 network contained a dominant component of 114 firms, each reachable by the others; by 1996 the dominant component numbered 119, and there were two minor components, one made up of 23 Japanese firms and one made up of 3 Italian firms. In both years, when we consider all interlocks, we find a dominant component that takes in most of the companies based in Europe and North America.

At increasing multiplicity, however, the picture changes dramatically. In 1976, considering only multiple-director (thick) lines, the dominant component contained only 25 companies – 24 of them European. By 1996 there was even less of a clustering of firms into components formed by thick lines, and no sign of a transnationalization of such clusters. The dominant component contained only 20 firms, 18 of them German and 2 Dutch. Considering only very thick lines (three or more shared directors), in 1976 the largest component numbered 15 (14 of them European); by 1996 the largest grouping was a predominantly French component of 7 firms, which included Belgian-based Fina. Consistent with our hypotheses, when we include thin lines in the analysis we find that a large North Atlantic component persisted across the decades and even expanded slightly; when we restrict the analysis to thick lines the components are smaller and more exclusively national – they involve predominantly European corporations, and they tend over time to become smaller.

Moving now to a somewhat more concrete level of analysis, Table 1.3 reports, for each of four regions, the mean degree of the four distinct kinds of lines that make up the entire global network.

This analysis tests H_3: when we distinguish between primary and secondary, thick and thin lines, how different are Continental Europe and Japan compared with North America and the UK? As we predicted, primary and thick lines predominate more in Continental Europe while thin secondary lines predominate in North America and the UK. The trend, consistent with H_2, is towards more thin, secondary lines in 1996, even on the European continent, while the degree of thick secondary lines and thin primary lines drops somewhat. The fall of thick primary lines – those most indicative of traditional organized capitalism – is most spectacular in North America and in continental Europe. In Japan and the UK the trend is reversed: here we find more primary interlocks in 1996 than in 1976. This latter trend leads us to believe that the national systems of corporate governance have converged to some extent, even if they have not fully integrated into a transnational regime. Contrary to what we expected, interlocking directorates involving Japanese firms are sparse and they do not live up to the expectation of a structure of finance capital that one would expect from the well-known pattern of inter-corporate cross-shareholding (Clarke 2007: 211). Even though the Japanese banks and insurance companies own some 40 per cent of corporate shares, they do not seem to monitor the corporations they partly own through a dense network of interlocking directorates. The lines that do involve Japanese corporations, however, are largely primary interlocks. The loose nature of the Japanese network should not, however, be mistaken for a lack of capital organization. As Gerlach has shown (1992), Japanese corporate capital has been primarily integrated through extensive cross-shareholding within *keiretsu*. Also, personnel exchanges among members of a given *keiretsu* tend to occur not as simultaneous cross-appointments but often as *flows* from one company to another, with the director or executive maintaining contact after being delegated, to return to the sending firm some time later (Westney 1996).

National and transnational interlocking

As we observed earlier, the entire global network consists of a combination of national lines (interlocks between companies headquartered in the same country) and transnational lines (interlocks between companies headquartered in different countries). Fennema (1982) found a substantial increase in transnational interlocking between 1970 and 1976, a period in which the network came into its own. How did the relative incidence and the patterning of national and transnational interlocks change over the subsequent two decades?

The most basic longitudinal comparison involves a simple tabulation of the

TABLE 1.4 National and transnational interlocks in the global network

	1976	1996
a. Total number of lines	368	355
b. N of transnational lines	84	88
c. 100* b/a	22.8	24.8
d. N of transnational lines within Europe	51	58
e. N of transnational lines: USA–Canada	9	5
f. N of transnational lines: Europe–North America	23	24
g. N of transnational lines: Europe–Australia	1	0
h. N of transnational lines: Europe–Japan	0*	1

Note: * The two ties that Fennema found in 1976 were carried by a person that was a member of an international advisory board of an American bank. These advisory boards have been excluded in our present analysis

number of intercorporate lines – whether thick, thin, secondary or primary – across the main regions of the world economy. We find in Table 1.4 that the total number of lines decreases by thirteen, but that the number of transnational lines increases by four, so that by 1996 one quarter of all lines traversed national borders. The number of companies with one or more transnational interlock nudges from 68 to 71. These changes are quite modest – not at all indicative of a qualitative shift in network structure. Nonetheless, they do support Hypotheses 1 and 5: there was a (slight) increase in transnational interlocking, but even in 1996 three-quarters of all the lines were contained within national borders.[3]

How are the transnational interlocks distributed among the major regions of the world? In rows d–h we find an increase in the number of transnational interlocks connecting firms based in Europe, a decrease in the number crossing the USA–Canada border, and otherwise little change. The major inter-regional axis links North America and Europe: in both years only one interlock ventures beyond the North Atlantic. Although the sample includes the largest corporations domiciled on the semi-periphery,[4] not a single interlock connects the boards of these companies with the corporate elites of Europe, North America or Japan. To the extent that interlocking directorates are an indication of transnational class formation, it is fair to say that van der Pijl's concept of an Atlantic ruling class remains apt well into the 1990s. The only notable development, not unexpected, is an increase in interlocking within Europe – the elaboration of a European corporate community, which is the subject of in-depth analysis in Chapter 7. This last observation, along with the lack of interlocks extending to Japan, refutes Amin's claim, stated without evidence, that 'capital interpenetration is no denser in inter-European relations than in the bilateral relations between each European nation and the United States or Japan' (Amin 2000: 14–15).

The network core and the transnationalists

Our analysis so far highlights overall trends in transnational and national interlocking that are relevant to our first four hypotheses, but it leaves unexamined the specific lines and firms that actually constitute the corporate network. Bearing in mind that the entire transnational network is constituted through the cross-border interlocks of approximately seventy firms, we now take a closer look at the specific firms and interlocks that are central to that network.

When we consider only the companies with *transnational* interlocks to three or more Top 176 firms, we find 24 such corporations in 1976 and 22 in 1996. That is, about 13 per cent of the entire sample participated extensively in transnational interlocks, forming a potential *centre* for the transnational network. These core companies accounted for 62 per cent of all the transnational lines in the network in both years; i.e. most of the entire transnational network was indeed focused around these corporations.

It is striking that, in both years, *banks were not particularly central in the transnational network*: the most transnationally interlocked boards have been those of industrial corporations. In both years, all of the firms with transnational ties to five or more firms (numbering four in 1976 and eight in 1996) were industrials. And, although financial institutions comprise 23 per cent of our sample, only 18 per cent of the 24 central corporations of 1976 were financials while the proportion in 1996 was 23 per cent. Whereas the pattern in national corporate networks has traditionally been one of bank centrality (Fennema and Schijf 1979), the transnational network seems organized along different lines. This may be explained by the fact that the transnational network is one of consensus and community building rather than of monitoring and control, as seems to be the case in the national networks – at least in continental Europe (Stokman and Wasseur 1985).

Figures 1.1 and 1.2 map the network among corporations most engaged in transnational interlocking. The actual density of interlocking at the centre of the transnational network remains essentially constant (.28 in 1976 and .27 in 1996). Yet only in 1996 do the 22 companies form a single component. In 1976 the 24 most central firms comprised a dominant component of 19, a chain of three Swiss and Italian companies, and two isolates, none of whose transnational interlocks involved other central firms. Although the centre was no denser in 1996, it was more connected at the same level of density, exemplifying our earlier observation of increasing network-wide efficiency. The dominant component of 1976 included three (Anglo-American) companies with only one interlock each: the largest block within this component consisted of 16 firms containing no cut-points. In contrast, the 1996 component not only included all of the central firms, but was itself a block, containing no cut-points, as each company was interlocked with two or more other firms. Indeed, with the exception of British-based HSBC, each company interlocked with at least three other

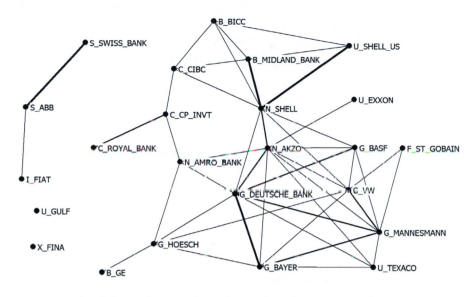

Note: Leading letters indicate country of domicile, as follows. B: Britain, C: Canada, F: France, G: Germany, I: Italy, N: Netherlands, S: Switzerland, U: United States, X: Belgium. Line thicknesses reflect the number of shared directors.

Figure 1.1 The core of the transnational network, 1976

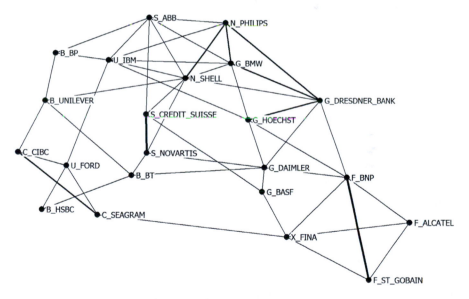

Figure 1.2 The core of the transnational network, 1996

members of the core network. By 1996, *firms with high degrees of transnational interlocks were tied to each other, comprising a well-connected core to which other firms were linked.*

In the dominant component of 1976, the key firms were Dutch (Shell and AKZO) and German (Deutsche Bank, Mannesmann, Volkswagen, Bayer, BASF), with Shell (and to a lesser extent AMRO Bank) bridging between continental and Anglo-North American firms. The German–Dutch grouping was clearly at the centre of the network, with extremely dense interlocking among the German corporations that extended to the three Dutch firms, to French-based Saint-Gobain, and to US-based Texaco.

The 1996 network shows less of a concentration of interlocking among a few firms, and more inclusion of French, Swiss, British and North American companies. One can still discern national clustering, however. The five German firms are still interlocked with each other, but at a lower mean degree (2.4 compared to 4.0 among the six German firms in the 1976 core network). Shell continues to serve as a transnational broker, connecting firms from Germany, Switzerland and the USA, but the same can be said of IBM, which is linked not only to Shell but also to Swiss, German, British and American firms. Another noteworthy change, already signalled, is the decline in thick lines. By 1996, the core network contained fewer such lines, and the number of shared directors comprising thick lines had fallen. This again suggests a transition in the role of interlocks from control to information exchange and community development.

What of our fourth hypothesis, that owing to the declining importance of voice-based corporate governance and the increasing importance of exit-based strategies, transnationalists in 1996 will tend to be outside directors compared to 1976? This hypothesis directs our attention towards the individuals who actually carry the national and transnational interlocks – the corporate directors who serve on two or more boards.

In 1976 there were 317 such people, 50 of whom held directorships across national borders, thus generating transnational interlocks. That is, 16 per cent of all interlocking directors were *transnationalists*. By 1996, the total number of interlocking directors had fallen to 270, with the thinning of interlocks, but the number of transnationalists had increased slightly to 53, comprising 20 per cent of all interlocking directors. If transnationalists had gained a bit more profile in the global network, the key question is how national networkers and transnationalists compare at the two times in terms of their status within firms in the sample.

Table 1.5 categorizes the interlocking directors in terms of the highest-status position they held in a sample company, using the categories employed in Fennema's 1982 study. In this categorization, occupancy of the top executive position is the highest status, occupancy of some other executive (insider) position is second highest, chairing the board of directors is third highest, and serving as only an outside director is lowest. The first two categories are indicative of an insider status with a Top 176 firm.

Overall, there is a tendency for the entire global network to be carried more

TABLE 1.5 Cross-classification of national networkers and transnationalists by highest status held (percentages)

	1976			1996		
	National networker	Trans- nationalist	Total	National networker	Trans- nationalist	Total
Outside director	46.8	28.0	43.8	47.3	58.5	49.6
Chair of board	12.4	24.0	14.2	11.1	9.4	10.7
Inside director	25.1	18.0	24.0	20.7	15.1	19.6
Top executive	15.7	30.0	18.0	20.7	17.0	20.0
TOTAL	100.0	100.0	100.0	100.0	100.0	100.0

by outside directors in 1996 compared with 1976. In the more recent year, half of all the interlocking directors held only outside directorships in the sample firms. (Some of these, of course, may well have been executives in companies beyond our sample.) What is striking, however, is *the trend away from insider status, or even the chairing of major corporate boards, within the category of transnationalists.* In 1976, only about a quarter of them were outside directors; most were engaged in some capacity of executive or board leadership in one of the Top 176 global companies, and nearly a third were top executives. Yet by 1996 well over half the transnationalists were outside directors. This shift is evidence of a tendency for the transnational network to become a site of class formation more than a structure of inter-corporate domination and control.

Conclusion

To sketch the lines of development in the global network and in the transnational corporate community, let us revisit our five hypotheses. Across the two decades from the mid-1970s, ties among the world's largest corporations continued for the most part to respect national borders; that is, the process of transnational class formation did not fragment national corporate networks but occurred in tandem with their reproduction (H_5). There was no massive shift in corporate interlocking, from a predominantly national to a predominantly transnational pattern. By 1996, three-quarters of all the lines linked companies domiciled in the same country, down only slightly from 1976. Even when we examine the twenty-odd companies with the most extensive transnational ties – forming the centre of the transnational network – we find nationally based clusters. Moreover, while in the 1990s national networks (with the notable exception of the USA – see Davis and Mizruchi 1999) continued to be organized around large financial institutions, industrial corporations predominated at the centre of the transnational network. All this suggests that *the transnational network is a kind of superstructure that rests upon rather resilient national bases*. As against those who, following Wallerstein (1974, 1980), see capitalism as a world system all along, we find that corporate governance still takes place predominantly within national frameworks. This also explains why it proved so difficult to create a European legal framework for corporate ownership and governance (Rhodes and van Apeldoorn 1998).

Consistent with H_2, however, there has indeed been a loosening of the global network, which we believe reflects the tendency towards exit-based rather than voice-based corporate governance. The network has come to include fewer primary and multiple-director interlocks, and more interlocks that are carried by single outside directors. By 1996, very few companies were ultimately linked by primary interlocks. Even so, the basic contrast between Anglo-American and European business systems remained evident. Our findings are in line with the common idea that continental European corporate governance is more voice based, while Anglo-Saxon corporate governance is more exit based. Our findings about Japan are less conclusive and need further investigation into the working of the *keiretsu*. We also find that continental European corporate governance became more exit based in the late twentieth century. By 1996, national systems of interlocking directorates tended to resemble each other more than they did in 1976. And yet the differences were still substantial, as we suggested in H_3, and corporate communities were still predominantly organized along national lines.

None of this is to deny the evidence we have found of a developing transnational corporate community. Although the early 1970s were a watershed in this regard (Fennema 1982), the decades that followed brought a consolidation of the transnational network, as large corporations were drawn into a structure knitted together mainly by thin, secondary interlocks and outside corporate directors (H_4). The network became more *efficient*: despite a slight drop in the overall density of interlocking, the connectivity of the global network increased. Moreover, the centre of the transnational network became more integrated yet no denser than it had been in 1976. While the total number of lines in the network decreased slightly, the number of transnational lines increased somewhat. There is thus some support for H_1 – that in the closing decades of the twentieth century, a transnational corporate community was in the making. While this support is very modest, the striking tendency by 1996 for transnationalists to be uninvolved in managing specific corporations supports our thesis that transnational corporate interlocking is less about inter-corporate control than it is about the construction of a transnational corporate community.

What is equally striking is the extent to which this community remained in 1996 centred upon the North Atlantic area. The modest proliferation of ties within Europe accounts entirely for the slight increase in the total number of transnational interlocks we have observed, while Japan, Australia and newly industrialized countries such as South Korea and Brazil remained effectively isolated from the transnational network. This raises the question of whether we are witnessing simply the consolidation of a European economic community and not a process of transnational class formation beyond that. The continuing pattern of trans-Atlantic interlocking, however, counters such an interpretation. This Euro-North American centricity is not surprising in view of the economic, political, cultural and geographical forces that had by the 1970s produced an 'Atlantic ruling class' (van der Pijl 1984) under American hegemony. Still, it underlines a certain disjuncture between class formation as a sociocultural process and the economic process of capital accumulation. The vast reach of today's TNCs and the increasingly integrated financial markets may be global, but as the century drew to a close the governance of corporations and the life of the *haute bourgeoisie* remained in important ways embedded in national and regional (including trans-Atlantic) structures and cultures.

2 | Forging a new hegemony: the transnational corporate-policy network, 1996

The process of transnational capitalist class formation, as van der Pijl reminds us, can be traced back as far as the eighteenth century, when, on the basis of such secular, non-statist networks as Freemasonry, a cosmopolitan bourgeoisie came to adopt a tendentially international perspective:

> Freemasonry provided a cover for developing the new identity on which the exploitation of members of one's own community is premised. By entering the masonic lodges, merchants and those otherwise involved in the long-distance money economy such as lawyers and accountants, realized the primordial alienation from the community which is the precondition for market relations, exploitation of wage labour, and abstract citizenship. (1998: 99)

The Freemasons point up a key aspect of transnational capitalist class formation, with deep historical roots: the extra-economic, elite networks that enable communication, coordination and the development of shared consciousness. If the Freemasons exemplify the early history of these networks, it is 'organized policy planning behind the scenes' which has been central to hegemonic integration in the era of modern capitalism (ibid.: 108). To the extent that at the close of the twentieth century a fully transnational capitalist class (TCC) was in formation, its social organization should be visible not only in a developing network of interlocking corporate directorships but in a network of overlapping memberships between corporate boards and such global policy planning boards as the Trilateral Commission and the World Economic Forum. In this chapter, we focus on the contribution that five leading policy groups made, through elite-level interlocks, to transnational capitalist class formation, as the twentieth century closed out.

A range of theoretical perspectives relevant to this issue now exists. In the 1980s, the Gramscian turn in international political economy, advocating a 'historically grounded conception of the dialectic totality of structure and agency' in processes of class formation and world order (Overbeek 2000), demonstrated that although the mechanisms of international trade and investment furnished structural conditions for global capitalist expansion, they could not provide the long-term vision needed for capitalist class formation. Van der Pijl (1998) and Overbeek and van der Pijl (1993) situate transnational class formation in the context of restructuring and stabilizing capitalist fractions (bank, commercial, industrial capital) under the global economic hegemony of neoliberalism. Of specific interest is the development of strategic vision in the social networks of the directors of corporations, banks and planning groups of various sorts (van der Pijl 1998: 5). Cox (1987), Gill (1990, 1992) and Robinson and Harris (2000), describing similar practices in relation to transnational state apparatuses, view the TCC as both an embodiment of transnational capital and an expression of political power manifested by transnational (or interstate) institutions such as the International Monetary Fund (IMF) and the WTO. 'World hegemony', as such, 'is describable as a social structure, an economic structure, and a political structure; and it cannot be simply one of these things but must be all three' (Cox 1983, in Overbeek 2000: 176). In a somewhat separate vein, as we saw in Chapter 1, Sklair (2001) places significant emphasis on the ideological awareness of transnational executives and views the dissemination of a culture-ideology of consumerism as integral to transnational capitalist class formation.

Robinson and Harris (2000: 14) draw on many of these perspectives to announce the emergence of a fully transnational capitalist class whose 'organic composition, objective position and subjective constitution [...] [is] no longer tied to the nation state'. As might be expected, the claim of such an epochal shift has forced a closer assessment of how the TCC is identified. Indeed, as we saw in this book's Introduction, the critiques that followed the article's publication bring to light several unresolved issues and questions, including the extent of the TCC's geopolitical scale – with particular emphasis placed on the recalcitrance of a North/South divide – and its alleged autonomy from national contexts.[1] From all sides of the current debate it is agreed that more direct evidence is needed.

Our analysis in Chapter 1 of elite inter-corporate relations in the twentieth century's closing decades showed that support for the claim that transnational capitalist class formation had taken a quantum leap is mixed at best. The network of corporate interlocks remained structured primarily around recalcitrant national patterns of organization; moderate increases in transnational integration via weak ties transecting national borders, however, intimated a tendency towards the further consolidation of a transnational business community. Such a community would, however, be a rather pallid affair if it were confined to the corporate boardrooms. In fact, given the persistence of national corporate networks, we might say that *the articulation of a transnational capitalist interest requires sites beyond the boardrooms* – places where business leaders can come together to discuss issues of shared concern, to find common ground and to devise strategies for action. Business activism of this sort would seem an integral aspect of community development at the higher reaches of corporate power. The significance of such arrangements is only enhanced by processes of globalization and the search for new forms of governance. Indeed, these conditions have prompted a range of scholarly attention on institutions of private authority and their self-regulatory potential (e.g. Ronit 2001: 562; Cutler 2010).

Building on the concept of a transnational corporate community, and recalling our basic premise that those who direct the largest corporations are the leading edge of a capitalist class, this chapter situates five global organizations of elite consensus-building within the larger structure of corporate power that is constituted through interlocking directorates. The elite policy-planning groups operate within an incipient 'global civil society' (Shaw 2000) that is distinct from both state power and economic power yet intimately linked to both. It is from these sites that the strategic and moral visions and policy frameworks informing a transnational capitalist interest have been forged. In this chapter, we shed light on the role global policy groups played in the formation of a transnational capitalist class in the late twentieth century. In Chapter 8, we revisit the analysis of policy groups, focusing on changes in the transnational corporate-policy network in the early twenty-first century.

Policy groups as construction sites for transnational hegemony

In the years since the Second World War we can trace the development of a neoliberal tendency within a differentiating global field of elite consensus formation. Set in motion with Friedrich Hayek's convening of the Mont Pèlerin Society in 1947 (Plehwe and Walpen 2006), its austere market-monetarist orientation gained a distinct, yet still marginal, voice in an organizational ecology dominated by corporate liberal tendencies – a regulatory strategy upheld at the time by the first truly North Atlantic planning body, the Bilderberg Conferences (first convened in 1952). Decades later, as it rose to dominance under the regimes of Reagan and Thatcher, undiluted neoliberal doctrine responded to structural shifts that beleaguered post-war Keynesian–Fordist regimes while accelerating the spread of transnational corporations, the expansion of foreign direct investment and the interpenetration of capital. Lending sanction to the emerging global regime were the policy imperatives of privatization, trade liberalization, deregulation, tax reform, and the introduction of market proxies and benchmarking into the public sector – a grouping of corrosive neoliberal initiatives that John Williamson (1990), World Bank Chief Economist for South Asia (1996–99), termed the 'Washington consensus' (see Weller and Singleton 2006).

Integral to the political and cultural reproduction of this new order was a synthesis of public and private elements from the states and civil societies of the capitalist core in several new private global policy groups, most notably the World Economic Forum (1971), the Trilateral Commission (1973) and the World Business Council for Sustainable Development (1995). While each group makes distinct strategic contributions to the field of transnational neoliberal policy, they share three critical attributes. They inhabit a space within civil society as 'embedded elements of a social network, within which neoliberal business activism [takes] shape and form' (Carroll and Shaw 2001: 196). They also act as vehicles of international elite integration, linking capitalists to a political-cultural community where class extremes are mediated and a 'collective will' thrashed out (van der Pijl 1998). Finally, all, to varying degrees, endeavour to 'translate class interests into state action by defining and promoting lines of policy that ensure the stability and reproduction of a system shaped by capitalist social relations' (Peschek 1987: 216). In these ways, neoliberal policy groups can be said to function as 'collective intellectuals' – 'deputies' or agents of the capitalist class 'entrusted with the activity of organizing the general system of relationships external to [...] business itself', as Gramsci described (1971: 6)

In the 1990s, the struggle to spread the neoliberal economic project on a global scale was far from straightforward. It experienced several major setbacks, including global recession and crises,[2] and the emergence of new forms of civil resistance crystallized around opposition to the legal incursions of capitalist globalization, including the Multilateral Agreement on Investment (MAI), the WTO, and World Bank and IMF initiatives. Increasing concern arose over how best to coordinate actions to promote and consolidate the project on different scales, 'with its social and environmental costs and their adverse political repercussions, and with identifying and pursuing flanking measures that would help to re-embed the recently liberated market forces into a well-functioning market society' (Jessop 2000). Indeed, by the mid-1990s neoliberal order was somewhat differentiated around the question of how best to assure long-term stability and reproduction of transnational capital.

For Robinson and Harris it is precisely this emergent strategic positioning within the neoliberal paradigm, and the tensions it created among globalizing elites, which gave rise to a transnational capitalist class defined both by economic structure and strategic-political rule – a class both in itself, and for itself.[3] Their analysis very usefully divides the globalist policy field into three neoliberal fractions, which we will employ to help frame our discussion of the projects of global policy groups. The first fraction is *free-market conservative*. Influenced by economist Milton Friedman, this fraction calls for a complete global laissez-faire, drawing on fundamental neoliberal tenets of monetarism, state deregulation, 'spontaneous order' of market relations, and possessive individualism. Reigning as neoliberalism's singular voice under the so-called Washington consensus, the project would be splintered and somewhat marginalized amid the global economic crises of the 1990s. Stemming from these actualities, the fraction that according to Robinson and Harris (2000) became dominant, *neoliberal structuralism*, advocates a 'global superstructure that could provide a modicum of stability to the volatile world financial system [...] without interfering with the global economy'. Following progenitors Bill Clinton and Tony Blair, its politics are distinctly 'Third Way' – 'finding a synergy between private and public sectors', as Giddens put it (1998: 99–100). Gill (1995a),

TABLE 2.1 Classification of five leading global policy groups

	Neoliberal variant	Agenda priorities	Organizational form	Core membership	Geopolitical reach
International Chamber of Commerce Est. 1919 Paris headquarters	Free-market conservative	Corporate self-regulated, global laissez-'faire	International business organization; government lobbyist; linking to locals	7,000 corporations from 130 countries	Global corporations & regional committees world-wide, including the Americas, Europe, the Middle East, Africa & the Asia Pacific
Bilderberg Conference Est. 1952 Geneva origin	Neoliberal structuralist	Economic order among 'heartland' states	Secretive policy-planning & elite consensus-seeking forum	115 national & inter-national corporate, govt, military & academic elite; no set membership	North Atlantic 'heartland', draws elite representation from western Europe & North America
Trilateral Commission Est. 1973 Washington, Paris, & Tokyo headquarters	Neoliberal structuralist	Economic order among 'triad' states	Policy-planning & elite consensus-seeking forum; research task forces; discourse producer	350 national & inter-national corporate, media, academia, public service, & NGO elite	The 'triad', draws elite representation from North Atlantic, Japan, ASEAN
World Economic Forum Est. 1971 Geneva headquarters	Neoliberal structuralist	'Global' economic order	Combined elite trans-national business organization, & policy-planning & consensus-seeking forum; research task forces; discourse producer	1,000 top trans-national corporations	Global, draws elite representation from Africa, North America, Latin America, Asia, & Oceania
World Business Council for Sustainable Development Est. 1995 Geneva headquarters	Neoliberal regulationist	'Global' environ-mental & economic reform	Combined elite trans-national business organization, & policy-planning & consensus- seeking forum; research task forces; discourse producer	123 top transnational corporations	Global, draws elite repres-entation from western Europe, central & eastern Europe, Africa, North America, Latin America, Asia, & Oceania

notably, has discerned a very similar policy shift in the 'new constitutionalist' discourse, launched during the G7 summit in Halifax, Nova Scotia, in June 1995. Responding to the Mexican crisis of 1994/95, G7 members opted to 'strengthen [economic] surveillance mechanisms under the aegis of the IMF, World Bank, and the BIS'. Contrasting with the position of free-market conservatives the new perspective held that 'ideology and market power are not enough to ensure the adequacy of neoliberal restructuring [...] [and must be] institutionalized at the macro-level of power in the quasi-legal restructuring of the state and international political forms' (ibid.). The third, and/or emergent, fraction is *neoliberal regulationist*. This current calls for a 'broader global regulatory apparatus that could stabilize the financial system as well as attenuate some of the sharpest social contradictions of global capitalism' (Robinson and Harris 2000: 43). World Bank senior vice-president Joseph Stiglitz's vision of a 'post-Washington consensus' – an international capitalist system which better contemplates the world's struggles over health and education, environmental preservation and equitable development – exemplifies this perspective (Stiglitz 1998). Although each globalist fraction is divided on the amount of structural interference that should occur in the new 'global economy', all three are neoliberal in that 'none question the essential premises of world market liberalization and the freedom of transnational capital' (Robinson and Harris 2000: 43).

Five key transnational policy groups

In this chapter we focus on five organizations that by the mid-1990s had come to comprise a field of global policy formation, two with long histories, and three whose origins lie within the recent wave of economic globalization. That field has taken a historically stratified and pluralistic shape as the groups developed around specific visions, issues and networks (see Table 2.1).

The Paris-based International Chamber of Commerce (ICC), founded in 1919, is the oldest of the business policy groups discussed here and the only one to maintain a primarily free market conservative strategic vision. It is also the largest, grouping some 7,000 member companies and associations from over 130 countries. As a forum for transnational capitalist consultation launched by investment bankers in the shadow of the First World War, the ICC has historically functioned as the most comprehensive business forum committed to liberalization, 'a triumphant lobbyist for global economic deregulation in fora such as the WTO, the G8 and the OECD' (Balanyá et al. 2000: 166).

The ICC's primary function is to institutionalize an international business perspective by providing a forum where capitalists and related professionals (e.g. law firms and consultancies, national professional and sectoral associations) can assemble to forge a common international policy framework in arenas ranging from investment to specific technical and industry-specific issues. Its secondary function is to knit national chambers throughout the world into a single global network through its World Chambers Federation (WCF). The WCF provides a vertical organizational link between the network of transnational capitalist interests carried by the ICC membership and the untold numbers of small- and medium-sized businesses active in local and national chambers of commerce. Through a combination of a free market conservative vision, the institutionalization of transnational business practices and the incorporation of local-level business into a global capitalist perspective, the ICC has come to occupy a unique niche within the organizational ecology of global policy groups.[4]

Offering a counterpoint to the austere, free market conservative vision of the ICC, the Bilderberg Conferences have facilitated more comprehensive, international capitalist coordination and planning. Founded in 1952, the Bilderberg, named for the Hotel de Bilderberg of Oosterbeek, Holland, 'assembled, in the spirit of corporate liberalism, representatives of Right and Left, capital and organized labor' (van der Pijl 1998: 121). Activities have typically revolved around issues of long-term planning and international order, and to this end Bilderberg Conferences have furnished a confidential platform for corporate, political, intellectual, military and even trade union elites from the North Atlantic heartland to reach mutual understanding. The group is run by a chairman and a small, permanent steering committee, which invites approximately 115 participants to the yearly conference.

Compared to the ICC, Bilderberg's lack of guaranteed membership, the breadth of its elite constituency, and its historically less doctrinaire political agenda have made it a more flexible vehicle for transnational class formation. A good indication of this is the group's migration from a predominantly corporate-liberal strategy to one that in recent years appears more aligned with neoliberal structuralism. Indeed, by the mid-1990s organized labour was all but excluded – the single invited delegate being John Monks, general secretary of the British-based Trades Union Congress. While labour was effectively shut out, neoliberal intellectuals – including Timothy Garton Ash of the Hoover Institute, Michael H. Armacost of the Brookings Institution and William W. Lewis of the McKinsey Global Institute – have attended in numbers.[5]

Emerging at the watershed of recent economic globalization in 1973, the Trilateral Commission (TC) was launched from within the Bilderberg meetings by David Rockefeller as a forum to foster effective collaborative leadership in the international system and closer cooperation among the core capitalist regions of northern Europe, North America and Japan – the 'triad'. It continues a consultative ruling-class tradition, bringing together transnationalized fractions of the business, political and intellectual elite during several yearly meetings, which it convenes at the national, regional and plenary levels. Unlike the secretive Bilderberg, however, the TC 'sought to develop a profile with greater transparency, public activities and sophisticated publications, responding to the greater sensitivity towards public relations' (ibid.: 124). Consistent with this strategy, its magazine, *Trialogue* (first published in October 1973), pioneered what has become a mainstay in the cultural arsenals of transnational business policy groups: the widespread dissemination of neoliberal opinion and analysis, as in the World Economic Forum's *World Link* magazine. A director, three regional chairmen and three regional executive committees guide the TC; its 350 members are chosen on a national basis.

In marked contrast to the ICC, the TC's attempts to enshrine the discipline of capital have generally favoured elements of regulation. In this regard, its influential 1975 report, *The Crisis of Democracy*, called for stronger economic planning measures, including job training and active intervention in the area of work, all in the service of 'sustained expansion of the economy' (quoted in Wolfe 1980: 298). Catalysed by the 1970s energy crisis and the formation of OPEC, the TC has also lobbied for integrating capitalism's (semi-)periphery into contexts of international regulation, including 'allowing the neocolonies a symbolically greater voice in organizations like the IMF, [and] tying neocolonial economies even closer to Western finance' (see Frieden 1980: 72). An influential series of 'Task Force Reports' (or Triangle Papers) on this issue has been delivered over its three-decade history (e.g. Watanabe et al. 1983). Overall, the TC's project is to institutionalize elite economic, political and intellectual/cultural bonds between the North Atlantic heartland and the Asia-Pacific and to expand the regulatory sphere of capitalist discipline to incorporate metropolitan labour and (more recently) peripheral states. These aims draw it in line with Robinson and Harris's (2000) neoliberal structuralist formulation.

Founded two years earlier, the World Economic Forum (WEF) convened Europe's CEOs to an informal gathering in Davos, Switzerland, to discuss European strategy in an international marketplace. Organized by renowned business policy expert Klaus Schwab, the meetings aimed to secure the patronage of the Commission of the European Communities, as well as the encouragement of Europe's industry associations. By 1982 the first informal gathering of 'World Economic Leaders' took place on the occasion of the Annual Meeting in Davos, bringing cabinet members of major countries and heads of international organizations (including the World Bank, IMF, GATT) together with a burgeoning core membership of top international capitalists.

The WEF moved beyond the TC to establish 'global initiatives' that distinguish it as the most paradigmatic example of neoliberal structuralism. Initially, the Forum promoted a free market conservative agenda, but by the mid-1990s persistent capitalist crisis forced it to adopt a more regulatory tack (van der Pijl 1998: 134). By early 1997 the new mood was expressed in a project on 'human social responsibility', followed by a litany of 'social issue' task forces culminating with the Global Health Initiative (2001) and the Global Governance Initiative (2001). These initiatives cross-cut with the widespread practices of Corporate Social Responsibility (CSR) among TNCs and the rise of a culture of 'global

43

corporate citizenship' which Sklair (2001) considers integral to transnational capitalist class formation.

Unlike the ICC, Bilderberg and TC, the WEF is organized around a highly elite core of transnational capitalists (the 'Foundation Membership') – which it limits to '1,000 of the foremost global enterprises'. Invited 'constituents', however, represent a variegated range of globalist elites, including members of the scientific community, academics, media leaders, public figures and various NGOs. Constituents populate a hodgepodge of policy working groups and forums, including the InterAcademy Council, the Business Consultative Group and the Global Leaders of Tomorrow. Like the ICC, however, the WEF actively extends its geopolitical reach and influence. It has done so primarily through yearly meetings apart from Davos and beyond the triad, as in the 1996 meetings in Turkey, China and India (*Annual Report*, 1995/96: 6), and more recently has defined a range of constituent 'communities', each organized through 'councils' and other bodies, such as the Network of Global Agenda Councils, which 'acts as an intellectual driving force for the Forum's Global redesign initiative'.[6]

The last group to have taken up a niche within the field of global elite policy planning by the mid-1990s is the World Business Council for Sustainable Development (WBCSD), founded in 1995. It is also the only group that can be characterized within Robinson and Harris's (2000) typology as neoliberal regulationist. Formed in a merger of the Geneva-based Business Council for Sustainable Development and the Paris-based World Industry Council for the Environment (a branch of the ICC), it instantly became the pre-eminent business voice on the environment. By 1997, WBCSD membership comprised 123 top TNC chief executives.

A child of the UN's 1992 Conference on Environment and Development (UNCED), the WBCSD reflects a maturing elite awareness that entrenchment and expansion of transnational enterprise must be coupled with consensus over environmental regulation. Drawing primarily on the expertise and prestige of senior transnational executives, it articulated a critical connection between neoliberalism and regulatory struggles over the environment, especially those associated with the UN Environmental Programme (UNEP) and the UN Conference on Trade and Development (UNCTAD). What makes the WBCSD unique in the global policy field are its efforts to surpass the prevailing dualism of 'business versus the environment' by forwarding a more comprehensive vision of capitalist social and moral progress – anchored in the late 1990s by its central axiom of 'eco-efficiency'.[7] Within this retooled version of sustainable development, business, governments and environmental activists make concessions around a general interest in sustaining both the health of the natural world and the 'health' of the global economy.

The discourses and strategies of the WBCSD work to advance a global regulatory perspective that moves beyond neoliberal structuralism. The WBCSD's reflexive discursive and organizational frameworks endeavour to draw realms that free market conservatives call 'externalities' – from employee relations to the health and safety of consumers – into an inclusive regulatory regime. The practices and discourses of corporate environmentalism – now employed by TNCs from Procter & Gamble and Mitsubishi to Monsanto and BHP Billiton – are vital in this regard, and have in their own right contributed to a persuasive globalizing capitalist ideology (Sklair 2001). What the WBCSD furnishes is a reflexive orchestration of these corporate initiatives into a class-wide hegemonic project.

With these five policy groups we see how variants of transnational neoliberalism have found organizational bases in the policy-formation field. Only the International Chamber of Commerce functions from the perspective of free market conservatism and speaks for and to a strictly business-centred constituency. The Bilderberg Conferences, Trilateral Commission and World Economic Forum in their own ways incorporate broadly neoliberal structuralist perspectives. The most recent addition to the field, the World Business Council for Sustainable Development, orients itself primarily in terms of neoliberal regulationism. Taken as a whole, these global policy groups can be regarded as agencies of transnational capitalist class formation. They provide intellectual leadership that is indispensable in the ongoing effort to transform transnational capital from an economically dominant class to a class whose interests take on a sense of universalism. The empirical questions to which we turn now concern the social relations that embed these groups within a structure of global corporate power.

The transnational corporate-policy network, circa 1996

Our empirical analysis in this chapter maps the social structure of the transnational corporate-policy network, the collection of leading corporate directors who participate on the five global policy boards described above. This elite is not coextensive with Sklair's 'transnational capitalist class'. His conception of the TCC goes farther and includes transnational executives, a globalizing state fraction, a globalizing technical fraction, and a globalizing consumerist fraction (2001: 17). Yet the transnational corporate-policy network does include the major capitalists who exercise the investment and top-level management functions within the world's largest corporations, as well as the organic intellectuals whose advice, as outside directors, is sought by the same companies. To date there has been no systematic study of the network of leading corporations and policy groups at the global level. Research carried out in national contexts suggests that corporate-policy interlocks contribute substantially to elite integration and to the hegemony of corporate capital (Useem 1984; Domhoff 2006 [1967; 1998]; Carroll and Shaw 2001). Case studies such as Gill's (1990) and anecdotal analyses such as van der Pijl's (1998) suggest that much the same applies in the global field. To explore this issue, this chapter poses three research questions:

TABLE 2.2 The nucleus of six corporate directors and their organizational affiliations

Name	Policy boards	Corp. boards	Corp. statuses
Paul Allaire	TC	Xerox	President
	Bilderberg	Sara Lee	Director
	WBCSD	Lucent	Director
		SmithKline	Director
Percy Barnevik	Bilderberg	ABB	President
	WBCSD	Dupont	Director
	WEF	GM	Director
Bertrand Collomb	Bilderberg	Aquitaine	Director
	WBCSD	Unilever	Director
	WEF	CIBC	Director
Etienne Davignon	Bilderberg	Fortis	Dep. chair
	TC	Generale Bank	Director
		Fina	Director
		BASF	Director
Minoru Murofushi	TC	Itochu	Chair
	WBCSD	HSBC	Director
	WEF		
Peter Sutherland	Bilderberg	BP	Vice-chair
	WEF	ABB	Director
		Ericsson	Director

TABLE 2.3 Eleven additional members of the core group and their organizational affiliations

Name	Policy boards	Corp. boards	Corp. statuses
Conrad M. Black	TC, Bilderberg	CIBC	Director
John H. Bryan	Bilderberg, WEF	Sara Lee	President
Livio D. Desimone	ICC, WBCSD	3M	President
George M. Fisher	TC, WBCSD	Eastman Kodak	President
Rokuro Ishikawa	TC, WBCSD	Kajima	Chair
Donald R. Keough	TC, WEF	Home Depot	Director
Henry Kissinger	Bilderberg, TC	Amex	Director
Helmut O. Maucher	ICC, WEF	Nestlé	Chair
Kosuka Morita	TC, WBCSD	Hitachi, Bank of Yokohama	Man. director
J. B. Prescott	WBCSD, WEF	BHP	CEO
Robert N. Wilson	TC, WBCSD	Johnson & Johnson	Vice-chair

1 *At the level of individuals*, who are the corporate directors at the centre of the corporate-policy network and how do their group affiliations create an inner circle of corporate governance and policy planning?

2 *At the level of organizations*, what is the basic shape and form of the interlocking directorates among the policy groups, and between them and the world's largest corporations?

3 What contribution do the global policy groups make to transnational corporate-elite integration?

The point of the analysis is to investigate one dimension of transnational capitalist class formation – the corporate-policy network – with an eye to what it tells us about the structural sources of elite integration as well as tension and possible fissure. Our empirical analysis maps the social structure of the leading corporate directors who participate in the network of 350 giant corporations and five global policy groups.[8] Our analysis is restricted to those directing at least one of the top 350 corporations and one other organization in our sample (whether corporation or policy group). These 622 individuals are a globally networked subset of the 6,751 directors of the world's major corporations as of year-end 1996.

Our first research question directs attention to the individuals who carry the transnational network: who are they and how do they create social structure through their group affiliations? We find that the network's *inner circle of cosmopolitans* consists of 105 corporate directors whose corporate affiliations span national borders, or link global policy boards to each other.[9] Through their networking, these 105 individuals make the most immediate structural contributions to transnational class formation. Indeed, the six most well-connected people create through their directorships a tightly knit nucleus of eighteen corporations and four policy groups (see Table 2.2). At year-end 1996, most of them sat together on multiple policy boards. Bertrand Collomb (president of Lafarge and 1997 'manager of the year', according to *Le Nouvel Economiste*) sat on all four policy boards and thus met Minoru Murofushi, chair of Itochu Corporation, on three of them. Within this nucleus, the integrative function of the policy boards is clear: without them, these transnationalists would be for the most part detached from each other; with them, they comprise an integrated social unit, with representation from the USA, Britain, Japan and continental Europe.

When we extend the analysis to all corporate directors with two or more policy-group affiliations, we add to the nucleus 11 individuals, 14 corporations and the remaining policy group (the ICC; see Table 2.3). This core group of 17 individuals provides all the direct linkages among the five global policy boards. Within it, the integrative role of the four highly networked policy groups stands out. For instance, all three Japanese directors in the core group sit on both the

TABLE 2.4 Distributions of companies and inner circle members by national domicile

Domicile	Percentage of firms	Percentage of inner circle	Difference
Canada	3.4	5.7	+2.3
USA	25.7	21.0	−4.7
Netherlands	2.6	7.6	+5.0
UK	9.7	16.2	+6.5
Germany	9.1	14.3	+5.2
France	7.1	11.4	+4.4
Italy	3.7	1.9	−1.8
Switzerland	2.0	3.8	+1.8
Sweden	.9	2.9	+2.0
Belgium	1.1	5.7	+4.6
Spain	1.1	1.9	+0.8
Norway	.3	0.0	−0.3
Australia	.9	1.9	+1.0
Japan	20.9	5.7	−15.2
Brazil	1.4	0.0	−1.4
Mexico	.6	0.0	−0.6
Venezuela	.3	0.0	−0.3
Argentina	.3	0.0	−0.3
Russia	.9	0.0	−0.9
Turkey	.3	0.0	−0.3
South Korea	3.7	0.0	−3.7
Hong Kong	.9	0.0	−0.9
Taiwan	.6	0.0	−0.6
Singapore	.9	0.0	−0.9
Malaysia	.3	0.0	−0.3
India	.3	0.0	−0.3
South Africa	1.1	0.0	−1.1
TOTAL	100.0	100.0	0.0
N	350 firms	105 persons	

TC and the WBCSD. Not only do these policy boards serve as transnational meeting points for the Japanese directors, equally these individuals serve as ambassadors between the fields of global policy work and Japanese corporate governance, while also linking the TC with the WBCSD. The core group shows an obvious Euro-North American bias. Corporations sited on the semi-periphery are entirely absent from it, and only five Asia-Pacific companies (four of them Japanese) are represented.

Although the inner circle's 105 members are indeed cosmopolitans, this does not render them rootless. On the basis of their corporate affiliations and other biographical details, we categorized each into a 'national' affiliation. For executives, we took the national domicile of their home firm to indicate their national base of operations; for outside directors we considered other biographical information, including the locus of their careers and residence. Table 2.4 compares the national domiciles of our sample of corporations with the national domiciles of the inner circle. At the centre of things, Europeans and North Americans entirely predominate. Although our sample includes the forty largest companies of the semi-periphery, corporate directors based outside the centre of the world system are completely absent from the inner circle. Any interlocks linking the network's inner circle to its margins emanate from the centre, not the semi-periphery, of the world system. It is also noteworthy that certain national sites are over-represented among the cosmopolitans – especially such middle powers as Belgium, the Netherlands, Switzerland and Canada, along with three major EU powers, Britain, Germany and France. Conversely, three advanced capitalist states are under-represented – the USA (slightly), Italy (more so) and Japan (extremely).

A rudimentary analysis of class positions revealed that 39 cosmopolitans were executives in a Top 350 corporation and 26 were executives in other companies. The remaining 40 were corporate advisers, 12 of whom were retired corporate executives serving as outside directors of various firms. The inner circle includes a sizeable contingent of corporate capitalists, directing some of the world's largest companies as well as companies not in our sample. Leadership in the policy domain has not been delegated to a separate stratum of organic intellectuals, or, put another way, top global capitalists serve also as organic intellectuals for their class.

Finally, a look at gender confirmed that male dominance continues to be the order of the day at the very top of the global corporate world. Only six members of the inner circle were women, and four of these were advisers to corporations, not executives.

The network as an inter-organizational field

We now move to a representation of the corporate-policy network as a set of inter-organizational relations. In Figure 2.1 the Trilateral Commission emerges as a central meeting point for the global corporate elite, but the WBCSD also plays a highly integrative role. In contrast to the other groups, the ICC's distinctive contribution to transnational class formation is to integrate global capitalism's centre with its margins; hence the ICC board blends a smattering of the global corporate elite with various representatives of national and local capital.[10]

If direct interlocks among policy boards provide some basis for elite consensus formation, another source lies in the extent to which the *social circles* of the policy groups intersect. A board's social circle is simply the set of other boards with which it is interlocked. An overlap between social circles means that the

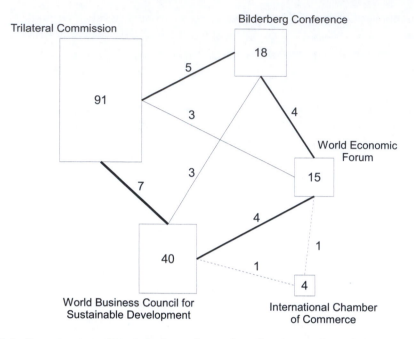

Trilateral Commission

Bilderberg Conference

World Economic Forum

World Business Council for Sustainable Development

International Chamber of Commerce

Note: Boxes are proportionate in size to the number of corporate-elite members affiliated with each group (indicated in each box). Line thicknesses reflect the number of shared elite members.

Figure 2.1 Number of interlocks among five global policy groups, 1996

same corporate boards that interlock with one policy group also interlock with the other. Table 2.5 lists the twenty-seven corporations maintaining at least three directorship interlocks with the policy groups. Heading the list is Zurich-based industrial conglomerate ABB (already shown in Figure 1.2 to be a part of the corporate network's core), whose directors serve on all five policy boards. Although there is no one 'nationality' that predominates in the policy-board social circles, the North Atlantic presence is striking. The 27 corporations, barely 8 per cent of our sample, account for 128 of the 305 directorship interlocks between all corporations and the 5 global policy groups. Moreover, corporations whose boards overlap with the policy groups also tend to be central in the network of corporate interlocks.[11] But 198 of our 350 corporations, including nearly all companies domiciled in the semi-periphery, share no directors with the policy groups. The only really salient regional fracture in the network is the massive divide between the world system's centre and its semi-periphery.

The integrative contribution of elite policy groups

To appraise the integrative impact of policy-board affiliations we calculated the extent to which corporate ties to the policy groups *reduce the distance between corporations* in the global network. To calculate this reduction we examined

TABLE 2.5 Numbers of directorships on five global policy boards

Corporation	Domicile	TC	WBCDS	BLD	WEF	ICC	Total
ABB	Switzerland	2	2	2	3	1	10
CIBC	Canada	4	1	2	1	0	8
GM	USA	1	3	2	2	0	8
Unilever	Holland/UK	3	2	1	1	0	7
Sara Lee	USA	2	1	3	1	0	7
Xerox	USA	2	3	2	0	0	7
BP	UK	1	2	1	1	0	5
Aquitaine	France	1	1	2	1	0	5
Nestlé	Switzerland	1	2	0	1	1	5
HSBC	UK	2	1	0	1	0	4
Fina	Belgium	3	0	1	0	0	4
Generale Bank	Belgium	3	0	1	0	0	4
Ericsson	Sweden	1	0	2	1	0	4
Kansai Energy	Japan	4	0	0	0	0	4
3M	USA	2	1	0	0	1	4
AIG	USA	3	0	1	0	0	4
Chase Manhattan	USA	4	0	0	0	0	4
Dayton Hudson	USA	2	1	0	0	1	4
Lucent	USA	2	1	1	0	0	4
SmithKline Beecham	UK	1	1	1	0	0	3
Deutsche Bank	Germany	1	0	1	1	0	3
Siemens	Germany	1	0	1	1	0	3
VW	Germany	2	0	0	1	0	3
Itochu	Japan	1	1	0	1	0	3
American Express	USA	1	0	2	0	0	3
Dupont	USA	0	1	1	1	0	3
Prudential	USA	3	0	0	0	0	3

the distances between points in the inter-corporate network, with and without the mediating ties provided by policy-group affiliations.[12] At this systemic level, the contribution of the policy groups to overall network integration is quite striking. Overall, the mean distance between corporations falls from 4.91 to 3.09 when we take into account directors' affiliations with policy boards. At the outer reaches of the network, the diameter (the largest distance between two points) drops from 15 to 9. These big shifts indicate that *the policy-board affiliations of the world's leading corporate directors effectively shrink the social space of the global corporate elite.*

A key remaining issue is how the broad pattern of participation in the policy groups draws corporate capital sited in particular locations in the world system

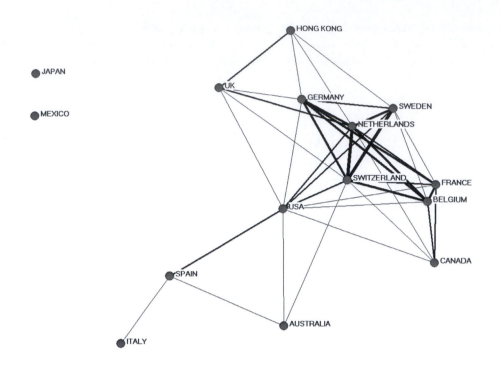

Figure 2.2 Mean international distances among 271 corporations, based on corporate interlocks only

into the transnational business community. To assess this we calculated the mean distance among corporations based in different countries, with and without corporate-policy board ties in the analysis. When only corporate interlocks are considered it is north-west continental Europe that is most transnationally integrated (see Figure 2.2).[13] Mean distances among the German, Dutch, Swiss, Swedish and Belgian networks are typically less than 3.0. We find firms based in Spain, Italy, Australia and Hong Kong in somewhat peripheral locations, and Mexican and Japanese corporations in very peripheral locations. The largest mean distances in the international network occur between Italian and Japanese firms (9.88) and between Mexican and Japanese firms (9.33).

In the second step (Figure 2.3), when we included the corporate-policy interlocks as indirect, mediating ties, mean transnational distances decreased sharply. Companies sited in the three Anglo-American countries – heavy participants on the policy boards – become fully integrated with the continental European bloc, whose own transnational distances fall further. Once the policy-board ties are taken into account, the mean distances between corporate Japan and firms domiciled in the North Atlantic plummet from a range of 6.15–8.00 to a range of 3.33–3.64, showing that for Japanese corporate directors, the policy groups offer a bridge into global governance. Firms domiciled outside the North

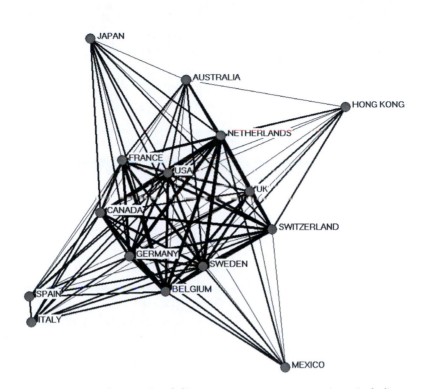

Figure 2.3 Mean international distances among 271 corporations, including paths mediated by five global policy groups

Atlantic heartland, however, remain relatively peripheral. Thus, the pattern of differential regional participation in the network persists, even as the absolute distances drop.

Conclusion

Let us first revisit our three research questions and take stock of what we have learned. The first question we posed concerned the role of key individuals at the centre of the network. We have found that as of 1996 a few dozen cosmopolitans – primarily men based in Europe and North America and actively engaged in corporate management – knit the corporate-policy network together by participating in transnational interlocking and/or multiple global policy groups. A mere seventeen corporate directors, some of whom serve on as many as four policy groups, generated a plethora of relations among the groups. As a structure supporting transnational capitalist class formation, the network was highly centralized in the individuals and organizations participating in it. Yet from its core it extended unevenly to corporations and individuals positioned on its fringes.

Our second question focused on the organizational level, at which we found that the neoliberal policy groups differ markedly in the extent to which the directors of the world's leading corporations participate on their boards. The International Chamber of Commerce (ICC), whose contribution to transnational capitalist class formation has been focused around the integration of the centre with its margins within a discourse of free market conservatism, was least involved at the core of the network. In contrast, the other four groups, advocating more structuralist or regulationist variants of neoliberalism, were deeply enmeshed within the global corporate elite. They were substantially interlocked with each other as well as with common corporate boards, a small number of which account for two-fifths of all the corporate-policy links. Most significantly, while the North Atlantic was especially well represented in the contingent of interlocked corporations, corporate capital domiciled outside the world system's core states was almost entirely detached, suggesting that van der Pijl's (1984) image of an Atlantic ruling class retained its cogency to the close of the twentieth century. Compared to this dominant pattern, other elements of possible segmentation – e.g. elective affinities that appear to attract financial capital to the Trilateral Commission (TC) and industrial capital to the World Business Council for Sustainable Development (WBCSD – see Figure 2.5) – barely registered.

Finally, in 1996 the neoliberal policy boards made a dramatic contribution to global corporate-elite integration. This additional layer of social structure, within which leading corporate capitalists step beyond their immediate economic interests to take up matters of global concern, pulls the directorates of the world's major corporations much closer together, and collaterally integrates the life-world of the global corporate elite. But if the policy groups broker and thereby strengthen inter-corporate relations they do so selectively, in a way that reproduces regional differences in participation. In 1996, as twenty-seven Japanese corporate directors, distributed among three of the five policy boards, pulled corporate Japan closer to the network's North Atlantic centre of gravity, that centre was even more tightly bound through the heavy participation of North Americans and Europeans on the policy boards.

These findings support the claim that by the closing years of the twentieth century a well-integrated transnational corporate community had formed, and that neoliberal policy groups, themselves vehicles of globalization, were instrumental in its formation. Whether this confirmed the arrival of a transnational capitalist class is partly a matter of semantics and partly a matter of substance. From one perspective, the selective participation in the corporate-policy network is striking, as is its centralized structure. Within an already elite group of leading corporations and corporate directors, those who actually constitute the network comprised a small core of cosmopolitan individuals and corporations, with a strongly Euro-North American bias. In contrast, most individuals participating in the global network did not hold elite positions beyond their home nation. As a mode of business activism, the network, centralized around a compact inner circle, evoked the image of a vanguard more than a mass movement. Yet as we have seen, it comprised a single connected formation, with considerable reach, and the policy boards effectively drew the national sub-networks into an integrated transnational structure. Moreover, claims about the formation of a transnational capitalist class do *not* depend exclusively on the structure of elite networks. Sklair (2001), for example, points to cultural practices – the worldly assumption of social responsibility, the shared ideology of consumerism – as integral aspects of transnational capitalist class formation. As Gramsci understood, class formation involves both structure and culture, and although network analysis gives some purchase on the former we have done no more than telegraph some of the discursive elements of neoliberal globalization as a hegemonic project.

One might at this point, however, make a preliminary assessment of the thesis of transnational class formation; conspicuously absent from the corporate-policy network, circa 1996, were corporations and capitalists based on the periphery and semi-periphery of the world system. In this sense, the network seemed to present one facet of a collective imperialism, organized to help manage global capitalism from the centre (see Steven 1994). In the blending of persuasion and coercion that such management entails, the policy groups clearly seek to persuade. They operate at one remove from the structural adjustment programmes, 'poverty reduction strategies' and other enforcement mechanisms, including military intervention, that are the province of statist bodies, whether national or international. They foster discussion of global issues among members of the corporate elite, often in combination with other influential political and professional elites. They facilitate the formation of a moving elite consensus framed within one or another variant of neoliberal discourse. They educate publics and states on the virtues of the neoliberal paradigm. In short, they are agencies of political and cultural leadership, whose activities are integral to the formation of a transnational capitalist class.

As the twentieth century drew to a close, the network of interlocks between neoliberal policy boards and the world's major corporations formed an important communication structure in this process. All five of the policy groups were embedded in the global network, and with extensive interlocking among four of them and a key elite-level connection between the most 'regulationist' and most 'free market' group,[14] there was no evidence of political fracture along the lines of Robinson and Harris's (2000) typology. By the same token, each group had its own modus operandi, occupied a unique niche in the organizational ecology of transnational neoliberalism, and found a distinctive location in the network. The ICC was comparatively marginal to the life of the global corporate elite as we have defined it, yet its policy work sustained a very broad network linking local capital from sites throughout the world system into the centre, in a hard-line project of free market conservatism. In contrast, the exclusively

Euro-North American Bilderberg Conference was well ensconced in the corporate network, and its gatherings brought business leaders together with political leaders in informal discussions that tended to promote a neoliberalism that retained a managerial role for the state. The World Economic Forum (WEF) and Trilateral Commission (TC), both strongly integrated with the corporate network, championed a similar project, but they rendered it more tangible in the activities of various working groups and the issuance of extensive policy documents and other texts. Both groups assembled agents and interests beyond the Euro-North American core and beyond the corporate elite per se, in explicit attempts to articulate a global political-economic interest. Finally, the WBCSD extended the general interest to the incorporation of nature into capital, and like the WEF and TC, drew Japanese business leaders into the network. Instead of political fracture, neoliberalism's own pluralism, as enunciated by the different groups, ensured that consensus would be a loose and variegated one, not a monolithic doctrine.

3 | Global cities in the global corporate network

Introduction

Corporate power never floats free, but is lodged in specific landscapes and geographies. This chapter takes up the spatial organization of the global corporate network at the end of the twentieth century. Since the 1980s two separate literatures have explored issues of hierarchy and networking within the global political economy. Stemming initially from Friedmann's (1986) conception of a 'world city hierarchy', a voluminous series of geographical investigations has branched into studies of *global cities*, which are interlinked in networks of trade and investment that disembed them from their national settings (P. J. Taylor 2004). A thinner line of sociological research, in which this investigation is centred, has followed from Fennema's (1982) study of the global network of interlocking corporate directorates, charting configurations of global corporate power. Both these lines of enquiry have offered insight into the social structuring of economic power within a globalizing world system. Pulling the two literatures together, we may ask, how have cities and interlocking corporate directorates been articulated into a global inter-urban network? The spatialized analysis this question provokes gives us a window on the organization of corporate power within the world city system.

Global cities: a networked hierarchy

In the literature on global cities we can, with P. J. Taylor (2004), trace a movement from hierarchy to network as the dominant metaphor. Friedmann (1986) viewed a city's location in the global hierarchy as issuing from the financial, headquarters and articulator functions assigned to it within the world system. Sassen (2001) has also emphasized hierarchy in her argument that globalization induces tendencies towards both conglomeration and decentralization of economic activities that give global cities such as Tokyo, New York and London a new strategic role as corporate command points, attracting the advanced producer services that power post-industrial accumulation. As a result, 'the more globalized the economy becomes, the higher the agglomeration of central functions in relatively few sites, that is, the global cities' (ibid.: 5). Sassen's more recent work embraces a dynamic, network approach while continuing to stress hierarchy. In the new system of 'global networks' and 'linked cities' places once on the periphery (e.g. Mexico City) have moved to the core, while certain industrial centres like Detroit have been peripheralized (Sassen 2002).

The morphology of global city networks has been shown to follow a hub-and-spokes pattern, whether the inter-urban tie consists of optic-fibre communications grids (Graham 1999), airline traffic (Smith and Timberlake 1995, 2002), the interconnected offices of advanced producer-service firms (Derudder et al. 2003; P. J. Taylor 2004) or global media firms (Krätke 2003), or the parent–subsidiary relations within transnational enterprises (Alderson and Beckfield 2004, 2007). The centrality of cities depends to some extent on what kind of inter-urban tie is measured. For instance, in the network of advanced producer services New York and London dominate (Taylor et al. 2002), but in the culture industries, Los Angeles and New York are important centres, although most world media cities are in Europe (Krätke 2003: 620), pointing to fundamental differences in the underlying practices that generate different types of inter-urban relations. Nevertheless, four cities stand out as particularly central across various criteria; namely, New York, London, Tokyo and Paris (P. J. Taylor 2004). But the centre of gravity in this geography of globalization is 'the northern transatlantic economic system (particularly the links among the European Union [EU], the United States, and Canada) [which] represents the major concentration of processes of economic globalization in the world today' (Sassen 2002: 10).

According to P. J. Taylor (2004: 200), these processes have been accompanied by a partial '"freeing" of cities from containerization imposed by states', as globalization of financial markets and of corporate investment undermines state regulatory capacities. Within the contemporary world economy, cities have become more than units within states. Operating through inter-urban networks that span national borders, cities 'are their own economic entity within the transnational spaces of flows' (ibid.: 52; cf. Castells 1996).

As important as the literature on global city networks has been in unsettling overly state-centred theoretical perspectives and in pointing to a worldwide configuration of inter-urban social relations, it suffers from empirical deficiencies. A continuing weakness is the relative lack of direct empirical evidence on connections among the world's major cities (Alderson and Beckfield 2004: 812). In P. J. Taylor's (2004) extensive and widely cited study, the strength of an inter-urban tie is *inferred* from the indirect evidence provided by a global service firm's presence in two cities. The founding assumption in this method is that 'the larger the office [in a given city] the more connections there are with other offices in the firm's network' (ibid.: 62). But no assessment of actual inter-urban connections occurs in Taylor's study. What Taylor taps into are the global strategies of financial, legal, accounting and management-consultancy firms as they maintain offices in various cities. He does not measure actual inter-urban connections but merely assumes that they occur in proportion to office size. Thus, even after Taylor's important contribution, the literature on global city networks continues to suffer from 'an evidential crisis' (ibid.: 39) based in a 'paucity of data' (Alderson and Beckfield 2004: 812).

Corporate networks and corporate power

This chapter explores the interlocking corporate directorship as an inter-organizational practice that actually *generates* a global inter-urban network. In contrast to other indicators such parent–subsidiary ownership or the producer–service relations that Taylor imputes, a director of firms based in different cities creates a durable, social relation, connecting corporate boards across the cities in which they hold their meetings. As an elite level, inter-organizational relation, the interlocking directorate provides us with a different kind of tie from that emphasized in Taylor's paradigmatic research. For him (2004: 61–5), what ties cities together are (imputed) *intra*-organizational relations among the offices of transnational producer-service firms. Interlocking directorates, in contrast, are *inter*-organizational, and they occur at the top echelon of the corporate power structure. They provide a different picture of the world city network, not geared to the functionality of economic production but to the social organization of a global corporate elite. If world cities comprise a system of power (Alderson and Beckfield 2004) and hierarchy (Sassen 2002), then the inter-urban ties that link the world's major corporations at the apex of corporate decision-making have great significance to our understanding of that system.

As with other practices underlying the world city network, corporate interlocking generates a *multi-level network* in which the firm, not the city, is 'the prime agency of production and reproduction' (P. J. Taylor 2004: 61). Global cities are sites for the two forms of corporate power discussed in this book's Introduction: instrumental and expressive. Location of a company's head office bears instrumentally upon its access to a pool of directors. Large metropolitan centres offer head offices 'ease of interorganizational face-to-face contacts, business service availability, and high intermetropolitan accessibility' (Pred 1977: 177). The tendency in advanced capitalism for major corporate head offices to gravitate to the largest metropolitan areas has meant that corporate elites tend to be spatially clustered. The well-researched case of the USA provides a good example. Studies have identified New York as the hub of an inter-urban corporate-interlock network that also includes semi-national subnetworks, particularly around Chicago, and regional groupings (Sonquist and Koenig 1975; Green 1983; Bearden and Mintz 1985). As for the expressive form of power, interlocking among firms based in the same city is a function of the presence of upper-class social clubs, suggesting that 'local upper-class clubs facilitate intense and intimate local elite interaction through which directors develop trust and thus lay the foundation for local interlocking' (Kono et al. 1998: 896).

The central issue we pursue in this chapter is that of capitalist class formation *across global cities*. Is it the case, as P. J. Taylor (2004: 214) avers, that by means of inter-urban ties a 'new network bourgeoisie' has formed, whose members constitute a global plutocracy? Can a configuration of key cities, linked at the level of corporate directorates, be shown to exist? If so, its shape and form may indicate the character of the new network bourgeoisie. What can a network analysis of inter-urban corporate-elite relations reveal about the structure of global corporate power and global cities at the close of the twentieth century?

Working hypotheses

The global-cities perspective of Sassen and Taylor suggests three working hypotheses that guide our analysis.

- H_1 First, if, as Sassen holds, global cities comprise the sites at which the 'central functions' of corporate business have become agglomerated, then *the network should be concentrated within the main global cities*.
- H_2 Second, if state–society complexes are giving way to more global, networked forms of organization then inter-urban ties should not be contained within state boundaries, but *there should be a substantial transnational network among the main global cities*. To the extent that the major global cities function both as sites for extensive intra-urban corporate-elite networks (H_1) and as nodes in a transnational inter-urban network (H_2), we could tentatively conclude that a 'new network bourgeoisie' has formed within and across the world's leading cities.
- H_3 Third, if economic globalization's centre of gravity lies in a 'northern transatlantic economic system' (Sassen 2002: 10), then *the inter-urban network should be most developed among the major cities of Europe, the United States and Canada*.

Participation and centrality in the transnational network

This chapter makes use of the same set of 350 leading corporations as analysed in Chapter 2; since our focus is on how the network of corporate interlocks articulates with the hierarchy of global cities, however, we do not consider elite ties between corporations and transnational policy groups. Although 6,751 corporate directors were identified for the 350 firms, 6,218 of them each directed only one firm in the Global 350. The global corporate elite – the directors who actually knit together the network of the world's largest corporations – numbers only 533. These individuals hold interlocking directorships in a total of 290 of the Global 350, the other 60 firms being isolated from the network. We first focus on a subset of this network, namely the *transnational elite relations that knit together global cities*. This network is carried by just 94 transnationalists: those whose directorships span national borders. They make up only 18 per cent of the global corporate elite and just 1.4 per cent of the directors of the Global 350. By abstracting this key group from the global corporate elite we can derive a clear sense of how firms and cities are positioned in the transnational network, uninfluenced by the purely domestic ties that actually predominate in the practice of corporate interlocking. Later, we bring in the 439 national networkers, who each sit on two or more corporate boards in a single country, but who do not engage in transnational interlocking. Their corporate interlocks contribute only to a city's prominence within its national network, not to its transnational connections.

In this way, the 'cosmopolitan' (i.e. transnational) ties that are particularly important to H_2 can be isolated from the more numerous 'local' elite ties that inscribe major cities within national networks. I will call the set of social relations carried by transnationalists the *transnational network* and the entire set of social relations carried by both transnationalists and national networkers the *global network*. The global network includes *all* interlocks among all Global 350 firms – it gives us the full, global, picture. The transnational network includes only those interlocks that are carried by transnationalists.[1]

The 94 directors who carry the transnational network hold 266 directorships in 122 corporations. That is, *only 122 of the Global 350 participate directly in transnational interlocking*, less than half of the 290 firms whose boards are interlocked with another Global 350 company. This underlines the relative rarity in 1996 of transnational interlocking, compared to the traffic among the boards of companies based in the same country. This rarity is not surprising, given the long history of corporate-elite formation at the national level and the relative

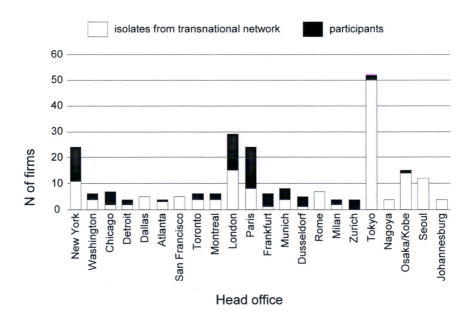

Figure 3.1 Participation in the transnational network, twenty-two cities

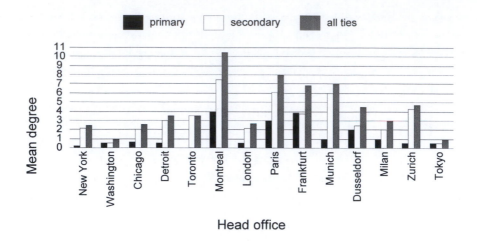

Figure 3.2 Mean degree of interlocking in the transnational network, fourteen cities

recency of transnational business organization (Scott 1997; Dicken 2003). The 94 transnationalists may seem like a small group, but they serve on boards with 275 additional members of the global corporate elite, who in turn direct an additional 85 Global 350 firms. Thus, most of the world's leading companies, and most members of the global corporate elite, participate directly in the transnational network or are linked to it at one remove.[2]

Now consider the distribution of transnational network participation across cities (see Figure 3.1) . The 22 cities that each host four or more corporations account for 241 of the Global 350. Four commonly cited global cities – Tokyo (52), London (29), New York (24) and Paris (24) – are host to a total of 129 corporate head offices. But cities vary tremendously in the degree to which the firms they host participate in transnational interlocking (the contingency coefficient for the relationship between the two variables depicted in the graph is .522). The transnational network is based overwhelmingly in the cities of the north-east of North America and the north-west of Europe, with Paris, London and New York claiming the most network participants.[3] On the North American side, the zone for what van der Pijl (1984) has called an Atlantic ruling class does not extend to Dallas or San Francisco; on the European side the zone does not reach Rome, although two companies based in Milan do participate. Within the zone of participation, certain cities – Zurich, Frankfurt and Paris, for instance – are particularly hooked into the transnational network.

Among participants in the transnational network, firms can be further differentiated as to their centrality. A basic measure of centrality is degree – the number of ties to other network members that a given member has, which in our transnational network ranges from 1 (28 firms are tied to only one other firm) to 20 with a mean of 4.59 and median of 3.30. In assessing centrality, however, we need to recall that not all interlocks are created equally. Recalling our discussion in the Introduction of the instrumental and expressive functions of directorate interlocking in the organization of corporate power, we can distinguish between primary and secondary interlocks: the former carried by corporate insiders, the latter by outside directors. Simply put, a situation in which, say, the CEO of Deutsche Bank sits on the supervisory board of Daimler has more substantive importance in the instrumentalities of corporate business than an interlock carried by an outside director of two companies, which likely serves no instrumental purpose for the firms, even as it contributes to elite integration.[4]

Mean centrality scores for firms based in fourteen cities are shown in Figure 3.2. Interestingly, firms based in New York, the centre of corporate power in the USA, are not particularly central in the transnational network: they average slightly more than two ties. The same goes for London-based companies and for other North American cities, with the conspicuous exception of Montreal, whose two participating corporations show the highest mean degree in the chart, averaging more than ten ties. The other cities that host relatively central corporations – Paris, Munich and Frankfurt – are on the European continent. Again, the differences hold for both primary and secondary interlocks. With the exception of Montreal, then, firms based in North American cities and London tend not to engage in primary interlocking on a transnational basis, reflecting the generally looser corporate networks in the Anglo-American business regime. Primary transnational interlocking is particularly common among firms headquartered in Paris, Frankfurt and Montreal, suggesting that instrumental relations of control, coordination and allocation may exist across these urban centres.

Mapping the inter-urban transnational network

At this point it is worthwhile condensing the corporate network into an inter-urban network. To do this we treat cities as points and the total number of interlocks between firms headquartered in two cities as a valued line (cf. Green and Semple 1981; Carroll 2001). Figure 3.3 displays the inter-urban interlocks between the forty-eight cities whose firms participate in the transnational corporate network. The thickness of lines indicates the number of inter-urban corporate interlocks carried by transnationalist directors. London, New York, Paris, Zurich, Frankfurt and Munich are all central; Osaka, Melbourne and Los Angeles are quite marginal. The ties that terminate in London, New York or Zurich, however, tend to be thin, while the ties linking the major Continental cities are thicker. There are marked between-country differences in the extent to which transnational interlocks connect to a range of cities or are focused on the main metropole. London and Paris dominate their respective countries as singular nodes: in Britain and France the network of transnational interlocks is effectively contained within these cities, consistent with H_1. In Germany and

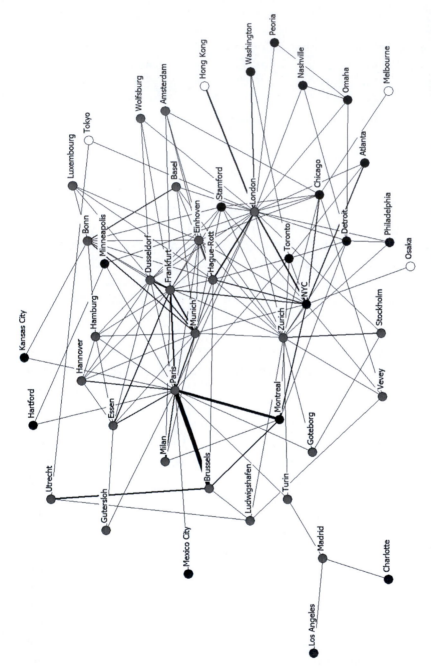

Figure 3.3 The transnational inter-urban network, showing all ties carried by transnationalists. Black circles indicate companies based in North America; grey, companies based in Europe; white, companies based in Asia-Pacific. Line thickness indicates the number of inter-urban interlocks

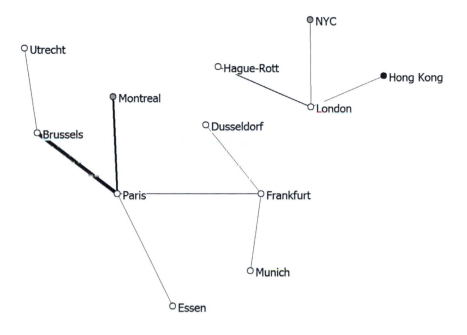

Figure 3.4 The transnational inter-urban network, cities linked by four or more interlocking directorships. For key, see Figure 3.3

the USA there is wider social space among a plurality of cities hosting corporations in the network. Another finding of note is the nearly complete fissure between American cities and certain major Continental cities – particularly Paris (effectively France). In 1996 there was only one director of both French- and American-based companies, namely Rand V. Araskog, former CEO of ITT and an outside director of Hartford Financial (based in Hartford), Dayton Hudson (based in Minneapolis) and Alcatel (based in Paris). For the most part, US-based corporate directorates hook into the European business community via London, and secondarily via Frankfurt and The Hague/Rotterdam. London certainly emerges from this analysis as a key articulation point in the North Atlantic network, in tandem with New York.

To get a clearer sense of the main inter-urban linkages we can reduce[5] the network to its most tenacious relations, by sequentially ratcheting up the criterion for inter-urban linkage. Two cities linked by virtue of a single interlock are connected only minimally at the level of corporate-elite relations. The single tie may be quite important to the interlocked boards, but it indicates only a low volume of elite social integration across cities. As we raise the bar, we reduce the inter-urban network to the thick ties involving numerous interlocks linking pairs of cities – the substantive bases for an inter-urban corporate elite.

Limiting the analysis to two or more interlocks between cities eliminates most

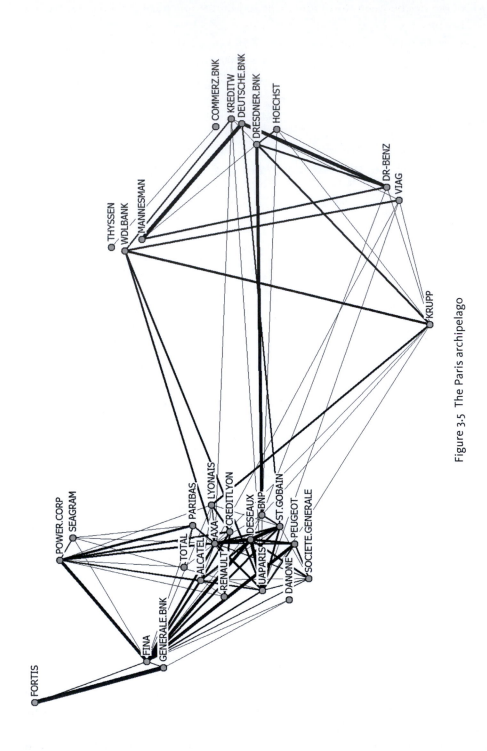

Figure 3.5 The Paris archipelago

of the ties between North American and European cities. Ten US cities become isolates from the network, with only four US cities retaining transnational ties. Washington and Omaha retain ties to London, Chicago retains a tie to Melbourne, and New York retains ties to London, Frankfurt, The Hague/Rotterdam and Montreal (as well as to Chicago and Atlanta). Besides New York, Montreal (with ties to Paris, Brussels and New York) is the only North American city that retains a central location in the global inter-urban network once the criterion is raised to two or more interlocks. The two major Japanese cities become isolates, as do Mexico City and three European cities (Amsterdam, Wolfsburg and Gütersloh). What remains as a connected component is a European-centred network that includes eight German cities, three Dutch and three Swiss cities, two Swedish and two Italian cities, Luxembourg, Paris, London, Hong Kong, Montreal, and five US cities (including Atlanta, which is tied only to New York).

Raising the criterion further to four interlocks (Figure 3.4) reduces the network to two intercity archipelagos, one centred around Paris and including Continental cities as well as Montreal; the other centred around London and including New York, Hong Kong and The Hague/Rotterdam, where Dutch-British Unilever is based.[6] Ultimately, the inter-urban network reduces to a Brussels–Paris–Montreal axis.

In Figure 3.5 the larger of the archipelagos from Figure 3.4 is depicted at the level of inter-corporate relations. By disaggregating the inter-urban network in this way, we can see what draws Montreal into the Continental network,[7] in the strongest instance of transatlantic interlocking. The key ties, linking Montreal-based Power Corporation to Brussels-based Petrofina and Paris-based Paribas, reflect the financial empire of the Desmarais family (of Montreal) and the Frère family (of Brussels). This partnership dates from the 1980s. In 1997 these families controlled, through their Swiss-based holding company Pargesa, major corporations in Belgium and France, and had recently forged a partnership with Germany's Bertelsmann media conglomerate (Leger 1997).

All but two of the twenty-eight firms in Figure 3.5 form a single connected component whose core is the densely integrated Parisian corporate network. Five Paris-based companies interlock with eight of the ten German-based companies, and the clear tendency at this seam in the transnational network is for financial institutions to interlock either with other financials or with industrial corporations, suggesting an integration of capital that stops short of inter-corporate control but that likely entails the exercise of allocative power. For instance, the tie between Paris-based BNP and Frankfurt-based Dresdner Bank, via two shared directors, reflects a 'cooperation agreement' that began in 1996 and was terminated (along with the interlock) in 2002. The Frankfurt-based financial institutions, including Deutsche Bank, clearly play an important role in knitting together the German network and connecting it to Paris. The links between Utrecht-based Fortis, a financial institution, and the two companies based in

Brussels are similar in kind to the relations that transect the Franco-German border. Although the tie from Montreal-based Power Corp to Brussels-based Fina is a vehicle for inter-corporate strategic control, those between Power Corp and the Paris-based financial institutions (AXA, Credit Lyonnais) are more likely based in credit relations. In short, the strongest configuration of transnational, inter-urban corporate ties suggests an integration of capital, and of top-level management, across several Continental cities, plus Montreal.[8] While this pattern is broadly consistent with H_3, it departs from the expectation, in H_2, that the inter-urban elite network would be most developed *among the leading world cities*.

Mapping the global network

Global cities are by definition centres of what Sklair calls transnational practices – 'practices that cross state borders and do not originate with state actors or agencies' (Sklair 2001: 107). By featuring only transnational interlockers and their corporate affiliations, our analysis to this point has focused on the elite ties at the heart of the global city network. This selectivity enabled us to discern the relative centrality of cities and the main inter-urban relations in the transnational corporate network. Yet in the entire global network, most interlocking corporate directors are 'locals', not 'cosmopolitans': they knit together firms based in the same country. How does the picture of inter-urban elite relations change when we consider the *global* network; that is, when we include *all directors* of the Global 350 corporations, adding to our transnational network of 122 corporations and 94 individuals another 168 firms and 439 individuals involved exclusively in nationally based interlocking?

In all, 88 cities serve as command centres for one or more of the Global 350 corporations. Although 18 of them have no board interlocks that extend to other cities, the other 70 are connected into a single inter-urban network. Table 3.1 lists the 20 most central cities, ranked according to intercity degree – the number of interlocking directorships that link firms based in a given city to firms based elsewhere. A city's overall degree in the global network is simply the sum of its intercity degree and its intracity degree.[9] Obviously, intercity and (even more so) intracity degree are functions of both the number of large firms based in a given city and the extent to which their boards are interlocked with other boards. Transnational degree refers to the subset of intercity ties linking firms based in different countries. These centrality measures enable us to define a city's degree of *introversion* as its intracity degree divided by its overall degree, and a city's degree of *extraversion* as its transnational degree divided by its overall degree.

Interestingly, American cities, which tend to be rather marginal in the transnational network, are well represented on this list. Leading the list is New York. The interlocking of New York-based boards produces an extensive local network with profuse ties into the loosely knit but wide-ranging American national

TABLE 3.1 Degree of interlocking, twenty most central cities in the global network

Rank	City	Intercity degree (A)	Intracity degree (B)	Transnational degree (C)	Intro-version 100 (C/(A+B))	Extra-version 100 (C/(A+B))
1	New York	165	92	22	35.8	8.6
2	Frankfurt	90	12	17	11.7	16.7
3	Munich	78	32	15	29.1	13.6
4	Paris	75	326	74	81.3	18.5
5	Chicago	57	?1	7	29.6	8.6
6	Düsseldorf	50	6	6	10.7	10.7
7	London	48	94	41	66.2	28.9
8	Detroit	46	4	4	8.0	8.0
9	Stamford	46	0	7	0	15.2
10	Tokyo	41	146	2	78.1	1.1
11	Washington	38	2	4	5.0	10.0
12	Montreal	36	16	21	30.8	40.4
13	Brussels	36	8	36	18.2	81.8
14	Bonn	33	6	10	15.4	25.6
15	Essen	33	0	4	0	12.1
16	The Hague*	29	6	21	17.1	60.0
17	Philadelphia	29	0	2	0	6.9
18	Zurich	28	2	18	6.7	60.0
19	Osaka	27	6	1	18.2	3.0
20	Dallas	26	2	0	7.1	0

Notes: All degrees are weighted by the number of shared directors; they therefore indicate the total number of interlocking directorships sited in a given city.
* Includes Rotterdam

network. New York's prominence in transnational interlocking derives mainly from the sheer number of corporate head offices it hosts as metropole of world capitalism's leading national economy. In its transnational degree, however, New York resembles Montreal and The Hague, and ranks only slightly ahead of Zurich and Frankfurt. Along with Chicago and the other five American cities in the table, New York scores rather low in extraversion. Like New York, Paris and London host many large corporations, to the point that their local networks entirely dominate their respective national networks. But these metropolises are also centres for transnational interlocks, some of which reach across the North Atlantic, albeit to different cities on the other side. Tokyo is, as we have seen, quite marginal as a site for transnational elite connections, yet it is absolutely central to the Japanese national network. Most interlocks involving Tokyo-based firms lead to other Tokyo-based firms, and most interlocks involving Osaka-based firms lead to firms based in another Japanese city, namely Tokyo. Indeed, in accordance with H_1, the intracity values in Table 3.1 identify precisely the

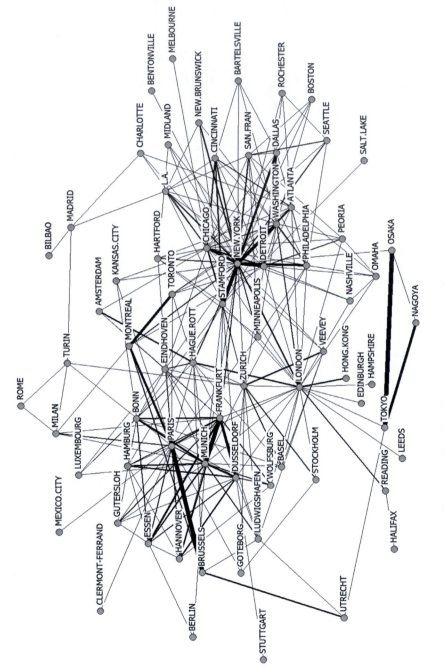

Figure 3.6 The global inter-urban network of seventy connected cities

four cities commonly cited as 'global', although the ordering is perhaps surprising: Paris, Tokyo, London and New York are the sites for extensive *intra*-urban corporate networks.

Several mainly European cities (Brussels, The Hague, Zurich, to some extent Montreal, Frankfurt and Munich) host a more modest number of large corporations and have weak local networks but extensive transnational connections. In contrast, secondary cities in the USA and Japan (Detroit, Stamford, Philadelphia, Dallas, Osaka) lack extensive local or transnational networks but are ensconced in their national networks. Part of the difference between the secondary cities of Europe and the United States has to do with the political division of continental Europe into many states (some of them rather small) in contrast to the integrated, continental political space that characterizes the United States. The ties linking Brussels-based companies to nearby Paris and Utrecht register as transnational interlocks, while the ties linking Philadelphia-based firms to New York and Washington, DC, are national in scope. In this regard, Germany – Europe's largest national economy – resembles the United States: its cities show extensive inter-urban ties but lower degrees of transnational interlocking. Overall, and consistent with H_3, transnational interlocking is concentrated among two North American and seven European cities with transnational degrees of 15 or more. Together these nine account for 51.8 per cent of all the transnational ties in the network of seventy cities.

In Figure 3.6 we present the entire inter-urban global network, which is clearly clustered along national lines. New York appears as the central hub of the US network (most of whose cities have no transnational links). New York's transnational ties lead primarily to London, which has the most cosmopolitan ties of any city and so dominates its network that other inter-urban ties within Britain are sparse and weak. Several inter-urban corridors provide strong bases for national integration – e.g. Tokyo–Osaka, Montreal–Toronto, Munich–Frankfurt. The last of these is especially interesting, as we have seen, for the way in which Frankfurt-based financial institutions are heavily interlocked with Munich-based industrials. But the German network is also densely linked to Paris, and to the extensive French network it houses. What stands out in this complete mapping of the global inter-urban corporate network is:

1 the Paris-centred intermingling of European corporate elites (compared, say, to the rather sparse ties between Canadian and American cities);
2 the close ties between Montreal, Paris and Brussels;
3 the very sparse ties between Paris and American cities;
4 the position of London as well as the Dutch and Swiss cities as *brokers* between the USA and continental Europe;
5 the marginality of Tokyo, Osaka and Melbourne; and
6 a nearly complete absence of cities from capitalism's semi-periphery.

TABLE 3.2 Primary and secondary interlocking in the global network

| Spatial span | Type of interlocking directorship | | Total | |
	Primary	Secondary	Column (%)	Number
Intracity (%)	34.8	65.2	37.2	838
Intercity and intra-country (%)	27.3	72.7	40.0	900
Transnational (%)	18.8	81.3	22.8	512
Total (%)	28.2	71.8	100.0	
Total number	634	1,616		2,250

Indeed, of the eighteen cities that host major corporate head offices but are entirely isolated from the global network, thirteen could be reasonably described as semi-peripheral (namely, São Paulo, Brasilia, Rio de Janeiro, Caracas, Buenos Aires, Moscow, Seoul, Pohang City, Taipei, Singapore, Kuala Lumpur, New Delhi and Johannesburg).[10]

Earlier in this chapter we distinguished between the primary interlocks (carried by inside directors) that have often served as vehicles of coordination and control across firms, and the secondary interlocks (carried by outside directors) that may contribute to elite integration and class hegemony without conducting instrumental corporate power. How, circa 1996, did primary interlocks appear in the global inter-urban network? In Table 3.2 it is clear that primary interlocking was most common among companies based in the same cities and least common among firms based in different countries. Less than a fifth of transnational interlocks involved insiders in one or both of the linked firms, but more than a third of intracity interlocks were primary. Interlocks predominantly linked firms in different cities but in the same country, followed closely by interlocks between companies based in the same city. Circa 1996, the transnational network was for the most part supplementary to the more numerous interlocks – many of them primary – that knit together the directorates of companies based in the same country and very often the same city. This pattern seriously qualifies our second working hypothesis. In 1996, interlocking directorships linking the world's cities across national borders comprised only 22.8 per cent of all interlocks in the global network, and were carried by outside directors, detached from the instrumentalities of strategic control and coordination.

Even so, to the extent that primary interlocks indicate functional relations it is worthwhile considering which cities, and which inter-urban axes, figure most prominently in these instrumental expressions of corporate power. Of the 70 connected cities comprising the entire global corporate network, 17 are isolated from the global network of primary interlocks. These cities, 6 of them American, 7 Continental and 3 British, hook into the global network only by means of secondary ties; their corporate elites seem uninvolved in the strategic coordination and control of corporate business across cities. The remaining 53 cities form a single connected network of inter-urban primary interlocks; 25 of them, however, lack any transnational ties. These include 12 cities with one tie each to another city in the same country, 8 cities with ties to two other cities in the same country and 5 cities with ties to three or more other cities in the same country.

Figure 3.7 maps the network of primary inter-urban interlocks among the twenty-eight cities that serve as sites for transnational primary interlocking (line thickness indicates the number of primary interlocks that span the cities, which varies from 1 to 5). All four commonly cited global cities participate in the network, although Tokyo has only a single tie to London. New York, a sociometric star in the connected network of six American cities, has only two (single) transnational interlocks, terminating in Montreal and Frankfurt – a much-diminished profile compared to its prominence in Table 3.1 and Figure 3.6. Overall, the American network becomes much smaller and sparser when we restrict attention to primary interlocks. As a marker of the extent to which the American network is carried by outside directors, New York's intercity degree plummets from 165 to 19 when only primary interlocks are considered. In contrast, the Continental European network remains well integrated by virtue of Paris and Frankfurt's centrality as well as the extensive primary ties among German cities and the less profuse ties between German cities and other Continental cities. Of sixteen Continental cities with primary transnational ties, fourteen form a connected component. Recalling our discussion of the Paris archipelago (Figure 3.5), it seems that many of the inter-urban primary interlocks on the Continent link major French, German, Belgian and other corporations into functional relations of strategic and allocative power, just as Montreal's strong ties to Paris and Brussels signify the participation of the Montreal-based Demaraises in a transatlantic financial group. But what of the other primary interlocks that make the network more then a pan-European configuration? Two examples will serve to illustrate the kinds of elite-level relations that are involved.

First, consider the three primary interlocks that link Washington to London. All three of these involved, in 1996, the exchange of directors between two giant telecommunications companies, MCI and British Telecom (BT). Peter Bonfield, president of BT, and Alan Rudge, vice-president, were outside directors of MCI; Bert Roberts, Jr, president of MCI, returned the favour by serving as an outside director of BT. At the time to which our data refer BT and MCI were partners in a joint venture underpinned by BT's 20 per cent stake in MCI. In 1997 BT acquired the remaining shares in MCI and relaunched itself as Concert. Second, consider the primary interlocks that in 1996 linked Kansas City to Bonn and Paris, and Paris to Mexico City. The presidents of Deutsche Telekom (Ron Sommer) and France Telecom (Michel Bon) each sat as outside directors on the

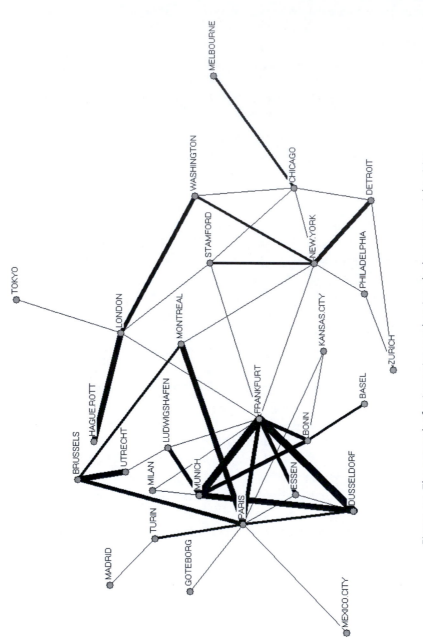

Figure 3.7 The network of primary inter-urban interlocks: twenty-eight cities with transnational ties

board of Kansas City-based Sprint Telecom, while another executive of France Telecom (Jean-Yves Gouiffes) was an outside director of Teléfonos de México. At the time to which our data refer, Deutsche Telekom and France Telecom each had a 10 per cent stake in Sprint, and all three companies were participating in the Global One joint venture. France Telecom owned a minority stake in Telemex, which it had acquired when the utility was privatized in 1990, although Grupo Carso (owned by Carlos Slim Helú, Telemex's chairman but not otherwise involved in the global corporate network) held a controlling interest. Not all transnational primary ties are so clearly interpretable in instrumental terms. For instance, the links between Zurich, Detroit and Philadelphia are carried by Percy Barnevick, president of Zurich-based ABB and an outside director of General Motors and DuPont. Here, no relation of strategic control is evident, and we can only speculate about possible instrumental motives. From company websites we learn that ABB had maintained close commercial relations with both GM and Dupont, and in the late 1990s established a joint venture with the latter to create fuel cells. ABB had also supplied GM with high-precision robots while employing Dupont's NOMEX insulation in its power transformers. These examples indicate that the network is based, in part, on specific relations of inter-corporate control and coordination.

Conclusion

Our findings suggest that the inter-urban network of corporate interlocks is structured somewhat differently from global cities networks that have been researched to date. As a transnational configuration of corporate elites, this network manifests its own specific form – a Euro-North American configuration in which Paris, London and New York, but also Brussels, Montreal, Frankfurt, The Hague and Zurich, are prominent. Tokyo, a principal global city in most analyses, is quite peripheral to the network, and New York's centrality derives substantially from its prominence within corporate America. Other American cities have rather little involvement with the transnational network, but Montreal, a second- or third-tier city by most accounts, is particularly prominent by virtue of its ties to continental Europe.

It is clear that the network is concentrated in a very few cities, reflecting the concentration of corporate power in command centres that in some cases entirely dominate their respective countries. This supports our first working hypothesis. Yet most interlocks link companies based in the same country, and the main global cities are not necessarily tied to each other. The network has a structure that is more nationally focused, and more complex, than that predicted by our second working hypothesis.

Strikingly, Paris is almost entirely detached from New York and other American cities, yet central on the Continent. If one were to seek a structural basis in the network for elite fractionalization, the New York–Paris fissure would merit closer scrutiny. Although, as predicted by H_3, the inter-urban corporate-elite network is essentially a North Atlantic formation (indeed, a configuration of the north-east of North America and the north-west of Europe), it seems, as of 1996, to have two segments, one Anglo-American and the other continental European. In keeping with regional patterns, the Paris archipelago is by far the more integrated. Yet what really stand out are two findings; in the first place, the marginality of cities outside the North Atlantic heartland – even those in southern Europe and western North America, let alone Asia, Latin America and Africa. If, as suggested in Chapter 1, the transnational corporate network exists as a relatively thin 'superstructure' atop more sturdy national networks, this chapter has further documented the exclusion from that superstructure of the semi-peripheral cities that house many of the world's people. In this respect, the 1996 network mirrors the well-known North–South pattern of global inequality, and cautions us about claims that the core/periphery structure of the world system is being transformed as semi-peripheral cities move into global capitalism's core (see Alderson and Beckfield 2004: 847–8). In the structure of global corporate power, the inter-urban corporate-elite network has not subverted the dominance of the developed capitalist core; it has reinforced it.

What also stands out, again in contradiction to our second working hypothesis, is the predominantly *national* character of most corporate interlocking, and especially of primary interlocking. Only on the European continent, in the ties connecting the Montreal-based Desmarais group to its European partners and in specific inter-corporate alignments spanning cities (e.g. in the rapidly centralizing telecom sector), do we find an extent and pattern of interlocking suggestive of instrumental elite integration across global cities. As a global and historical macro-structure, the inter-urban elite network seems to have arisen through a plurality of socio-historical processes as well as spatio-temporal constraints. Instead of an integrated configuration of elite-level ties among the world's major cities (H_2), we find a patchy, uneven network that has likely been shaped by several interrelated factors:

1 Transnational political-economic structures and institutions that have set the context for international business activity, and for elite-level relations. Beginning with the Marshall Plan of 1947, the North Atlantic has been consolidated as a 'heartland' for the international circulation of capital and commodities (van der Pijl 1984: 148–50; 1998: 89; Sassen 2002: 10–12). More recently, and partly as a competitive response to challenges posed by both the USA and Japan, Europe has been evolving into a confederation, knitted together not only by legal statutes, trade relations and a common currency but by elite groups such as the European Round Table of Industrialists, which we consider in Chapter 7. The rest of the world tends either to be integrated *into* the Euro-North American heartland or detached from it.

2 Nationally specific legal frameworks and business systems. Here, the contrast is between the voice-based, organized form of corporate capitalism that evolved on the Continent (with propensities towards extensive board-level functional relations between firms) and the exit-based Anglo-American business system which has been structured more around the stock exchange, resulting in lower propensities to interlocking (especially primary interlocking) among American and British firms (Doremus et al. 1998; Whitley 1999).

3 Linguistic/cultural affinities – evident in the Montreal–Brussels–Paris configuration (which includes a transnational financial group headed by French-speaking patriarchs based in Brussels and Montreal), but also in the extensive secondary ties linking American cities with London.

4 The structure of political space – the division of continents into nation-states whose boundaries establish the very basis for distinguishing 'national' from 'transnational' relations. The vast size of the United States as a continental nation-state contrasts sharply with the division of Europe into many states, with the upshot that inter-urban ties within North America tend to occur *within* the same state while many inter-urban ties in Europe are transnational.

5 The physical constraints of geographical space. The business of boards generally requires physical co-presence of directors, monthly or several times a year. Despite advances in long-haul transportation, travel times between, say, Melbourne and New York still present obstacles to interlocking. As if to confirm this, in 2004 Rupert Murdoch's News Corp., one of the world's largest media corporations, with major investments in the USA, moved its head office from Adelaide, Australia, to New York.

In combination, these factors can account for the proximities of cities within the corporate network and the departure in our findings from a hypothesized scenario in which the network would be most developed among the leading global cities (H_2).

The second factor has specific relevance to the inter-urban corporate network and the tenacity of nationally bound relations within it. The practices that generate this network have to do with the management and control of corporations and the exercise of strategic and allocative power within particular contexts (Scott 1997). To be sure, nationally and regionally specific business systems have engendered path dependencies in the transition to globalized capitalism (Whitley 1999), which are evident in our findings.

For quite different reasons, corporate interlocking is a less common practice in Japan and the USA, and this partly accounts for the relative marginality of many Japanese and American firms (and cities) in the network. In Japan, corporate capital has been organized into tightly knit groups within which strategic and allocative power is centralized on the basis of cross-ownership of shares (Gerlach 1992), but corporate directorates tend not to interlock very extensively.

Instead, companies send executives to each other, who later return to the original posting – the 'interlock' exists as a temporal flow of personnel (Westney 1996). This practice, no doubt combined with language barriers, the historical exclusion of Japan from the North Atlantic heartland (van der Pijl 1998) and the disincentives posed by Japan's spatial location, helps explain why Japanese-based corporations – and thus Japanese cities – are so marginal in the network. American capitalism has been structured more around the stock exchange than around the institutionalized relations of organized capitalism. Because allocative power has been less institutionalized in close financial–industrial relations, the American corporate network has been loosely knit (Scott 1997; Windolf 2002). It became looser in the 1980s and early 1990s as changes in corporate finance and governance weakened bank hegemony (Davis and Mizruchi 1999). Britain has also had a diffuse business system (Scott 1997), but the City has long held a central position in international finance, and capital ties to the nearby European continent (especially the Dutch connection), together with a colonial legacy linking London to Hong Kong, raise London's transnational profile.

It is on the European continent that we find the densest clutch of transnational interlocks (including most of the primary ties), spanning mainly across cities of the north-west. Elsewhere, I have reported that the mean degree of interlocking among the eighty-one dominant corporations domiciled in the north-western corner of the European continent is actually higher than the mean among the ninety US-based firms in our Global 350. In this sense, 'the corporate elite of northwestern Europe is more socially integrated than the American corporate elite' (Carroll 2004: 142). Partly an upshot of the political division of Europe into many states, the Continental network is more than just a recent by-product of the formation of the European Union, as important as that may be. Its path dependencies – as in the propensity for strong ties between financial and industrial forms of capital – reach back to the inception of organized capitalism (Doremus et al. 1998). In Germany, France and other Continental countries, strongly institutionalized credit relations centred on banks and the interweaving of shareholdings have tended to produce dense interlock networks, reflecting the structure of strategic control and allocative power (Scott 1997: 142–69). As national borders within Europe weaken, capital relations deepen, particularly along a Franco-German axis. Canada bears some resemblance to Europe in its more centralized banking apparatus with a history of dense ties to industry, and in its corporate empires based on inter-corporate ownership (Carroll and Lewis 1991), one of which now links Montreal to Brussels and Paris in the strongest set of transatlantic ties, a veritable transnational financial group.

These considerations take us well beyond our working hypotheses and provide a more nuanced view of the structure of global corporate power and global cities at the close of the twentieth century. The network of inter-urban interlocking is indeed concentrated within the main global cities (H_1), and centred upon

Sassen's northern transatlantic economic system (H_3), but the major global cities do not necessarily connect with each other (contradicting H_2), and certain second-tier cities are surprisingly prominent. If economic globalization has effected a partial 'freeing' of cities from the spaces defined by nation-states (P. J. Taylor 2004), at the level of corporate elites the network remains strongly focused, and largely contained, within statist boundaries (which themselves are shifting, with the political integration of Europe).

What, then, do our results imply for the 'new network bourgeoisie' – the transnational capitalist class? It would be difficult, from the evidence presented here, to characterize the new network bourgeoisie as the predominant fraction within the global structure of capital and class. The transnational inter-urban network is carried by a small number of directors, and involves a minority of the world's largest companies. Its ties are predominantly indicative of expressive rather than instrumental inter-corporate relations – although important instances of transnational strategic and allocative power relations are evident. The highly uneven participation and centrality of global cities within the network, and the overall salience of within-country ties, casts doubt upon the notion that with globalization and the rise of global cities, state–society complexes and nationally integrated corporate elites have been 'disorganized' and 'disarticulated' as transnational linkages proliferate (Scott 1997: 241). In short, as an integrated formation the new network bourgeoisie seems to be very much in its infancy.

On this issue, however, one major caveat must be registered. Interlocking corporate directorates give us one window on global corporate organization. Primary interlocks trace relations of strategic and allocative power; secondary interlocks may be unrelated to such inter-corporate instrumentalities, yet they weave corporate directors into a solidaristic business community, enhancing their capacity to exercise political and cultural leadership. But other kinds of ties might serve similar instrumental and expressive functions for a new network bourgeoisie.

In Chapter 2 we saw that participation of corporate directors on the boards of global policy-planning groups plays a dramatic role in integrating the global corporate network. A new network bourgeoisie may be integrated by these kinds of expressive relations, which complement interlocking corporate directorships while projecting the business activism Useem (1984) studied within national settings on to a transnational field. The global network of corporate boards and policy groups provides an additional layer of social organization in the life of the corporate elite, and, to the extent that groups such as the World Economic Forum exercise some modicum of cultural power and political influence, this additional layer may serve a hegemonic function.

An important study by Alderson and Beckfield (2004) makes a similar point with regard to the *operational* form of corporate power. As noted in the Introduction, elite-level connections across boards have no relevance to operational power, yet this power, exercised *within* corporations, is absolutely integral to the functioning of global capitalism. Within each transnational corporation, operational power radiates from head office and extends, via subsidiaries, into labour processes in various cities and countries. Alderson and Beckfield's study of the global network of parent–subsidiary relations within the world's 500 largest transnational corporations provides a partial mapping of global operational power that complements the elite-level analysis presented here, and reveals further nuances in the inter-urban network. At the centre of the network, these researchers found a densely connected block of four cities: Tokyo, New York, Paris and London – the host cities for many of the world's largest companies. What Alderson and Beckfield's study reveals is that the four leading cities are linked, via parent–subsidiary relations, in a global network of operational power that 'comes close to approximating an idealized *core/periphery* structure' (ibid.: 847). Just as we have found for the corporate-elite network, this structure is concentrated among the major cities of capitalism's core. One major difference stands out, however. For reasons elaborated above, Tokyo and New York appear in the global corporate-elite network as less central than London and Paris. Yet they are absolutely central in the network of transnational operational power (ibid.: 830). Indeed, Tokyo (followed by New York) is the most central point in the entire inter-urban network of parent-to-subsidiary relations. Quite independently of the elite network analysed here, the transnational structure of operational power provides an extensive basis for a 'new network bourgeoisie', centred in the four main cities of the triad but extending through parent–subsidiary relations to more than three thousand cities worldwide. Important though they are in the organization of strategic, allocative and hegemonic power, elite-level relations give us only the top tier, the most visible aspect, of a more extensive structure. If we include within the new network bourgeoisie the executives who manage the many, dispersed branch plants of TNCs – as does Sklair (2001) in his definition of the transnational capitalist class – then its organizational basis seems much more substantial.

PART TWO

Into the twenty-first century: the changing organization of corporate power

4 | Transnational accumulation and global networking

Into the twenty-first century

Corporate power is organized in part through the elite relations that constitute the object of this study. Yet the *material basis* for corporate power lies not in these relations but in the ongoing process of accumulation that reproduces capitalism's class relations on an expanding scale. Refracted through the world's largest corporations, the accumulation process is visible in a shifting composition at the top of the hierarchy of firms. In Chapter 1, we noted the late twentieth-century recomposition of the leading corporations, as American dominance faded and as tertiary-sector activities gained prominence. This chapter takes us into the twenty-first century, with a more in-depth examination of the changing composition of the world's 500 leading corporations (G500). Our primary interest is in exploring the shape of these shifts and their implications for global corporate power.

Here and in the four chapters that follow, we draw upon a single database assembled first by designating the G500 corporations, at two-year intervals, beginning at year-end 1996 and continuing through 2006. The data, consisting of the directorships of individuals and the attributes of both individuals and organization, are similar to data analysed in Chapters 1–3, but the selection of firms differs slightly. The starting point was *Fortune* magazine's Global 500, published each July and incorporating financial data from the end of the previous year. The *Fortune* list offers a consistent time series, good coverage across the entire range of industries and corporate domiciles, and additional data on country of domicile and industry for each listed firm. It consists of the 500 largest corporations, ranked by total revenue in $US. As a measure of size, revenue favours commercial and industrial capital (firms with high volumes of sales) over financial capital (firms whose assets may be vast but whose revenue consists in interest, dividends and the like; Carroll and Fennema 2004). To ensure adequate representation of financial capital, we adopted the procedure used in previous comparative studies of corporate networks (Stokman et al. 1985; Windolf 2002) and stratified selection of firms so that in any year 20 per cent were financial institutions and 80 per cent non-financial corporations. The G500, then, includes a G400 (the largest industrials, ranked by revenue) and a G100 (the largest financials, ranked by assets).[1]

For each company of adequate size, at two-year intervals beginning in 1996 and ending in 2006, we obtained names of directors from corporate annual reports, available electronically at official corporate websites or in the Mergent Online database.[2] The resulting file of verified corporate affiliations for 22,551 individuals and 804 corporations enables us to track the changing organization of corporate power over the decade.

Recomposition of the accumulation base

The G500 are the units of capital that form the global corporate elite's 'accumulation base' (Carroll 1982), and we are particularly interested in shifts in their spatial and sectoral distribution. Such shifts are a source of change in the corporate network, as firms gain or lose standing in capital's global league table. Previous research using similar samples of Global 500 companies has confirmed the continuing predominance of corporations based in capitalism's core, the 'triad' (North America, western Europe and Japan/Australia/New Zealand), although Sklair and Robbins (2002) have made the case for a growing if still modest segment of global corporate capital based in the South. In these comparisons, it is illuminating to divide the Global 500 into its two basic components: the 100 largest financial institutions and the 400 largest non-financial (hereafter 'industrial') firms. The former, as we have argued, are key centres of *allocative* power in global capitalism (Mintz and Schwartz 1985); they gather money capital from various sources and (in theory at least) steer it towards the most promising ventures. The latter are the organizations within which actual

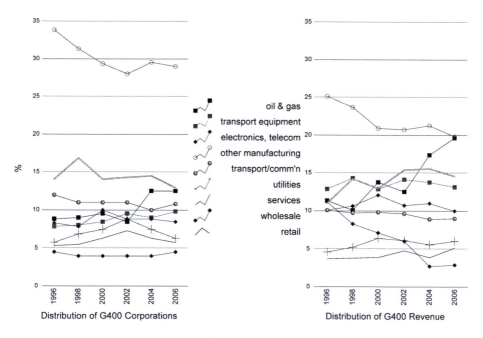

Figure 4.1 Industrial composition of the G400, 1996–2006

commodities are produced and marketed. In this case, corporate power asserts itself at place-specific points of production and in marketing practices aimed at wholesale or retail buyers.

Figure 4.1 charts the changing composition of G400 industrials. The intricate technical division of labour in contemporary capitalism creates a complex structure of industry, which we have reduced to nine manageable categories. The first four involve manufacturing processes; the next two involve industrial services (transport and communication, utilities); the last three encompass tertiary activities of sales and other services. Across the decade, the number of G400 firms producing oil and/or gas grew substantially, as did the complement of manufacturers of transportation equipment, while the number of retailers, after an initial increase, showed a net decline. Other sectors exhibited no clear-cut trends, except for the overall decrease in the broad category of other manufacturers. The chart's right panel weights the 400 cases by revenue. Here we find evidence of a massive concentration of capital in a decreasing number of retailers, as their share of total revenues grows to nearly 15 per cent. The concentration of capital in retail sales contrasts sharply with the trend in wholesale; five Japanese and two South Korean trading companies (including Mitsubishi Corp., Mitsui, Itochu, Sumitomo and Samsung) shrink dramatically.

The oil and gas sector accounts for the other major shift. In 2006, the revenue claimed by fifty G400 firms in this sector equalled that of 116 other manufacturers. In these shifts we can discern the effects of (1) the 1997 Asian financial crisis, which hit Korean and Japanese corporate capital hard, (2) the skyrocketing price of oil after 2001 (with growing security concerns in the wake of September 11), and (3) the consolidation, under control of giant retailers like US-based Wal-Mart, of the 'global supermarket' (Buckman 2004). Across the decade, corporations specialized in oil/gas production, transportation equipment manufacture and retail sales increase their share of G400 revenue from 35.2 per cent to 47.3 per cent. The trends depict a global capitalism chronically reliant on fossil fuels, automobility and ever-expanding consumerism.

Global corporate capital is unevenly distributed not only industrially, but spatially. Figure 4.2 charts the Global 500 both by economic sector and by domicile of head office. It contrasts the G100 financials with the G400 industrials, and groups domiciles into six categories: three zones of the core and three zones of the semi-periphery (S-P).[3] The right-hand panels show the amount of the total capital represented by firms based in the six zones, reckoned in current US dollars.

For the world's 100 largest financial institutions (shown in the lower panels), the story is familiar: *in 1996 every head office of these centres of allocative power was located within the triad*. Two ensuing developments are notable. North America and particularly Europe consolidate their status as the locus for the lion's share of head offices and financial assets, while financial capital based

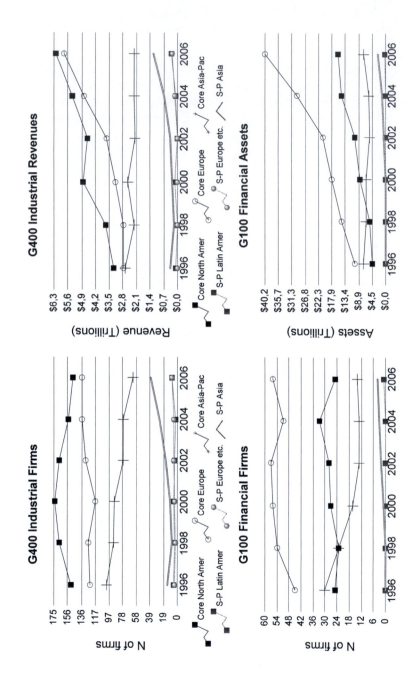

Figure 4.2 Regional trends in capital accumulation, 1996–2006

in Japan loses position. Second, semi-peripheral Asia (specifically, China and South Korea) emerges as the one locus outside the core for giant financial institutions, as the Bank of China, the Industrial and Commercial Bank of China, the China Construction Bank and the Kookmin Bank (of Seoul) enter the G100.[4] When we consider the assets controlled by these 100 financial institutions, the growing concentration of the command of capital in Europe and North America is even sharper. The share of total assets controlled by giant financials based in Japan crashes to 9.3 per cent; the share controlled in Europe (expanding to a remarkable 60.8 per cent) and North America reaches 84.8 per cent. The world's leading sources of allocative corporate power remain ensconced mainly in Euro-North America, but increasingly in Europe.

A closer analysis shows that Europe's rising stature as a centre of finance is attributable particularly to UK-based firms, whose share of G500 assets nearly doubles from 8.7 per cent to 15.1 per cent, but also reflects the growing assets of financials based in France, the Netherlands, Switzerland, Sweden, Spain and Ireland. The dramatic gains by UK-based finance, whose thirteen G100 members represent $10 trillion in assets in 2006 – only $4 trillion less than the nineteen US-based financials – enhance London's status as an alpha global city.

To some degree, the same holds for the world's 400 largest non-financials, although the place-specific character of commodity production favours the location of many head offices near production sites. Here we do find a few corporations domiciled on the semi-periphery in 1996, and the same pattern of recent growth in the Asia-Pacific semi-periphery combined with a somewhat less pronounced decline in corporate Japan. Once again, the increasing dominance of Euro-North America is accentuated when we consider the distribution of capital (in this case, total revenue), as opposed to firms, registering the size differential between giant corporations of the core and those of the semi-periphery. But in this instance corporate North America keeps pace with Europe, while the accumulation of Southern-based industrial capital is vigorous.

Looking within the broad regional categories, several nuances become evident. Within North America, the mild decline in the number of G400 industrials from 151 to 148 masks divergent tendencies in Canada and the USA, as the complement of industrials based in Canada rises from five to nine. If we include Bermuda-registered firms as effectively US-based, corporate America's share of the G400 drops from 167 to 158. This decline is concentrated in the more industrial sectors of the G400: across the decade, the number of US- (and Bermuda-) based service/trade firms grows from 35 to 44 but the number engaged in industrial activity falls from 111 to 96. In comparison, for the core European region, the number of firms engaged in industrial activity grows from 97 to 110. Within Europe, industrial capital based in Britain (dropping from 30 to 24 G400 firms) and Italy (dropping from 9 to 6) declines while the Nordic countries (rising from 3 to 12), Spain (from 3 to 8) and the Netherlands (from 5 to 11) gain head

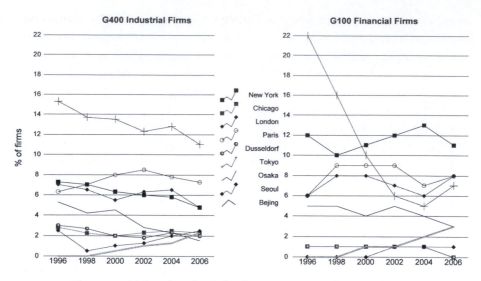

Figure 4.3 Main urban domiciles for G500 corporations, 1996–2006

offices. On the semi-periphery, the pattern of capital accumulation is especially uneven. In 1996, only four G400 firms were based in semi-peripheral Europe, the Middle East and Africa, and only five were based in Latin America (three in Brazil). Semi-peripheral Asia hosted fourteen companies, eleven of them domiciled in South Korea (with another two in India). The East Asian financial crisis of 1997 decimated South Korean corporate capital, and ultimately opened opportunities for North American and European corporations to acquire part of South Korea's industrial base at a song, courtesy of IMF conditionalities. By 1998, only seven firms based on the Asian semi-periphery remained in the G400, and only three of these were domiciled in South Korea. Yet the following eight years witnessed a recovery of South Korea-based corporate capital (from six industrials in 2000 to twelve in 2006). Even more significantly, China-based firms entered the G400 in numbers, as large Chinese business organizations adopted the corporate form (Clarke 2007: 215–17). Absent from the G400 as recently as 1998, Chinese firms numbered thirteen by the end of 2006. At that end-point, thirty-eight of the world's largest industrial corporations were based in semi-peripheral Asia. Besides China and South Korea, only two countries served as major hosts – India and Taiwan, with five firms each. But among all these, only Chinese capitalism had attained a significant, and significantly state-organized, combination of large-scale financial and industrial capital.

Other zones of the semi-periphery manifest much more modest incursions into the G400, and as we have seen, register no major financial institutions by 2006. In Latin America, where the total 2006 complement of G400 firms came to seven, the number headquartered in Brazil stayed at three; only Mexico gained stature as host to four corporations. As for the rest of the world, which housed eight G400 companies in 2006, only Russia evidenced a major carbon-fuelled gain, from one in 1999 to five in 2006. Africa lost its single firm with Anglo-American Corporation's move from Johannesburg to London in 1999.

In 2006, the pre-eminence of the USA among nation-states remained striking. With 154 G500 corporations (135 of them industrials), the USA towered above all other host countries. The erosion of American dominance we noted in Chapter 1 continued, however. By year-end 2006, 192 G500 firms (136 of them industrials) called Europe home. Accompanying this shift towards Europe was both the rise of the South and the fall of corporate Japan – particularly its financial sector. The accumulation of capital within giant corporations based on the semi-periphery was focused in a few countries – China, South Korea, Taiwan, India, Russia, Mexico and Brazil – which in 2006 accounted for fifty-two of fifty-eight G500 corporations based in the global South.

Figure 4.3 depicts the percentage of major firms with head offices in nine key cities, each of which served as a host for at least ten G500 head offices in either 1996 or 2006. These charts show highly mixed secular trends. The four alpha global cities – New York, London, Paris and Tokyo – claimed 35.9 per cent of the G400 and 46 per cent of the G100 in 1996. By 2006, the respective proportions were 27.8 per cent and 34 per cent. Most of the emptying out involved Tokyo, whose G100 complement shrank by 70 per cent after 1996. For Osaka, Japan's other omnibus business centre, the decline in giant industrials was particularly steep.

Interestingly, London and New York also declined as head office locations for the world's largest industrials. In finance, these cities show divergent trends, with London posting a net gain of two major financial institutions by 2006, and New York a net loss of one. In contrast, Paris is the one alpha global city that registered gains in the command of industry and finance. Two secondary cities of the core, Chicago and Düsseldorf, show gentle declines as command centres while Beijing manifests the strongest and most consistent increases on both industrial and financial sides. By 2006, it has overtaken Osaka and Chicago, though it remains decidedly secondary to the four alpha cities. The only other city of the semi-periphery that clears the bar for this analysis, Seoul, collapsed as a business centre with the 1997 Asian financial meltdown, but thereafter recovered lost ground, even adding one financial institution, as several Korean corporations rose from the ashes. Overall, the nine major centres account for a much-reduced share of the G500 by 2006 (a decline from 251 to 194 companies). Much of the emptying out from these nine urban centres reflects the collapse of corporate Japan after 1997. The decrease in G500 corporations headquartered in Tokyo and Osaka, forty-nine, nearly matches the net decrease of fifty-seven. The shift also marks, however, the increasing prominence of several beta global cities.

Indeed, what the decade appears to bring is a modest *dispersion* of corporate

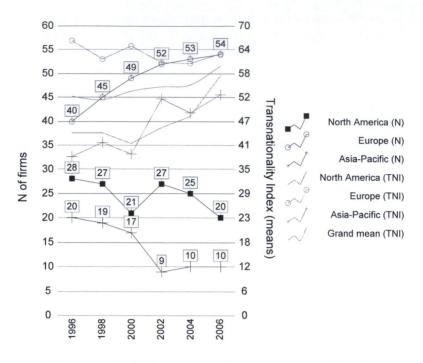

Figure 4.4 UNCTAD transnationality among G400 industrial
corporations of the triad

command centres. Within the core, the gains are mostly in the smaller states of Europe. Most spectacularly, Stockholm comes to host five industrial and four financial giants (up from two industrials in 1996). Madrid gains three industrial head offices (from a base of four in 1996) and retains Santander Bank as a major financial institution, while Zurich registers the same net gain of three head offices to host eight in 2006. Amsterdam's clutch of head offices grows by three, to seven; Dublin moves from obscurity to host four corporations; and Helsinki, home base for one G500 firm in 1996, hosts three at year-end 2006. The Anglo-American tax haven Bermuda, which we have classified as part of North America, attracts three G500 corporations with strong ownership and management ties to the USA, to host four head offices in 2006. On the other hand, three beta cities of the core decline, as Washington, DC, loses three head offices to retain four, Detroit sheds two to retain three, and Kobe loses three to retain only one. On the semi-periphery, besides Beijing and Seoul, Taipei gains G500 head offices (adding four to host five) as does Mumbai (moving from zero to three), Moscow (from one to four), Mexico City (from one to three) and Shanghai (from zero to two). A host of semi-peripheral cities became domiciles of single G500 corporations, contributing further to the global dispersion. In 1996, only 13 semi-peripheral cities hosted any G500 firms; by 2006, 23 did (13 of which hosted one G500 firm each).

The slow but steady dispersion of head offices is not the only trend, accompanying recent globalization, that has recomposed the G500. The firms themselves have continued to transnationalize their capital circuits. This can be seen in the tabulations of corporate 'transnationality', published by the United Nations Conference on Trade and Development (UNCTAD) in its *World Investment Report*. There are various markers of corporate transnationality, e.g. size of foreign assets or sales, ratio of foreign to total assets, number of foreign subsidiaries, proportion of subsidiaries that are foreign, number of countries in which a company has subsidiaries (UNCTAD 2008: 26–9). Since 1993, UNCTAD has published a Transnationality Index (TNI), 'a composite of three ratios: foreign assets to total assets, foreign sales to total sales, and foreign employment to total employment', which assesses 'the degree to which the activities and interests of companies are embedded in their home country or abroad' (ibid.: 28). In Marxist terminology, the TNI gives a serviceable indication of the extent to which a firm's constant capital (assets), variable capital (employment) and commodity capital (sales) are located outside of its national domicile – that is, the extent to which it accumulates capital in circuits that are transnational and not simply contained within the home market. For the 100 largest non-financial TNCs worldwide, UNCTAD reports that the TNI increased by 14 points between 1993 and 2006 (ibid.: 28). Matching the UNCTAD 100 with our G400s, we find that the latter includes most but not all of the former. In 1996, 90 of the 100 firms identified by UNCTAD were in the G400; by 2006, 89 were. These companies are overwhelmingly located in the triad[5] – increasingly in Europe (see Figure 4.4). Moreover, enterprises in the UNCTAD 100 that call Europe home show higher mean TNI scores than firms based in North America or Japan/Australia, although increasing transnationality in the latter two categories narrows the difference by 2006.

For a more dynamic view of change in the global corporate elite's accumulation base, we can track the 'careers' of G500 firms by grouping them into three categories:

1 'Top Dogs', numbering 252, consistently rank among the G500;
2 'Fallen Angels', numbering 213, disappear from the G500 after 1996;
3 'Rising Stars', also numbering 213, count among the G500 in 2006, having entered the ranks of the world's largest corporations after 1996 (see Carroll and Klassen 2010)

These three trajectories account for 84.3 per cent of the 804 companies that were at some point in the G500 between 1996 and 2006. The remaining cases fall within two residual categories. They include firms too small to qualify for the G500 of 1996 and 2006, but large enough at some point in the interim to qualify (ninety-one companies), and firms large enough for the G500 of both 1996 and 2006, but not large enough to qualify in the intervening years (thirty-five companies). What the distinction between Top Dogs and Fallen Angels/Rising Stars gives us is a rough-and-ready division of global corporate capital into its most institutionally stable fraction and a more volatile fraction encompassing institutional change through differential rates of capital concentration, or major instances of restructuring and centralization.

Not surprisingly, the Top Dogs of global capitalism reside in the triad. North America (97 firms), western Europe (97 firms) and Japan/Australia (54 firms) are home to 98.4 per cent of all G500 Top Dogs. These giant corporations form an institutionally stable core for the organization of global economic power. On the other hand, the vast majority of semi-peripheral corporate capital appears as 'Rising Stars' (44 firms comprising 64.7 per cent of all Southern companies in the G500 at some point, 33 of which are domiciled on the Asian semi-periphery). Within the triad, corporate Japan's decline is plain in its 68 Fallen Angels, replaced by only 13 Rising Stars. Net decreases of this sort are also evident in Italy (10 Fallen Angels, 4 Rising Stars) and the USA (71 Fallen Angels, 58 Rising Stars), while in Canada (2 and 8), Australia (0 and 2) and much of western Europe more firms enter the G500 as of 2006 than exit after 1996. In five European states there are no disappearances, but only companies rising into the G500 – Sweden (6), Spain (5) the Netherlands and Ireland (4 each) and Denmark (2). With France gaining five G500 firms as its 16 Rising Stars replace 11 Fallen Angels, and the other major European states showing little net change, western Europe witnesses a gain of 85 Rising Stars as it loses 64 Fallen Angels.

These patterns tell a story of continuity and change, of continuing dominance by the world's largest monopolies, combined with uneven trajectories in the concentration and centralization of capital. Only 5 of the 213 Fallen Angels (4 based in the USA, 1 in Japan) fell so far as to go bankrupt after 1996. In many cases, companies simply failed to concentrate capital at sufficient rates to remain among the G500. Ninety-eight firms, 40 based in Japan, 28 in North America, 22 in Europe and 5 on the Asian semi-periphery, fit this description. Most of the other Fallen Angels disappeared in major corporate reorganizations that centralized capital into still larger units. Sixty-eight firms (32 in North America, 25 in Europe and 11 in Japan) were taken over by other G500 companies. Twenty-three disappeared in 'mergers of equals' between G500 corporations. Such mergers were especially important in reshaping Japan's corporate landscape, as ten financial institutions were consolidated in a sequence of mergers into three giant banks.[6]

The changing global corporate-interlock network

Consider now the directoral links among the world's largest 500 corporations. Across the decade, the total number of interlocking directorates between pairs of G500 corporations *falls* from 1,604 to 1,086. Expressed as network density, i.e. the percentage of all possible ties that actually exist, the drop is from 1.286

per cent to 0.871 per cent. That is, *the global network is thinning* – a trend that accentuates the trajectory from the 1970s, charted in Chapter 1. Coincident with the network's thinning has been the shrinking of corporate boards – a process that leaves fewer possibilities for interlocking directorships. In the most recent decade, the average size of corporate boards drops from 20.3 to 14.0, with much of the decrease occurring in the first four years (by 2000 the mean board size was 16.52). This substantial decline reflects the implementation of corporate governance reforms in various countries, favouring the exit-based, market-oriented Anglo-American model of smaller boards with fewer inside (executive) directors over the voice based, network-oriented regimes of Europe and Japan (Clarke 2007: 100–104, 138).

The background to this is complex, but a major impetus issues from the ascension in the 1980s of investor capitalism (Useem 1996; Bieling 2006: 432–3), wherein the high profit rates demanded by institutional investors are supposedly facilitated by slimming corporate boards to 'leaner, meaner' proportions while increasing board oversight capacities by appointing outside directors (Carroll 2004; Heemskerk 2007). The movement to reform corporate governance also gained impetus from high-profile financial scandals and failures in the USA and the UK, the most spectacular being that of Enron in 2001 (Clarke 2007: 152–8; Soederberg 2010). By 1999, in the wake of the Asian financial crisis, the OECD had enunciated its Principles of Corporate Governance as a universal framework. Elaborated further in 2004, the Principles attempt to raise standards worldwide for accountability, transparency and shareholder rights. Among other things, they mandate that 'board members should be able to commit themselves effectively to their responsibilities' (OECD 2004: 25) – a commitment discouraging 'service on too many boards' (ibid.: 65).[7] Corporate capital's organic intelligentsia in management science voiced the same concerns. An indicative study, evidencing anxiety about multiple directorships and elephantine directorates, used a Fortune 500 sample in attempting to demonstrate the pitfalls of multiple board memberships and overly large boards for monitoring CEO and corporate performance (Young et al. 2003). As discussed in Chapter 1, the Anglo-American model contrasts with more relational regimes of corporate governance, for which Germany provides the classic exemplar, with its large boards bearing many interlocks to associated corporations and financial institutions, as in Rudolf Hilferding's (1981 [1910]) notion of finance capital. Overall, the trend for both financial institutions and industrial corporations in Figure 4.5 continues to be towards the Anglo-American model, in the sense of smaller boards and therefore fewer directors available for interlocking.

The situation becomes clearly more complicated, however, as we consider the particular regions that the companies call home and the forms of capital (financial or industrial) they subtend. Although financial institutions continue to have larger boards than industrials, the decrease in board size is sharper

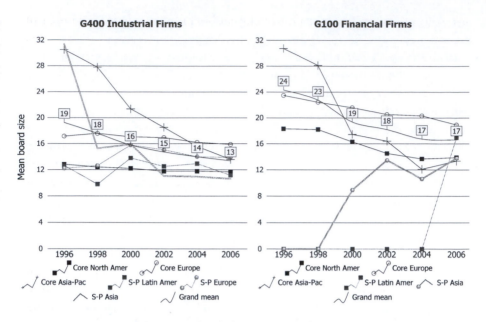

G400 Industrial Firms

G100 Financial Firms

Figure 4.5 Mean board size for G500 corporations, 1996–2006

among the former. The decline in mean board size is modest among industrial corporations based in the North Atlantic, and drastic among firms based in Asia. These regional differences intimate nationally specific processes. Much of the overall drop reflects radical governance reforms in Japan and South Korea, in the wake of the 1997 Asian financial crisis (Ahmadjian and Song 2004). Board size for industrial firms based in South Korea plummets from the highest (37.1) to one of the lowest (9.9) national means. The drop among financials in Canada is also sharp (from 29.8 to 16.5) as Canada's big banks adopt new norms of governance after the mid-1990s (Carroll 2008a). Yet in Germany, there is little change, as industrials and financials maintain boards respectively averaging 25.2 and 27.6 directors in 2006, only slightly diminished from a decade earlier. In part owing to the organizational inertia in the co-determination system, German corporations continue to have boards more than twice the size of their US counterparts, giving little evidence of harmonization down to an American norm. In this respect, the difference between Continental and Anglo-American forms of corporate governance persists.

Our main interest here is in the *national and transnational interlocks* that in the first case bond large corporations into national corporate communities and in the second bridge borders, creating the basis for a transnational corporate community. In this chapter, we focus on the level of the corporation, on ties among the world's largest companies, within and across national borders. These elite linkages are, however, always effected through individual directors, the focus of the two chapters that follow. At the corporate level, as the average directorate has been shrinking, the mean degree of national interlocking (the number of firms with which a given firm maintains interlocks) has indeed been falling, worldwide (see Figure 4.6). For the entire G500, mean degree drops from 6.42 to 4.34. This basic measure contains two additive components – the national and the transnational. As the graphs show, *the downward secular trend is wholly attributable to a decline in national interlocking*. Despite shrinking directorates, the degree of transnational interlocking actually increases slightly across the decade.[8]

In reading these trends, it is as well to note some peculiarities of the data. In the first place, a firm's degree of national interlocking is constrained by the number of other G500 firms domiciled in the same country. In 2006, for instance, six countries were hosts to single G500 firms. Although these firms could very well be centrally located within their respective national corporate communities, our singular focus on the largest firms in the world does not make these communities visible. Within the domain of the G500, such firms engage in no national interlocking. Much the same holds for firms domiciled in countries that contribute only a few firms to the G500, and thus for most of the semi-periphery, with the exception of South Korea and China (see Figure 4.2).[9] For this reason, in charting the regional trends in national interlocking, we show only the regions of the triad, plus semi-peripheral Asia. As we survey those regions, the thinning of national networks in North America (effectively the USA, since mean degree in the Canadian network declines only slightly, from 2.67 to 2.53) is striking. The trend in Europe is gentler, so that by 2006 the extent of national interlocking in the two regions of the North Atlantic has converged. Of course, the very large American network offers far more opportunities for interlocking, while in Europe the national division of economic space limits such opportunities (and creates more opportunities for transnational interlocking; see below). Strikingly, in 2006 Germany, with forty G500 firms, shows a mean national degree of 9.20, more than twice the mean degree for US-based corporations (4.10). On the other hand, Japan, which accounts for the lion's share of G500 firms based in the third leg of the triad (in 2006, sixty-nine firms, compared to Australia's eight) shows a very low degree of national interlocking in 1996, which drops even further after the Asian financial crisis, to a mean of one. On the Asian semi-periphery there are signs of national corporate interlocking among G500 firms only in India (2006 mean national degree = 1.60) and South Korea (2006 mean national degree = 0.46).

Transnational interlocking tells an altogether different story. Firms based in western Europe are by far the most extensively engaged in this practice, but as measured by mean transnational degree, the trend among them is initially upward and then gently downward from 1998 on. This is also the overall trend for the G500. Firms based in North America average just under one transnational interlock, while those domiciled in Japan or Australia rarely share directors transnationally. The trends among firms based in Latin America and the European

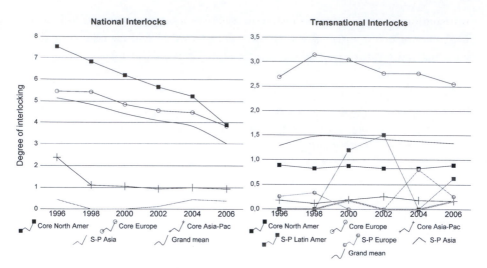

Figure 4.6 Degree of national and transnational interlocking for G500
corporations, 1996–2006

semi-periphery (including Africa) are erratic, as firms from different countries
enter and leave the G500, but transnational interlocks remain rare. The slight
overall increase in mean transnational degree, despite net decreases among
western European firms and flat trends elsewhere, reflects the shifting composition of the G500, as the complement of European-based industrial and financial
companies increases at the expense of the USA and Japan (see Figure 4.1).

These trends in central tendency, however, give us only one representation
of the global network. Another approach, which takes into account the shifting
regional composition of the G500, is to consider how much of the total volume
of interlocking is accounted for by firms based in specific places. In Figure
4.7, the large number of US-based firms and the continuing coherence of the
American network mean that *an enormous portion of the entire global network
is fixed in the nationally bound interlocking of US-based companies*. The US share
of all national interlocks does fall from 51 per cent to 42 per cent, but even in
2006 the American corporate community claims the largest share of national
networking, by far. In this sense, *capitalist interests based in the USA retain a
dominant position in the global network, despite trends in capital accumulation, and
even corporate interlocking, that subvert that dominance*. Meanwhile, the national
networks of France and especially Germany come to claim a great share of the
total volume of national interlocking, while corporate Japan's decline sees its
share cut by two-thirds. With the British national network, never more than a
rather loose formation (Scott 1997; Windolf 2002), claiming 5 or 6 per cent of
the total, the G5 holds a commanding presence, accounting for 94 per cent
of the entire volume of national interlocking in 1996, and 89 per cent in 2006.

If corporate America claims the lion's share of national interlocking, on the transnational side corporate Europe dominates the scene. About four-fifths of all transnational interlocking involves firms based in the seven national domiciles that account for at least 5 per cent of transnational interlocks in either 1996 or 2006. In this domain, the large complement of American firms leaves a footprint in the network similar to that of the much smaller complement of French companies. As of 2006, corporations based in the three major European states – France, the UK and Germany – account for over two-fifths of all transnational interlocks. The ten firms based in Switzerland (representing 2 per cent of the G500) account for 7 per cent of the transnational network, with Dutch firms showing a similarly strong propensity towards transnational interlocking.

These complementary analyses reveal the global corporate network to be a social formation still centred in 2006 upon the North Atlantic. Overall, the degree of interlocking decreases across the decade, as corporate boards slim down and as directors reduce their multiple directorships, in accordance with new norms of corporate governance. And, although as a proportion of all interlocks transnational ties increase from 19.9 per cent to 30.9 per cent, the global network remains to some extent a collection of (thinning) national networks (with the American corporate community still claiming pride of place), linked transnationally by companies based in the North Atlantic (with European firms playing the lead role).

What these schematizations, based on means and overall counts, do not reveal is how the *distribution* of interlock degree changes over the decade. Interlock degree, both national and transnational, is distributed over the G500 in anything but a normal, bell-curve shape. At one end of the distribution, the number of isolates from all interlocking (degree = 0) jumps from 69 to 120,

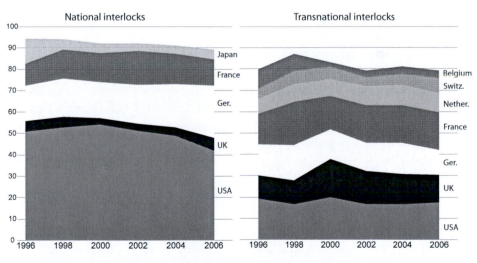

Figure 4.7 Proportions of national and transnational interlocking, key countries, 1996–2006 (%)

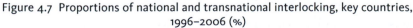

owing partly to the increased complement of Southern-based companies that do not interlock with any G500 corporations, but also to the increasing isolation of Japanese corporate boards.[10] In the same ten years, however, the number of isolates from transnational interlocking actually falls, from 313 to 266. While fewer G500 firms participate at all in the global network, reducing overall degree, among those that do, the participation rate in transnational interlocking increases substantially, from 61.7 per cent to 82.4 per cent. By 2006, the boards of the world's major corporations seem bifurcated between insular directorates, isolated from the global corporate network, and directorates that interlock on both a national and (increasingly) transnational basis.

At the other end of the distribution of transnational degree from the isolates, the number of firms with extremely profuse interlocks drops sharply after 1998. In 1996, thirteen firms (ten of them European), each with ten or more transnational interlocks, accounted in themselves for 26.2 per cent of all transnational links, yet by 2006 only four firms (all European), accounting for 8.5 per cent of the transnational network, were so heavily engaged. Across the decade, *transnational interlocking becomes less the preserve of a few internationally well-connected companies, and more a general practice in which nearly half of the world's largest firms participate*. The result is only a slight change in the mean transnational degree, masking a significant development: unlike national interlocking, which shows a general decline, transnational interlocking becomes a more common board practice, and the transnational component of the global network becomes more broadly based. By 2006, it is becoming a typical corporate practice to maintain directorate interlocks across borders – presumably engendering a more cosmopolitan ethos in the boardroom. This finding points to a broadening of transnational capitalist class formation, reinforcing Clifford Staples's (2006) argument that an important aspect of that process is the increasingly multinational composition of major corporate boards.

Once again, however, when we look more closely we find that the overall trend is not a summation of homogeneous regional trends. As of year-end 2006, most firms based in North America continue to have no transnational interlocks. Even here, however, the tendency is uneven, as 9 of the 15 G500 companies based in Canada are engaged in transnational interlocking compared to only 68 of the 154 US-based corporations. Meanwhile, in Europe it is by 2006 unusual for a major corporate directorate *not* to be interlocked transnationally. Fully 70.3 per cent of G500 firms based in western Europe participate in transnational interlocking, compared to only 5.8 per cent of Japanese-based firms and 44.2 per cent of US-based firms.

Transnational interlocking is not only spatially focalized on corporate Europe; it is very much the business of the world's most transnationalized companies. Across the decade, there is a weak correlation in each year between a firm's score on the UNCTAD TNI and its degree of transnational interlocking.[11] The extent to which companies are transnationally extraverted correlates more strongly with TNI scores.[12] Among large non-financial corporations that accumulate capital on a relatively transnational basis, the more transnationalized a company's circuitry of accumulation, the more transnationalized is its directorate interlocking. As a group, the ninety-odd G400 industrials that UNCTAD identifies as the most transnationalized large corporations in the world participate heavily in transnational interlocking. In 1996, 60.0 per cent of G400 firms in the UNCTAD 100 had board ties spanning national borders, compared to 28.1 per cent of G400 industrials not in the UNCTAD 100. By 2006, the proportions were 78.6 per cent and 36.7 per cent, respectively. In both years, firms on the UNCTAD list accounted for roughly half of the total volume of transnational interlocking involving G400 corporations. Recalling that western Europe is the locus for an increasing preponderance of heavily transnationalized firms (see Figure 4.4), it is not surprising that at year-end 2006, fifty-four highly transnationalized European industrials accounted for fully 40.4 per cent of the total volume of G400 transnational interlocking. In the same year, the 116 US-based industrials that remained relatively non-transnationalized, relying primarily on the vast American home market, accounted for 34.4 per cent of all national interlocks involving G400 firms. Without exaggerating the differences between the two, one might infer that the unique position of American capitalism in the world system, as the largest zone of affluence and political security for capital, has reinforced among US-based corporations a stronger home-market orientation, also expressed in the more nationally focused pattern of interlocking directorates. Large corporations in Europe, embedded in smaller home markets, have been obliged to expand internationally, and with that, they have created more transnational directorate networks. We shall explore the case of corporate Europe in Chapter 7.

To get a more dynamic view of change in the global corporate power structure, let us consider how firms showing different trajectories as Top Dogs, Fallen Angels and Rising Stars hook into the network. Since most of the enterprises of the global South that appear in the G500 by 2006 are Rising Stars, this variable functions more like a constant in the world beyond the triad. Within the latter, however, some interesting differences are notable.

- In 1996, in Europe, but not in North America or the Asia-Pacific, G500 companies that would go on to be Top Dogs in the ensuing decade networked more extensively, both transnationally and nationally, than corporations fated to fall from the G500 before 2006.[13] The extent to which a large company maintained interlocks, nationally and transnationally, at the beginning of the decade forecast its likelihood of continuing to dominate global capital's league table. In Europe, elite networking appeared to make a difference in the accumulation process.

- By 2006, in all three zones of the triad, Top Dogs held central positions in their respective national networks, compared with Rising Stars,[14] and in Europe and the Asia-Pacific, this difference also applied to transnational interlocking.[15] European Top Dogs showed especially high levels of transnational networking, averaging 3.37 interlocking directorates compared to a mean of 1.75 among Europe's Rising Stars. Remarkably, Europe's Top Dogs claimed half of all transnational interlocking directorates in 2006 (49.0 per cent, up from an already remarkable 46.9 per cent in 1996).

These findings suggest that *corporate interlocking and successful capital accumulation are mutually reinforcing processes*, and that, particularly in Europe, transnational networking 'makes a difference', in both directions. Highly networked firms tend to remain near the top of the global corporate hierarchy, and the boards of firms that have managed to stay near the top tend to interlock with other giant companies. In this way, the corporate network is reproduced as an elite within an elite: at any given time, it is the well-established firms which dominate the network.[16]

To summarize these findings, three factors – region of domicile, transnationality and corporate survivorship – help explain the differences in degree of national and transnational interlocking among G500 firms. Degree of interlocking is, as we have seen, distributed among the world's leading corporations in distributions that are quite skewed, with increasing numbers of firms disengaged from the practice of interlocking directorates and with relatively few companies heavily engaged. Although such skew severely tests the robustness of statistical procedures such as analysis of variance (ANOVA), in an attempt to appraise how the three factors interact in shaping a firm's position in the global network, we conducted a series of ANOVAs, using 2006 data. The results must be interpreted with caution, and for that reason will not be presented in detail. We found the effect of region[17] was definitely the strongest of the three factors, both for national and transnational degree, and it was the most robust when the other factors (and, later, interactions between factors) were included in the model as statistical controls. On its own, region explained 19.2 per cent of the total variance in transnational degree and 15.4 per cent of the total variance in national degree. Once the other factors and their interactions with region and with each other were included, region explained 11.9 per cent and 8.3 per cent of the variance, respectively. On the other hand, the effects of corporate survivorship[18] were more modest (accounting for 7.2 per cent of national and 3.1 per cent of transnational degree), and dropped effectively to zero when the three factors were considered together. The full factorial ANOVA showed that it is mainly in interaction with region that corporate survivorship influences transnational degree: European Top Dogs in particular are the most transnationally networked firms. Finally, transnationality[19] on its own explained much more variance in transnational degree (14.8 per cent) than in national degree (7.4 per cent), but once the other factors and interactions were included, its effects diminished to 2.2 per cent and 1.3 per cent, respectively.

What these results point to is a pattern of national interlocking that favours Top Dogs based in North America and Europe, and a pattern of transnational interlocking centred upon transnationalized Top Dogs of the triad, particularly those headquartered in Europe. Indeed, Europe not only hosts the largest contingent of highly transnational corporations that have consistently dominated capital's global league table since the mid-1990s (55 of 91 such firms), but that select group of 55 averages four transnational interlocks each, three times the grand mean. Highly transnationalized Top Dogs of North America also manifest a mean transnational interlocking (1.44) above the average for corporations of that region (0.89), as do the most transnationalized Top Dogs of Japan and Australia (0.91, compared to 0.24).

Although the twenty-three Rising Stars of the core Asia-Pacific zone do not figure at all in transnational interlocking, in other regions some firms that rise into the G500 become major players in the transnational network. The sixty-nine North American Rising Stars tend not to be transnationalized in their accumulation strategies, but four that do appear on UNCTAD's list average 2.5 transnational board interlocks, with Montreal-based Alcan linked to five non-Canadian G500 companies and New York-based Goldman Sachs linked to three non-American firms. Another twenty North American Rising Stars that do not make UNCTAD's list of major transnationalized firms do participate in transnational interlocking in 2006, averaging 1.95 such ties. Similarly, Europe's 85 Rising Stars include 27 firms that are not highly transnationalized in accumulation but which participate in transnational interlocking (averaging 2.22 interlocks) and 24 highly transnationalized firms that heavily participate in the transnational network (averaging 3.71 interlocks). On global capitalism's vast semi-periphery, Rising Stars number 44, but only 3 are sufficiently transnationalized to appear on UNCTAD's list. Although 25 of the 44 are isolates from the global network, 10 participate in transnational interlocking, averaging 1.2 interlocks.

Finance capital and directorate interlocking

If the global network is a configuration linking the major organizational sites within which corporate capital accumulates, a key issue is how the structure of board interlocking corresponds to the circuitry of accumulation. This is at its heart a question of the *instrumentalities of corporate power*: of how the elite network of interlocking corporate boards is implicated in the control of capital as it moves through its various forms – financial, industrial, commercial – in cycles of valorization. There are numerous ways in which such articulations can occur – e.g. an institutionalized commercial relation (purchase/sale) may be supplemented, and cemented, by a directorate interlock, or two firms launching a joint venture may in appointing directors to the board create a meeting point for directors from the parents. Social scientific investigations of corporate networks have concentrated on two forms of articulation between corporate interlocking and capital accumulation. These are:

• financial-industrial relations, through which credit is allocated by banks and other financial institutions to industrial corporations in need of financing; and
• inter-corporate ownership relations, which, when sufficiently concentrated, enable some firms to exert *strategic power* over other companies (Carroll and Sapinski 2011).

In the remainder of this chapter, we explore the first of these forms of articulation as they appear in the global corporate network (for an analysis of the latter see Carroll 2010).

In the classic case of finance capital, financial institutions wield an *allocative power* over agents dependent on credit, particularly large industrial firms, whose vast size means that major new investments require funds far exceeding the stream of short-term profits. Big banks, however, in need of outlets for their own accumulating financial capital, are also dependent on their large industrial clients. For this reason, the relation between financial and industrial capital evolved as a *symbiosis*, expressed in the typically profuse board interlocks between banks and non-financial corporations that formed that focal point for national corporate communities throughout much of the twentieth century (Fennema and Schijf 1979). The resulting integration of capitals under the aegis of a financial-industrial elite came to be known as *finance capital*, after Rudolf Hilferding's (1981 [1910]) volume of the same name. A raft of subsequent sociological investigations of interlocking directorates in various advanced capitalist countries confirmed the strong tendency towards bank-centred capital integration, although the specific forms of integration varied cross-nationally, as distinctive regimes of finance capital (see Scott 1997: 103–203).

As I have suggested elsewhere, however, since the 1980s, changes in financial investment and ownership, the most recent of which fall under the rubric of *financialization*, have transformed the capital relations that undergird corporate-elite networks, modifying the form of finance capital (Carroll 2008a: 45). Most significantly, the concentration of capital within institutional investors frantically concerned to boost the value of their shares destabilized the 'patient money' relations between corporations and banks, and led financial institutions to shift from low-yield (but also low-risk) relationship financing to higher-yield (and higher-risk) transaction-based financing, weakening the financial–industrial nexus constitutive of finance capital. In the past three decades, as banks moved from financing production to speculation in asset-backed commercial paper, derivatives and the like, and as institutional investors become important centres of allocative as well as strategic power, the relationship between financial institutions and non-financial corporations became looser and more episodic (ibid.: 56). Consistent with these developments, several studies of national corporate networks in the 1980s and 1990s evidenced a weakening in bank centrality (Davis and Mizruchi 1999; Carroll 2004; Heemskerk 2007). The implications for the global corporate network remain unexplored.

According to the simplest indicator of centrality, the number of G500 boards with which a firm shares one or more directors, such a weakening did occur in the global network after the mid 1990s. In 1996, G100 financial institutions averaged 5.77 national interlocks and 1.43 transnational interlocks, compared with respective means of 4.98 and 1.24 among G400 non-financials. By 2006, the slight overall difference in national degree, favouring financials, had reversed: financials maintained 2.73 national and 1.41 transnational interlocks; non-financials maintained 3.08 national and 1.32 transnational interlocks.

Beyond bank centrality within the interlock network, the notion of finance capital implies a clustering of interlocks *between* financial institutions and non-financial corporations. An appropriate measure of such clustering is density: the proportion of pairs of firms in a network or in a segment of a network that are directly linked to each other. In 1996, the overall pattern in the global network fitted the model, although the differences were not sharp. The density of interlocking between financials and industrials (0.015) was slightly above that among industrials (0.012) or financials (0.011). By 2006, there was no difference in the first two values (both stood at 0.009), but financials tended to be sparsely linked to each other (0.006). Overall levels of interlocking for the global network, however, tell us nothing of country-specific trends, or of the relative incidence of financial–industrial interlocks that are 'national' compared to those that transect national borders, as in Andreff's (1984) notion of internationalized finance capital.

To explore whether national financial–industrial axes have been receding and transnational ones emerging, we can compare the density of interlocking within and between countries. For clarity's sake, we restrict the analysis to the G7 countries – a group whose finance ministers have been meeting since 1976 to coordinate policy, and which provides one narrow operationalization of the major advanced capitalist countries. These seven national domiciles accounted for 86 per cent of G500 corporations in 1996 and 73 per cent in 2006. Figures 4.8 and 4.9 show the density of interlocking for financial institutions and industrial firms, within and between the G7 countries. These aggregated sociograms consist of fourteen nodes – two for each G7 country. Each node represents the set of G500 financial institutions or industrial companies domiciled in a given country at a given time. Lines indicate the density of interlocking between two sets of firms (e.g. financial institutions in Italy, It_finan, and industrial corporations in

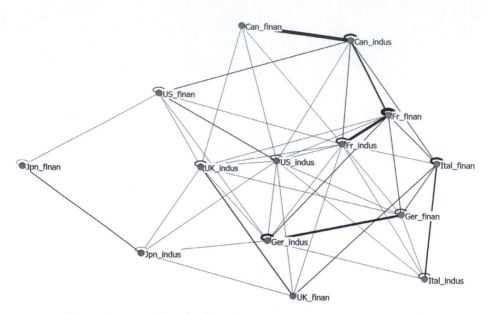

Figure 4.8 Financial and industrial interlocks among G7 countries, 1996

Germany, Ger_indus). Intra-sectoral densities within the same country appear as reflexive ties or 'loops' (e.g. the density of interlocking among German-based industrial corporations). Line thickness indicates the density of interlocking, which, as expected, decreases generally over the decade.[20]

In 1996, national financial–industrial axes are quite evident. The strongest ones integrate the command of financial and industrial capital in Canada (density = 0.45), France (0.36) and Germany (0.26). Financial–industrial interlocking is weaker in Italy (density = 0.15), Britain (0.10), the USA (0.07) and Japan (0.02), but even in these cases the financial–industrial nexus is comparatively dense. Also robust are the interlocks that integrate certain national sectors of industry or finance. The French (0.47) and Italian (0.27) financial sectors, and the Canadian (0.30) and German (0.27) industrial sectors, show high levels of internal cohesion. Some of the national differences in this regard reflect variant corporate-governance norms; for instance, in Canada, banks have long been prohibited from sharing directors, whereas in France and Italy such practices have been common (Carroll 1986; Stokman et al. 1985). Although most of the lines that cut across national borders are thin, French financial institutions interlock with Canadian industrials (density = 0.17) at a rate higher than national financial–industrial interlocking in four of the seven countries. Sparser transnational ties pull together the financial sectors of Germany, France and Italy.

By 2006, national financial–industrial axes are still evident, if diminished in density, in Germany (density = 0.19), Canada (0.18), France (0.12), Italy (0.11) and Britain (0.08); such interlocking in the USA and Japan, however, has receded to no more than background level (0.03 and 0.01 respectively). The Canadian

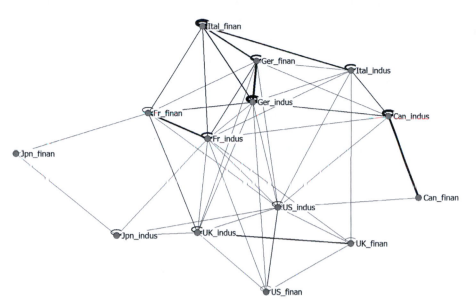

Figure 4.9 Financial and industrial interlocks among G7 countries, 2006

and German industrial sectors each remain internally cohesive, as does Italy's financial sector; interlocks among French financials, however, have dramatically decreased in density. The major lines of transnational interlocking run between Italian financial institutions, on one side, and German financial/industrials as well as French financials on the other. Overall, these comparisons reveal *an attenuated persistence of national financial–industrial axes in Europe and Canada*, and some evidence of increasing transnational elite relations of this sort on the European continent. Although financial institutions' prominence as network 'hubs' (Mintz and Schwartz 1985) had by 2006 disappeared, the financial–industrial nexus continued to shape the interlock network, but in an uneven, regionalized manner.

The international network, 1996 and 2006

Despite what we have shown to be a modest and selective extension of the transnational network to the global South, its continuing focus upon the triad, and particularly the North Atlantic, is visible in Figures 4.10 and 4.11. These blocked sociograms aggregate the network to the level of the countries that host large corporations. In these international networks, which show core countries as circles and semi-peripheral countries as squares, the thickness of lines connecting two countries indicates the *number* of interlocking directorates between the G500 firms of one country and the other. The sociograms depict the distribution of the entire set of transnational interlocks at the two end-points of this analysis. In each year, the set of transnational interlocks, when aggregated to the level of countries, yields a single, connected network; several countries, however,

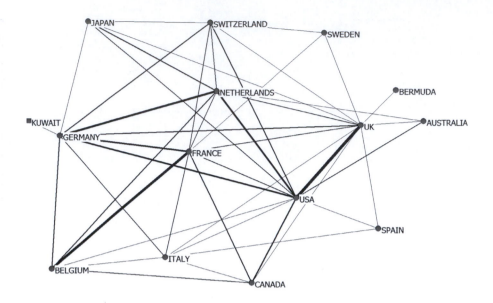

Figure 4.10 The international network of transnational interlocks, 1996

are isolated from the network (eleven in 1996 and seven in 2006) because the G500 companies they host do not participate in transnational interlocking.

In Figure 4.10, showing the state of play in 1996, we can discern the network's basic architecture as a combination of North Atlantic ties and ties within Europe. The latter are particularly profuse between corporations based in Germany and the Netherlands, France and Belgium and Germany and France, suggesting that in 1996 these four countries hosted the core of Europe's corporate community, while Britain played the role of entrepôt across the North Atlantic. Fifteen national domiciles are represented in this network, nine of which are western European and only one of which is semi-peripheral (Kuwait). The network is quite dense and compact; 43 per cent of its nodes are directly connected, and only two nodes (Kuwait and Bermuda) are pendants, bearing (weak) ties to a single node.

By 2006 (Figure 4.11), the international network is much larger, but less dense and compact. Twenty-five countries are represented by firms whose interlocks span national borders, including seven semi-peripheral states and thirteen countries of western Europe. The former domiciles, however, inhabit the network's margins, for the most part as pendants, each with a single interlock to one corporation headquartered in a core state. The network's more extensive reach (which also includes Finland, Norway, Ireland and Austria, domiciles not represented a decade earlier) makes for a reduction in overall density to 0.233 and an increase in the diameter of the network, from three to four (the latter being the distance from Austria to Brazil, Turkey and Russia).[21]

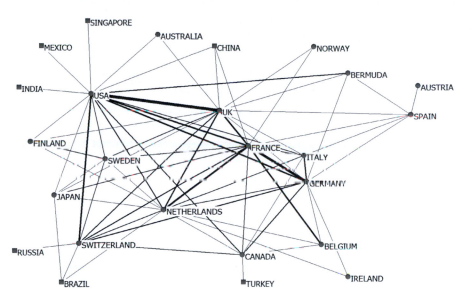

Figure 4.11 The international network of transnational interlocks, 2006

Despite greater inclusiveness in membership, the configuration remains centred upon the North Atlantic, with a proliferation of interlocks across the borders
of western Europe. Corporate Britain's special relationship with American capital
is only moderated attenuated, but British ties to corporations based on the
European continent (especially France and the Netherlands) have expanded, and
the Franco-German axis has strengthened. The directorates of French, German,
Dutch and British companies are especially interlocked, but the heart of the
network also includes corporate America, Canada, Switzerland, Sweden, Italy
and Belgium.[22] At both end-points, 92 per cent of transnational interlocking
directorates in the sociograms occur between companies based in the North
Atlantic. What happens in the interim is a redistribution of ties away from Japan
and Australia, whose ties to the North Atlantic drop from twenty-four to twelve.

These interlocks, however, are dispersed among an increasing number of
cities. The number of cities linked by interlocking directorates into a dominant component grows by 14 to number 109, while the proportion of interlocks
accounted for by ties among firms domiciled in the 12 most central cities falls
from 24 per cent to 20 per cent. The upshot is a global network that by 2006
is slightly more dispersed across many cities, even as it retains a Euro-North
American centre of gravity.[23]

Clearly, the decade straddling the turn of the century produced a great deal
of change in the global corporate network, as corporations rose into and fell
from the G500, enhancing or diminishing the profile of their domiciles as sites
for the command of corporate capital. In various ways, the patterning of capital

accumulation, in specific corporations, economic sectors and regions of the world economy, shaped the ongoing processes of class formation. At the same time, corporate governance reforms tended to loosen national networks while processes of globalization amplified the volume of transnational interlocks, without, however, introducing any major displacement of the network from its Euro-North American centre of gravity. Indeed, the more things changed, the more they seemed to stay the same – as in the continuing prominence of Top Dogs at the centre of the network and the attenuated persistence of financial–industrial axes in several major advanced economies. What this analysis of continuity and change at the corporate level has not considered are the human agents who carry the national and transnational interlocks that compose the global network. That is the focus of our next two chapters.

5 | Transnationalists and national networkers

A transnational capitalist class implies more than a global network of inter-locked corporate directorates. Given the duality of interlock networks – their existence on both corporate and personal levels – a transnational capitalist class should be discernible as a distinct segment within the global corporate elite. In exploring this aspect of class formation in the most recent years, we shift our attention from the inter-corporate network to the *interpersonal network* of interlocked corporate directors. This chapter examines the national and trans-national segments of the global corporate elite.

According to the leading proponent of the thesis of transnational capitalist class formation, this class is '*trans*national because it is tied to globalized cir-cuits of production, marketing and finances unbound from particular national territories and identities and because its interests lie in global over local or national accumulation' (Robinson 2004: 47). Through mechanisms that include cross-national mergers, strategic alliances, interlocking directorates and global outsourcing, what were formerly national capitals with international holdings 'fuse [...] in a process of cross-border interpenetration that disembeds them from their nations and locates them in new supranational space opening up under the global economy' (ibid.: 54). In this way, 'the locus of class formation [shifts] from national to emergent transnational space' (ibid.: 54).

A key issue in appraising the extent to which formerly national capitalist agents have become disembedded is the trajectory of national and transnational corporate elite segments. Has the increasing density of transnational capital circuits, through which commodities and money transect national borders, been accompanied by a proliferation of the elite connections that constitute a transnational segment within the global corporate elite? Has the global elite become less clustered around the national corporate networks that, in an earlier era of capitalism, provided the basic architecture for capitalist classes' top-tier leadership (Fennema and Schijf 1979; Stokman et al. 1985)? To what extent is the global corporate elite's centre of gravity shifting from national to transnational segments and agents?

Earlier chapters in this volume have provided rather limited support for Robinson's position. The changes in the global corporate interlock network we observed in Chapter 1 between 1976 and 1996 confirm only a modest ten-dency towards increased transnational interlocking among the world's largest corporations. In Chapter 2 we showed how corporate interlocks with global policy boards create an additional layer of elite sociality and an additional mechanism of transnational class formation; in Chapter 3 we established that the global corporate elite is highly regionalized, i.e. spatially concentrated in the global cities of the North Atlantic. The analysis of transnational accumulation and the global inter-corporate network in Chapter 4 did evidence a decline in national networking and a geographically uneven increase in transnational interlocking in the most recent decade. We found, however, that the ties that proliferated between 1996 and 2006 were largely focused upon western Europe and the northern trans-Atlantic. Such a pattern suggests, in contrast to Robinson, that transnational capitalists remain partially embedded in national and regional configurations, even as they operate in an emergent supranational space.

This chapter complements the previous one. Our focus here, on the directors rather than the corporations they direct, allows us to pose two research questions:

Q1: Can we trace the formation, within the global corporate elite, of a *transnational segment*: a set of directors whose transnational interlocks connect them to each other, forming *an inner circle of cosmopolitans*?[1] Or is the pattern of transnational interlocking haphazard and dispersed, with national networks continuing to form the major clusters and transnationalists simply serving as incidental bridges between them?

Q2: How does the regionalized character of global capitalism structure the global corporate elite in its national and transnational segments? Do transnationalists link *within* or *across* the major regions of global capitalism; i.e. is transnational interlocking intra- or inter-regional in character? How do specific regions figure in elite social organization – does the elite remain centred upon the North Atlantic; how, if at all, are emerging sites of corporate command, such as China, incorporated into the network?

In exploring the interpersonal, as distinct from inter-corporate, network, we restrict ourselves in this chapter to the 'inner circle' of the global corporate elite: the directors of the world's largest 500 corporations (G500), who at a given time sit on at least two G500 directorates (see Useem 1984). This definition combines two criteria – positional superiority within the hierarchy of command and sociality in the network of inter-corporate relations. As directors of mega-corporations, these individuals participate in the strategic direction of corporate business; as interlockers they 'carry' the corporate network, creating a basis for elite solidarity, strategic coordination and, ultimately, class hegemony (Sonquist and Koenig 1975). Given the division of the world into nation-states, we can, as we did earlier, distinguish two segments of the global corporate elite. Directors whose corporate affiliations are all contained within the same country are *national networkers*. Those who direct G500 corporations domiciled in different countries, i.e. that interlock across national borders, are *transnationalists*.

Q1: How do transnational and national segments appear within the global corporate elite?

In Figure 5.1, we see that over the decade the total number of G500 corporate directors diminished. The decline was particularly precipitous among non-interlocking directors (who are not members of the global corporate elite), but even the corporate networkers thinned from 845 to 696. Comparing across categories of region, the most dramatic drop is in the complement of directors of Japan-based firms – both interlockers and directors with single affiliations. This reflects two important shifts that occurred over the decade. The slow rate of accumulation in corporate Japan throughout the 1990s and into the new century (Ikeda 2004) reduced the number of Japanese-based firms in the G500 from 124 to 69.[2] Just as significant was the widespread but selective adoption of US-style corporate governance in Japan, in an attempt to reap efficiencies from 'leaner' corporate directorates. Initiated by Sony's decision to cut its board from thirty-eight to ten in 1997, and quickly emulated by other large Japanese firms, this had a major impact on board size, and thus on the number of directors of Japan-based companies, though not on other aspects of governance in these enterprises (Ahmadjian 2000). Besides the thinning ranks of Japanese directors,

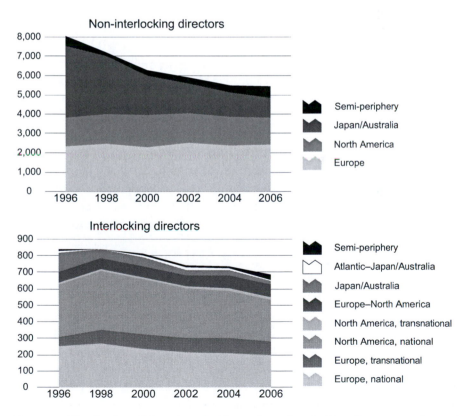

Figure 5.1 Distribution of G500 interlocking and non-interlocking directors, 1996–2006

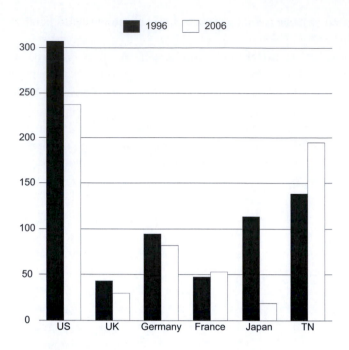

Figure 5.2 Numbers of interlockers: national (G5 countries) and transnational

the rise to economic prominence of several semi-peripheral states means an increase in the number of directors of firms based in the global South.[3] Most of that increase, however, registers among the non-interlocking directors.

Among the interlocking directors – the members of the global corporate elite – there is a tendency in all three regions of the triad – Japan/Australia, western Europe and the USA/Canada – for the number of national networkers to decline. Concomitantly, the number of transnationalists increases by a hefty 41 per cent, from 142 in 1996 to 200 in 2006. But what is perhaps most striking about the distribution of the global elite is its Euro-North American centrism: the bottom five strata of the area chart, depicting the multiple directors of firms based in western Europe or northern North America, account for the lion's share of the global elite.[4]

In light of the declining number of interlocking directors of G500 corporations, a question worth asking is whether this set of directors actually constitutes a single, connected network, and whether the network shows signs of decomposition. The answer, from an analysis of the participation rate in the dominant component (the largest network in which all members are directly or indirectly linked to each other), is clear. In 1996, the dominant component included 96 per cent of all G500 interlockers; by 2006 it took in 98 per cent. It is in this very basic sense that we can speak of a *global corporate elite* – a connected network of the directors of the world's largest firms.

Certainly, the basic trends in Figure 5.1 – growth of the transnationalist elite segment amid the thinning ranks of national networkers – lend some face validity to Robinson's hypothesis on the expansive character of the TCC. Although the global elite actually shrank in the most recent decade, this stems from the decline in the segment of national networkers. Indeed, comparing national networkers for each G5 country with the segment of transnationalists (Figure 5.2), not only is there a precipitous drop in Japan, but a decline in three of the other four countries. Only in France does the number of national networkers grow (modestly). By 2006, the transnationalist segment of the elite overshadows all national networks in the G500 but that of the USA.[5]

A strong version of the thesis of TCC formation, however, would predict not only growth in the complement of transnationalists, but *increasing cohesion among them*. In John Scott's view (1997), as globalization disarticulates national corporate networks it rearticulates elite relations transnationally. If this were so, we would observe transnationalists becoming more cohesive than the national networkers.

A simple way of approaching this issue is to compare the number of contacts that occur within different segments of the elite. On average in 1996, transnationalists sat on boards in common with 7.0 other transnationalists, but that value falls to 5.3 by 2006. That is, on average, each transnationalist encounters five other transnationalists on G500 boards. This is a not inconsiderable level of cohesion, greater in fact than the mean number of contacts for national networkers in Japan (2.7) and Britain (3.3) in the same year, but somewhat below levels in France (6.7), the USA (8.6), and especially Germany (14.5). In short, transnationalists do connect with each other, but at a rate that is below that in some of the larger national networks. Most strikingly, the German corporate elite in 2006 is nearly three times more interlocked than the segment of transnationalists.

The increasing number of transnationalists in the global elite suggests their growing presence in the social circles of individual elite members. This is visible in the rising proportion of immediate contacts that are transnationalists. For the elite as a whole, the average proportion of contacts who are transnationalists rises from 0.200 to 0.310; among national networkers, the mean proportion of contacts who are transnationalists increases from 0.159 to 0.252. Over the decade, transnationalists gain a greater presence in the social circles of national networkers, indicating that they are not forming a stratum unto themselves. What is equally interesting is *the strong propensity for transnationalists to sit on boards with each other*. By 2006, the social circles of transnationalists contain, on average, 45.5 per cent transnationalists (up from 40.4 per cent), signalling a real social cohesiveness. Transnationalists are not simply serving as bridges between national networks, but are sitting together on corporate boards.

A more systematic assessment of cohesiveness is afforded by the E-I index

TABLE 5.1 Internal and external ties for major segments of the global corporate elite

	1996				2006			
	In-ternal	Ex-ternal	Total	E–I	In-ternal	Ex ternal	Total	E–I
Europe	2,712	939	3,651	−0.486	1,704	861	2,565	−0.329
North America	4,102	587	4,689	−0.750	2,102	431	2,533	−0.660
Japan/Australia	848	11	859	−0.974	52	7	59	−0.763
Global South	32	0	32	−1.000	50	9	59	−0.695
Trans-nationalists	1,148	1537	2,685	0.145	1,038	1,308	2,346	0.115

(Krackhardt and Stern 1988). For a given network segment the index subtracts the proportion of all the Internal ties (connecting segment members to each other) from the proportion of all the External ties (connecting segment members to non-members). It ranges from −1, indicating that the segment is completely introverted (with all ties linking members to each other), to 1, indicating that the segment is completely extraverted (with all ties linking members to non-members). A value of 0 indicates that half of all ties are internal and half are external.

In Table 5.1, the entire global elite is divided into five segments: the trans-nationalists, national networkers whose corporate affiliations are contained within each of the three regions of the triad, and national networkers whose affiliations are contained within the rest of the world ('global South'). Each pair of individuals sitting together on a board in common creates a tie, which is internal if they belong to the same elite segment, and otherwise external. The distinction between internal and external ties is a revealing one when paired with the distinction between transnational and national elite segments. It enables us to explore the extent to which transnationalists interlock with each other as compared with the extent to which they interlock with national networkers located in different regions. Is the transnational segment of the elite effecting a disarticulation of national networks and a rearticulation of corporate power into a transnational configuration; or, perhaps, do the transnationalists serve as 'articulation points' (Harary 1969) or *brokers*, bridging between national segments that remain structurally well integrated?

Except for the global South, which clearly occupies a quite marginal position in the network, the total number of ties decreases over the decade, with the sharpest decline in Japan/Australia, followed by North America. This general decline in interlocking is consistent with findings from earlier chapters. The global interpersonal network has been thinning not only in its ranks but in its density of interlocking. In 1996, the density of interlocking[6] among all 846 members of the elite was 0.0169; by 2006, for an elite of 695 individuals, it was 0.0161.

The two most instructive comparisons in Table 5.1 are between the transnationalists and the national networkers, and, within national networkers, between the Europeans and the North Americans. Let us consider them in turn.

Compared to national networkers in the three regions of the triad, the transnationalists show much smaller decline in their total number of ties, so that by 2006 they account for 38.1 per cent of all connections in the global corporate elite, up from 29.3 per cent in 1996.[7] Comparing E-I indices, the transnationalists emerge as the only extraverted elite segment. In the aggregate, however, their interlocks are only moderately more externally than internally oriented, and the E-I index shifts away from extraversion over the decade, as the number of internal relations among transnationalists decreases only slightly compared to relations between transnationalists and national networkers. National networkers, in contrast, are markedly introverted, particularly in 1996. They become somewhat less introverted, however, which is to say that they come to include more transnationalists among their contacts. Still, there is a persistent difference between the national networkers and the transnationalists. As national networkers come to interlock more with transnationalists they retain their internal linkages. The transnational elite segment is internally integrated, but not as a group unto itself. It appears more as a bridge, with growing internal cohesion, across persistent national networks.

As for the comparison of European and North American national networkers, it is the former who tend to sit with transnationalists on common corporate boards. In fact by 2006, European national networkers are involved in 66 per cent of all the ties linking national networkers to transnationalists, with most of the rest involving North Americans. Clearly, the European national networks are much less introverted than the North American or other national segments. At the same time, however, the main locus for elite interlocking shifts from North America to Europe. Over the decade, the national networks of North America lose nearly half of their internal ties, while losses in Europe (both internal and external) are much more modest. By 2006 the national networkers of Europe are, overall, slightly better connected than those of North America, and the transnationalist segment is not far behind the two major regions of national networking. In that year, these three segments accounted for 98.4 per cent of all the ties that knit together the global corporate elite.

These findings beg us to explore the regional dimension of elite structure in greater depth, but there is one further empirical entailment to our first research question. The thesis of TCC formation implies that the transnational elite segment is becoming more socially integrated, as it gains the capacity to act as a class-for-itself (Robinson 2007). Component analysis offers a more structural measure of whether transnationalists cohere as a social category within the global corporate elite. *Considering only the connections among them,* do transnationalists form a connected network (a component), all of whose members can reach each other either directly or through other transnationalists? Or are transnationalists fractured into disjoint networks? In both years, most transnationalists form a single, connected network, with a participation rate in the component of approximately 90 per cent (92 per cent in 1996 and 90 per cent in 2006). In their corporate affiliations, transnationalists not only span national borders; they affiliate with each other in a connected network that is embedded within the global corporate elite.

More stringently, within the connected component, we may ask how many transnationalists form a 3-core, i.e. a component whose members each connect with at least three other 3-core members, creating a relatively thick sociality. In 1996, 105 transnationalists (74 per cent of the entire segment) comprised a 3-core; in 2006, 152 (76 per cent) did, bringing three-quarters of the transnationalists into a well-integrated network that cuts across the national borders of the capitalist world order. These results lend credence to the thesis that transnationalists are, increasingly, a well-connected elite segment with a growing capacity to develop consciousness of kind and, perhaps, political solidarity.

Q2: How does the regionalized character of global capitalism structure the global corporate elite in its national and transnational segments?

The topography of the global corporate elite can be represented by means of a set of spatialized categories highlighting the position each director holds in the network. The key conceptual distinctions are between

- national networkers and transnationalists;
- North (the advanced capitalist triad or Wallersteinian 'core'[8]) and South (for present purposes, the semi-periphery – not surprisingly, G500 companies do not locate their head offices in any peripheral countries); and
- the three macro-regions of the North.

This enables us to consider how national networkers of different regions are positioned in the global network, and how transnationalists link within and across those regions. Although these distinctions logically imply fourteen categories, *intra-regional* transnationalists appear almost exclusively within (western) Europe and (northern) North America, and North–South transnationalists are so uncommon that it makes sense to treat them as a single category; thus the global elite can be grouped into the ten categories shown in Figure 5.3.[9]

Most members of the elite are national networkers of the triad; their numbers decrease, however, and in the case of Japan-Australia, plummet. The collapse of the Japanese network leaves Euro-North America as the elite's centre of gravity. With the entry of more Southern-based firms into the G500, semi-peripheral national networkers appear but remain quite rare within the global elite, which

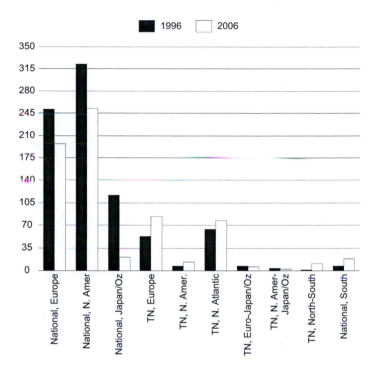

Figure 5.3 Typology of corporate interlockers in the global network

is firmly rooted in national corporate networks of the United States, Canada and western Europe.

Now, considering the fourth, fifth and sixth pairs of bars, there is a prodigious growth in the number of European transnationalists, whose multiple directorships pull together corporate Europe. In contrast, the number of transnationalists within North America grows only slightly, and, contrary to the European trend, this growth does not indicate a further continental integration of corporate elites.[10] An implication of these trends is that the number of global corporate elite members based in Europe (either as national networkers or as intra-regional transnationalists) overtakes the number of elite members based in North America. Transnationalists whose affiliations span the North Atlantic, already numerous in 1996, continue to augment, reinforcing Euro-North America's prominence within the global configuration. Indeed, there are very few transnationalists whose directorships establish inter-regional elite ties beyond the North Atlantic heartland, although the number of transnationalists who connect centre to semi-periphery does grow from one to twelve.[11]

Weighting the frequencies in Figure 5.3 by the number of G500 directorships held by each individual yields an even stronger tendency towards Euro-North American predominance, and a shift, within that block, towards western Europe. Between 1996 and 2006, the percentage of all global elite directorships held

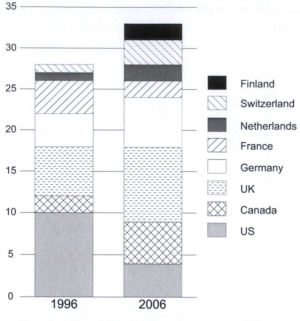

Figure 5.4 Domicile of principal corporate affiliation,
trans-Atlantic linkers

by directors of firms based in Europe or North America grew from 84.9 to 91.5
– reflecting in part the eclipse of the Japanese national network. The percentage of all directorships held by European national networkers and European
transnationalists grew from 37.2 to 42.8; the percentage held by those directing
only North American firms shrank from 38.7 to 36.3; the percentage held by
North Atlantic transnationalists grew from 9.0 to 12.4. What also stands out is
the sparseness of ties linking the North Atlantic elite to the rest of the world.
There is an increase in both national and transnational directorships involving
the South, but by 2006 only 4.0 per cent of directorships in the elite network
include firms domiciled in the global South.

Further evidence of a network shift towards corporate Europe can be discerned
from a closer analysis of the participation rates in the connected component
of transnationalists. We saw earlier a strong tendency for transnationalists to
form such a component, through their mutual corporate affiliations. Over the
decade, however, *fewer* North American transnationalists come to participate
in the connected component of transnationalists (falling from 87.5 per cent to
53.8 per cent), indicating that their intra-regional affiliations tend not to connect
them to the larger transnational formation. In contrast, more than nine-tenths
of European transnationalists participate (92.9 per cent in 1996 and 91.9 per
cent in 2006). Given how integral interlocks across the Atlantic are to global
elite organization, it is not surprising that North Atlantic linkers, already heavy
participants in 1996, become nearly unanimous in their component member-

ship by 2006 (an increase in the participation rate from 92.2 per cent to 97.5 per cent). From this analysis, it seems clear that *the segment of transnationalists is predominantly a well-connected combination of the European and North Atlantic transnationalists.*

There is a further sense in which one might speak tentatively of a shift towards Europe. Interlocking directorships can be said to have directionality, if one directorship can be taken as the director's principal corporate affiliation. This is typically the case when an executive or chairperson of one corporation sits as an outside director of another. We determined which directors have a principal affiliation with one G500 firm, by serving as an executive, chair or major shareholder in that firm. In the practice of corporate strategic power, those with principal affiliations fulfil a more 'inside' function; conversely, outside directors typically sit on the board in an advisory capacity. The elite segment that is worth scrutinizing in this regard connects Europe and North America (see Figure 5.4). In 1996, 28 of 64 members of this segment had identifiable principal affiliations within the G500; 36 were exclusively outside directors. In 2006, 33 of 80 had identifiable principal affiliations. Strikingly, those with identifiable affiliations tend to be based in Europe, and over time, the presence of US-based insiders drops to 5 of 34 while the presence of insiders based in Britain, Germany and Canada grows to 9, 6 and 5 consecutively. If there is directionality to North Atlantic elite relations, it increasingly runs from Europe to the USA.

A long-recognized virtue of network analysis is its capacity to help us visualize social structure (Moreno 1934; Freeman 2005). Our typology of interlockers enables a dissection of the global elite network into its macro-regional *subnetworks* and (inter-)regional *bridges*, creating an overall map of the global corporate elite, attuned to its spatiality. This allows us to ask how the regional subnetworks compare with each other; to what extent the bridges pull them together; and who the key transnationalists are, linking the North Atlantic with the rest of the world.

Figures 5.5 and 5.6 present step-wise mappings of the entire network, beginning (in step 1) with the national networkers who form the backbone of subregional elite networks that are nested within the global corporate elite. In step 2, the transnationalists whose corporate affiliations are contained within one macro-region (whether Europe or North America) are superimposed upon the map. In step 3, the transnationalists whose affiliations span across macro-regions are superimposed.[12]

Beginning with Figure 5.5, which dissects the network as of 1996, in step 1 a pronounced clumping of national networkers into their respective components is evident. The major countries of the triad (and the only Southern-based network, South Korea) have been labelled, with G5 states particularly prominent. Among the larger national networks, directors of German firms are densely interlocked,

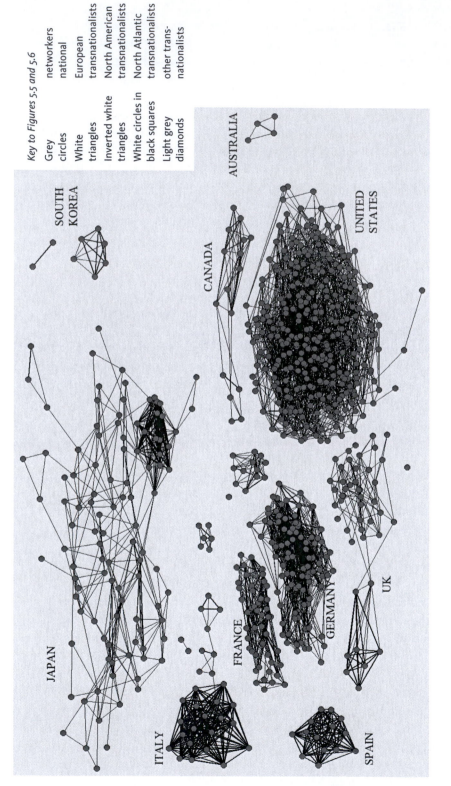

Figure 5.5 National networkers and transnationalists in the global corporate elite, 1996

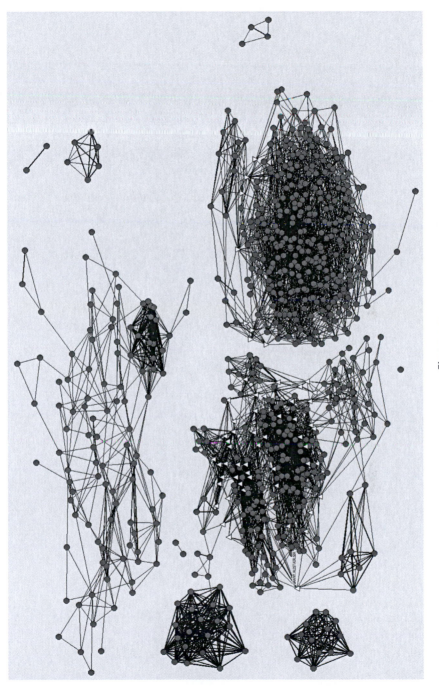

Figure 5.5a

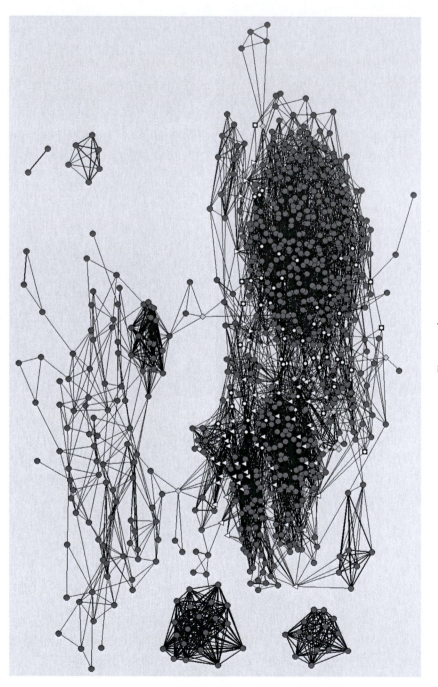

Figure 5.5b

as are directors of American companies, the British less so. The small Spanish network is generated by two firms sharing fourteen directors (Endesa S.A. and SEPI, which held controlling interest in Endesa). Except for directors associated with the South Korean chaebols LG (represented by two directors) and Samsung (represented by six directors), the global South is absent from this sociogram, in large part because in 1996 only South Korea had a sizeable complement of corporations (eleven in all) with revenues large enough for the G500.

In the second step, each North Atlantic region becomes integrated by virtue of the *intra-regional* transnationalists, who are represented with white triangles on the European side and with inverted white triangles on the North American side. In North America, eight such directors bridge between the Canadian and US national networks. In Europe, fifty-six such directors link the national networks of continental western Europe, in particular Germany and France, into a dense configuration, with Britain and especially Italy somewhat marginal and Spain entirely isolated. Overall, at this step, the European elite segment appears nearly as integrated as the North American one.

When the seventy-eight *inter-regional* transnationalists are introduced into the sociogram, in the third step, the effect is to unite Europe and North America into a single entity. The North Atlantic transnationalists, represented by white circles enclosed in black squares, carry the ties that create one big network. Other inter-regional transnationalists, represented by light grey diamonds, are few and far between, but they provide important bridges between the North Atlantic heartland and the rest of the world. The entire Japanese national network is linked to the heartland by two people. Yasuyuki Wakahara, chair and president of Asahi Mutual Life, sits on the boards of Fujitsu and of Dutch-based Fortis, linking the Japanese network to the European segment. Masataka Shimasaki, an outside director of Nippon Life, also directs Lehman Brothers of New York. The small network of Australian-based directors connects to the US network through James J. O'Connor, president of Unicom, director of two other US firms (First Chicago NBD and UAL Corporation), and a director of BHP, the jewel of the Australian mining industry. But beyond these key points of articulation, the non-North Atlantic transnationalists change the picture only slightly.[13] The global network of 1996 was primarily a North Atlantic configuration.

Ten years on (Figure 5.6), that basic configuration is still unmistakeable, and if anything, more pronounced. Beginning again with the national networkers (step 1), what stands out in its modesty is a much-diminished and quite sparse Japanese component. Sparser ties are, in fact, evident in most of the surviving national networks, with the conspicuous exception of Germany. The Italian and Spanish components are no longer big enough to merit a label in the sociogram. Notably, the number of national networkers based in Italy has dropped from twenty-eight to three. But with an increased presence of G500 firms based in the semi-periphery, there is a commensurate increase in national networkers

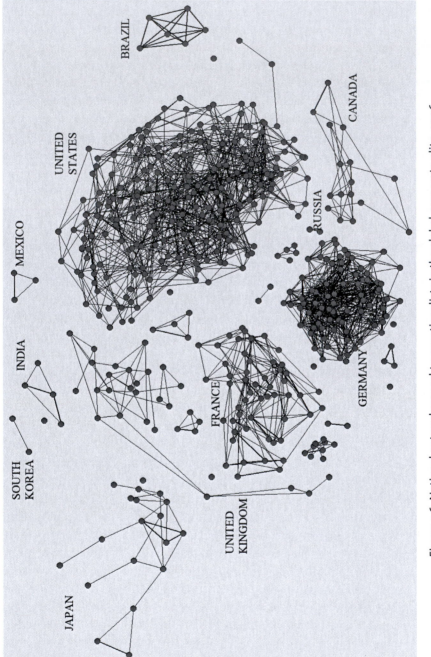

Figure 5.6 National networkers and transnationalists in the global corporate elite, 2006

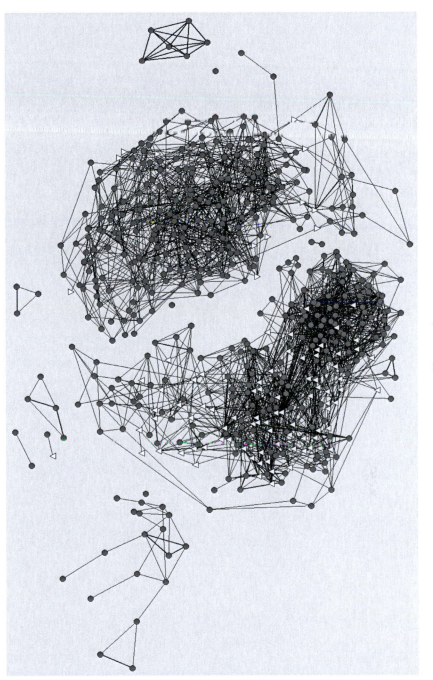

Figure 5.6a

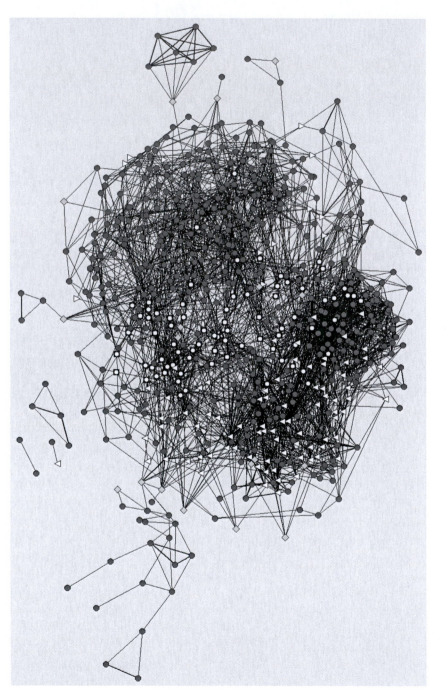

Figure 5.6b

based in India, Mexico, Brazil and Russia. Two Russian recruits to the global elite sit on the boards of entwined energy giants Rosneft and RAO UES. Energy is also the common denominator for the four new recruits from India, who together direct four oil and gas companies. Three directors of Mexico-based firms are focused more in the telecommunications sector: all sit on the board of Carso Global Telecom, and two direct America Movil, but one directs cement monopoly Cemex. Finally, six Brazilian-based directors serve on the boards of Banco Itau and its major shareholder, holding company Itau. In contrast to these emergent mini-networks, after radical restructuring of chaebols following the Asian financial crisis of 1997, the South Korean presence has been reduced to two directors, each associated with a surviving chaebol (LG and SK), who sit together on the board of Kookmin Bank.

In the second step, the addition of *intra-regional* transnationalists creates a well-integrated European network, but elite ties between US and Canadian networks are less extensive, so the national networks remain easily discernible. The European network is organized not only around 200 national networkers but very much around the eighty-six European transnationalists. As a mark of European consolidation, although Spanish national networkers now number only five, there are seven transnationalists that draw Spanish business leaders (isolated in 1996) into the European corporate elite. Similarly, corporate Italy, with only three national networkers, is linked to corporate Germany via eight European transnationalists.

Once again, the third step – the addition of *inter-regional* transnationalists – produces a highly integrated North Atlantic component, with precious few ties to the rest of the world. A single point of contact afforded by the board of Sony Corporation links the Japanese elite network to Europe. Peter Bonfield, a director of UK-based Astrazeneca and the Swedish firm Ericsson, sits with Yotaro Kobayashi, Akishige Okada and Fujio Cho on the Sony directorate. Ensconced within the European region of the sociogram, however (and therefore not clearly visible), is a small component of four directors – all of them transnationalists – who represent a significant capital relation between Europe and Japan but do not sit on other G500 Japanese boards. Since 1999 Renault has owned a controlling interest in Nissan, and as an implication, four directors of Nissan also sit on boards of European companies, most notably Renault.

Two other points of contact extending beyond the North Atlantic are readily seen in the sociogram. The triad of Mexico-based directors hooks into the US network via Lorenzo Zambrano, chair of Cemex, whose seat on the IBM board puts him in contact with seven US national networkers and one North Atlantic linker. Sergio de Freitas, a director of Banco Itau, provides a comparable North–South linkage for the small Brazilian component, through his seat on Rotterdam-based Arcelor Mittal – the world's largest steelmaker, whose Indian-born owners exemplify another aspect of transnational capitalist class formation (Lenard 2006). Less visibly, the dyad of directors based in Russia is hooked into the European elite through Hans Rudloff, vice-chair of Swiss-based Novartis, who sits on the Rosneft board. Despite these instructive instances, the continuing predominance of the densely networked North Atlantic region is quite clear.

Note, however, that this chapter's focus on the corporate elite rather than the corporations imposes a stringent standard on what counts as a point and a line in the network. The sociograms depict only ties among directors who are members of the global elite. This means that a member of the elite who sits on G500 boards that do not contain any *other* members of the elite will appear as an isolate, and that a national segment will appear only if at least two directors sit together on the board(s) of one or more firms domiciled in a given country. China is absent from the network for this very reason. Its statist capitalism does not require much in the way of board interlocks (there is only one director of the sixteen China-based companies who sits on two boards, and hence, no national interpersonal network). By 2006, however, three directorships do link China to the North Atlantic heartland. John Thornton, a director of US-based Intel, sits on the board of Industrial and Commercial Bank of China. Frederick Anderson Goodwin, president of the Royal Bank of Scotland, directs the Bank of China. Baron Levene of Portsoken, who directs UK-based Lloyds TSB and French-based Total, also sits on the board of China Construction Bank. These three directors are North–South transnationalists, but the ties they carry to China are not visible. The same holds for another North–South transnationalist, Dipak C. Jain, who directs both Reliance Industries (of India) and Deere & Co. (of the USA). Since Jain does not sit with elite members on any other G500 corporate boards based in India, his tie to India is not visible in the sociogram.

Rounding out the list of inter-regional relations not visible in Figure 5.6 are three directors of Australia-based companies and two directors of firms based in Japan, none of whom sits with other elite members on their respective Australian and Japanese boards. Solomon D. Trujillo, president of Australian telecom firm Telstra, also directs US-based Target Corp.; John Buchanan (see note 9) directs BHP Billiton as well as two British and one American company; Roger Campbell Corbett, president of Woolworths (Australia), accepted a seat on the board of Wal-Mart late in 2006. Although they do not interlock with other members of the Japan-based elite, Kenji Matsuo and Hiroshi Tada do link corporate Japan to business elites in two other regions. Matsuo, president of Meiji Yasuda Life, also directs French bank Société Générale; Tada is an outside director of both Mitsui & Co. and Brazil-based mining giant CVRD.

These particular trans-regional ties add nuance to the picture, but they do not seriously qualify the extent to which the global corporate elite remains centred in the North Atlantic zone.

Conclusion

Distinguishing national and transnational segments, this chapter has explored recent changes in the composition and structure of the global corporate elite. Without doubt, transnationalists have gained prominence. Increased numbers and cohesiveness coincide with their growing presence in the social circles of national networkers. By early 2007, transnationalists were firmly embedded in the global network, through their extensive ties to each other and to various national components. These results lend credence to the thesis that transnationalists are, increasingly, a well-connected fraction with a structural capacity to develop consciousness of kind and, perhaps, political solidarity. Discovery of interlocks, however, does not tell us how such connections are actually used by directors and corporate boards (Mizruchi 1996). Data of a more ethnographic character would be required to make stronger claims about cosmopolitan solidarities in the consciousness and action of the transnationalists. But given the profuse contacts between transnationalists and national networkers, such solidarities are unlikely to be seriously at odds with the perspectives of business leaders within the major advanced capitalist countries. In the inner circle of the global corporate elite, transnationalists and national networkers intermingle extensively, 'national' and 'supranational' spaces intersect, and whatever common interest takes shape is likely to blend 'national' and 'transnational' concerns.

For their part, national networkers, despite thinning ranks and sparser interlocks, continue to form the backbone of the global corporate elite, and remain on balance introverted (i.e. nationally cohesive). Our focus on directors of the G500 highlights only the very peak of each national elite network. For the broader networks underneath those peaks, the transnational segment likely functions less as an agent of disarticulation than as a resource for coordinating the national with the transnational. Such coordination should not be mistaken for a benignly technocratic exercise in optimizing efficiencies. Overall, the shift within the global elite towards the transnationalists can be seen on the one hand as promoting further integration of the global economy and on the other 'as the source of concentration of economic and political power which threatens democracy, social welfare and cohesion' (Nollert 2005: 310).

Regionalism is a powerful force in the global corporate elite's social organization. Although transnational interlocking has grown, the notion that the elite is becoming disembedded from national moorings and repositioned in a supranational space underestimates the persistence of national and regional attachments. Indeed, according to Kalb (2005: 178), 'globalization rhetoric notwithstanding, territory and space have become more important as signifiers of patterned bundles of social relationships and institutions rather than less'. The basic structure of the elite is highly regionalized. Most members are national networkers; most transnational interlocking integrates corporate Europe or links across to North America. Step-wise comparisons of sociograms show how extensively Euro-North America dominates the global field as a highly integrated bloc, and how modest the 'rise of the capitalist South' has been in the world of the global corporate elite, despite the appearance of major semi-peripheral corporations (Sklair and Robbins 2002). With the sharp diminution of the Japanese network, the elite has become centred even more strongly upon the North Atlantic; with its growing regional cohesiveness, corporate Europe has gained prominence within that heartland. Eurocentrism in the network of transnationalists derives in part from the importance of pan-European inter-locking in the very constitution of corporate Europe and in part from recent corporate governance reforms in the USA which reduced the size of boards and the extent of interlocking (Chhaochharia and Grinstein 2007), in an effort to restore competitiveness.[14] Yet also, within trans-Atlantic elite relations, it is European capitalists who sit on American boards, intimating an intriguing reversal of scenarios for American hegemony in Europe that were posited in the late 1960s by writers like Ernest Mandel (1970: 20–26).

The shift towards Europe in elite organization, while consistent with the widely acknowledged decline of American hegemony (Go 2007), should not be read in terms of the instrumentalities of power. Elite interlocks are relationships of class hegemony, of solidarity and coordination, more than domination. And they give us only one vantage point on the question of transnational capitalist class formation, a view detached from the governing boards of many thousands of lesser units of capital, from the parent–subsidiary relations that constitute TNCs as hierarchical networks of corporate command centred upon global cities (Alderson and Beckfield 2007), and from the actual circuitry of capital as it moves through surplus value production, realization and (re)investment. Moreover, research has shown that other kinds of relations – mediated through shared positions on major policy boards – are crucial to elite cohesion, whether in integrating corporate Europe (van Apeldoorn 2002; Nollert 2005) or in bring-ing the third leg of the triad more closely into the global formation (Chapters 2 and 8, this volume).

Still, a mapping of interlocking corporate directorships helps specify the process of transnational capitalist class formation at its higher reaches. It has been taking shape not so much as an abstractly 'global' or even triadic config-uration but through further consolidation of an Atlantic ruling class, consoli-dated under American tutelage in the post-war years (van der Pijl 1984), but increasingly based in parity between business elites on both sides of the ocean. The trends point to the declining predominance of US-based capitalists in the top tier of global capitalism. The shift towards Europe registers the successes, from a business standpoint, of European integration, along with the decline of American hegemony. But it may also be located within the *longue durée*. Already in the early years of capitalist development, Europe's elite was 'closely tied by culture and concrete interests to a pan-regional international class' (Halperin

2007: 551). For the ruling class, the roots of European integration go deep. In any case, the shift we have observed is only a relative one, within an increasingly integrated North Atlantic bloc – the centre of gravity for a transnational capitalist class that remains embedded within the persistent national business communities of the global North.

6 | Billionaires and networkers: wealth, position and corporate power

Capitalist class formation has been, since the nineteenth century, coincident with the amassing of great fortunes by prominent families. The rise of a trans-national capitalist class invites an enquiry into how such fortunes appear in the structure of global corporate power. Throughout most of the twentieth century, 'millionaire' evoked a strong image of super-affluence, semiotically bundled with notions of the 'sixty families' whose fortunes dominated national societies (cf. Lundberg 1937; Campbell 1963; DiDonato et al. 1988) and the 'very rich'. In delineating the economic component of the American power elite, C. Wright Mills (1956) placed the latter alongside the 'chief executives' and the 'corporate rich' (cf. Domhoff 2006 [1967; 1998]). Stanislav Menshikov entitled his 1969 book on the American bourgeoisie's monopoly fraction *Millionaires and Managers*, to connote the confluence of power based on property ownership and power based on the operational control of enterprises, a confluence that remains at the heart of capitalist class power.

Personal fortunes of 1 billion US dollars were not unheard of before the 1980s – Henry Ford, Andrew Mellon and Howard Hughes come to mind. Reckoned in contemporary dollars, the fortune of John D. Rockefeller, the world's first billionaire, would dwarf that of Bill Gates (Klepper and Gunther 1996), although the difference in part reflects the relative size of the American economy a century ago and today (Broom and Shay 2000). Indeed, by the late twentieth century long-range inflationary tendencies had combined with rising overall income levels and ongoing processes of accumulation to raise the bar for super-affluence. From the 1980s onwards, neoliberal policies – particularly the shift away from progressive taxation, the reduction in rates of taxation, and the deregulation of investment practices – enabled massive fortunes to proliferate. These policies fed a 'paper boom' (Stanford 1999) that inflated the prices of financial assets and the wealth of those owning them. Nowhere was this more evident than in the United States. *Forbes* began to track American billionaires in 1982, when its research detected twelve such fortunes. By 1987, when forty-nine US billionaires made the list, *Forbes* had begun to count billionaires outside the USA, who numbered ninety-six.

Just as corporate elites have long been under the microscope of social scientists, there is a research literature on the super-affluent. Our interest in this chapter is in the positions that the wealthiest families and individuals hold within the structure of global corporate power, and on this issue the literature offers several preliminary insights. A century ago, Watkins's (1907) seminal study of the growth of large fortunes emphasized that 'abstract property' – paper assets such as corporate shares and bonds – empowered the very rich to concentrate ownership and control through compounding interest, asset appreciation and the capture of an 'unearned increment' quite distinct from industrial profit. A century later, whether they spread their holdings across a number of corporations or focus them upon a single firm, the bulk of the wealth of the super-rich is stored in corporate shares (Broom and Shay 2000).

There is an indelible relation between the accumulation of corporate capital and the production and reproduction of great fortunes. Such fortunes are, of course, a pivot point in the intergenerational reproduction of the capitalist class; hence the findings, from Canterbury and Nosari's (1985: 1079) classic study, that 40 per cent of the richest 400 Americans are heirs to fortunes and, in a multiple regression, that inheritance accounted for 43 per cent of their mean wealth. Similarly, Broom and Shay's (2000) multivariate analysis of the determinants of extreme wealth identified kinship ties as one of the strongest predictors, as individuals tied by kinship were much wealthier than isolated individuals.[1]

If kinship matters, then so does gender. The relationship between family, patriarchy and private property is ancient (Engels 1977 [1884]), but one contemporary implication is that men vastly outnumber women on the lists of the very rich (cf. Canterbury and Nosari 1985; Broom and Shay 2000). The gendered character of opulence is also evident in the manner in which fortune is secured. Consistent with a division of labour that has tended to marginalize women vis-à-vis capital and the state (Zeretsky 1976; Fox 1989), inheritance, in 1980s America, played the dominant role in shaping the size of the fortunes of women, while a combination of inheritance and active entrepreneurship seemed more significant for men (Canterbury and Nosari 1985: 1080). Not surprisingly, Broom and Shay's longitudinal analysis (1982–99) of the American super-rich found that women comprised only 12 per cent of the total population of individual wealth holders ($n = 918$), that only seven of the 113 super-affluent women did *not* inherit great wealth, and that only one (namely, Oprah Winfrey) amassed her fortune independently of a husband, sibling or offspring.

An equally telling determinant of great wealth is one's location in the geography of accumulation (including consumption of luxury goods). Within the relatively well-researched United States, the super-rich tend to cluster in certain states, chiefly New York, Texas, California and Florida (Canterbury and Nosari 1985: 1078). Globally, billionaires tend to reside in high-GDP countries, and in states with high levels of corruption (Torgler and Piatti 2009), the textbook example of the latter being the post-Soviet Yeltsin regime (see Goldman 1998). Beaverstock et al. (2004: 402) observe that the super-affluent are increasingly adept at 'positioning themselves beyond the jurisdiction of nation-states', as in offshore tax havens – although the neoliberal tendency towards reduced personal and corporate taxes everywhere has muted this tendency. Their account of the world's fifty richest, based on the *Forbes* 2003 list of billionaires, provides a sketch of the geography of the super-rich:

> Perhaps unsurprisingly, it is the high-income economies of the West who provide the most names on the list, with North America accounting for 19 of the fifty, and Europe for another 17. Beyond this global core, the majority are drawn from the oil-rich states of the Middle East; there are no names on the list from Africa, South America, or for that matter Australasia, but Hong Kong and India do make appearances [...] (p. 403)

Such a regional pattern is indeed unsurprising, but it raises the related issue of how billionaires participate in practices and processes of globalization. On the one hand, there is recent evidence that 'globalization enhances super-richness' – that a country's capacity to guarantee the free movement of capital and commodities is 'a key ingredient in enhancing the accumulation of extraordinary wealth' (Torgler and Piatti 2009: 11). On the other hand, many of the very rich live not as residents of specific nation-states but as transnational subjects, global in cultural orientation and business outlook and *hypermobile* in their extreme mobility (which typically includes multiple residences). In this sense, the super-rich may be regarded as 'a genuinely transnational faction of the global elite' – even if their activities may centre less on cross-border corporate interlocking and more on governance of foundations, charities, advisory councils and think tanks (Beaverstock et al. 2004: 405).

Billionaires and networkers

Clearly, the power base of the super-affluent is distinct from that of corporate directors. The latter, including the networkers who are the focus of this study, participate in what Guglielmo Carchedi (1977) has termed the *function of capital*: the control and surveillance of commodity production and circulation that enable surplus value to be appropriated and realized. In organizational terms, corporate directorates wield sovereign authority over specific firms. They exercise the function of capital at the highest level, even as lower levels of operational management also participate in practices of control and surveillance that form part of what Carchedi has termed the 'collective capitalist'. Billionaires, however, do not necessarily inhabit corporate boardrooms or otherwise participate in the function of capital, although their incomes derive from appropriated surplus value. Put another way, billionaires, particularly heirs to fortunes, may have an essentially passive relation to the accumulation of capital. They may be coupon-clipping *rentiers*, whose affluence appears as a mere by-product of the vagaries of the market and the efforts of others. *Rentier* billionaires hold paramount positions in capitalism's relations of distribution, but they are at one remove from the relations of production. Conversely, directors of the world's largest corporations hold authoritative positions in production relations; and those who network across borders are especially engaged in transnational practices of corporate governance and accumulation.

There is good reason to believe, however, that within the structure of global economic power, billionaires and boardroom networkers overlap and intersect. Studies of corporate business and capitalist class organization have documented many instances of participation by major shareholders in the top management of large corporations, sometimes as unitary interests, sometimes as members of more diverse controlling constellations (Scott 1997). Research on corporate ownership around the world reveals that, contrary to Berle and Means's (1932) thesis of separation of ownership and control, even the largest corporations tend to have controlling shareholders.

> These controlling shareholders are ideally placed to monitor the management, and in fact the top management is usually part of the controlling family, but at the same time they have the power to expropriate the minority shareholders as well as the interest in doing so. (La Porta et al. 1999: 512)

Even in the USA, long held to be a bastion of management control over large corporations, the vast majority of publicly traded corporations have controlling shareholders (Holderness 2009). Comparative research shows that in most capitalist countries, firms with major shareholders (holding 10 per cent or more of voting shares) have boards on which those shareholders are represented by substantial minorities or majorities (Dahya et al. 2007: 83). There is also evidence from Australia that more than a third of the largest post-war fortunes 'were associated with leadership of public companies, in the capacity of directors and executives' (Gilding 1999: 179).

But if the research literature suggests that some of the world's billionaires may be active participants, as major shareholders or even directors, it is silent on how the super-affluent are positioned within the global corporate elite.[2] In this chapter, we take up four broad positional issues:

- How do the major regional differences we have discerned – North/South, inter-triadic – pertain to the world's billionaires, and to billionaires in the global corporate elite?
- Given long-standing patriarchal norms surrounding property inheritance, how does gender figure in the positioning of billionaires within the corporate elite? Do women continue to inhabit the margins of economic power?
- How do other social relations, beyond the corporate boardroom, embed the world's billionaires within the global power structure? In particular, does kinship organize the super-affluent into tightly knit groups around specific firms; does billionaire participation on transnational policy boards create bridges that span across these groups?

- Are billionaires, in their corporate affiliations, likely to be rooted in national domiciles, wherein they control a single giant firm and its subsidiaries; conversely, which billionaires are more transnational in their network positions?

Forbes billionaires and G500 billionaires

Our criterion for billionaire status comes directly from *Forbes*, which draws on public records and business intelligence in annually assessing the net worth of wealthy individuals and families.[3] Fortunately for this research, *Forbes* adopted a rule in compiling its 1997 list which was applied consistently thereafter. Noting that the booming stock markets of the day had conjured a good many newly minted paper billionaires, *Forbes* revised its selection criterion: 'A billion bucks no longer gets you in. You've got to have made it yourself, or you've got to be actively managing it.'[4] In effect, these criteria removed many *rentiers* from the list. The *Forbes* lists considered here feature billionaires who are or have been actively engaged in the accumulation of capital. Any individual listed as a *Forbes* billionaire in the years 1997, 1999, 2001, 2003, 2005 or 2007 was deemed eligible for inclusion in this research.

Forbes sometimes lists fortunes by families and sometimes by single patriarchs. We follow this convention in designating as 'billionaires' all individuals on the *Forbes* list. Where a fortune is, according to *Forbes*, 'shared' by several family members, we apportion it equally among them. But we then widen the designation to include any family members on G500 boards, based on further biographical research. Other family members are generally close relatives – spouses, siblings, parents, offspring, occasionally a cousin.[5]

Understandably, billionaires make up only a tiny fraction of the world's leading corporate directors. Of the roughly 20,000 people who at some point in the decade served on a G500 board, billionaires comprised only 1.2 per cent (235 individuals), and members of immediate families added another .5 per cent (95 individuals). A further 11 billionaires and 6 more family members served on G500 boards, but not when the companies were in the G500, bringing the grand total to 347.

Figure 6.1 shows that from 1996 to 2006, although the number of billionaires active on G500 boards increased from 91 to 126 people,[6] the population of billionaires grew much more frenetically, from 225 to 946.[7] Thus, by early 2007 proportionately *fewer* of the world's billionaires were active on G500 boards. In 1996, nearly a quarter of these fortunes were directly represented by a family member on a G500 board; by 2006 barely 10 per cent were.[8]

Several factors are relevant to an interpretation of these trends. Many billionaires control large firms that do not rank among the 500 largest in the world,[9] and it is likely that inflation of asset prices swelled the ranks of billionaires with fortunes based in firms that did not clear the bar for G500 membership, which itself has been rising along with the ongoing concentration and centralization of capital.[10] Other billionaires own private companies, unlisted on stock exchanges and so secretive that they remain outside the realm of observable cases for a study of this kind.[11] Still other billionaires may appoint non-kin representatives to the board of the firms they control (Dahya et al. 2007). Finally, a great many wealthy capitalist families in control of some of the world's largest companies are multimillionaires but not billionaires. Indeed, Haseler (1999) views those with more than $1 billion in net worth of investable assets as the smallest of four factions within the world's super-rich. In this respect, our focus on billionaires establishes a very high bar in exploring the relationship between propertied wealth and representation in the global corporate elite.

A more stringent criterion for elite membership requires that an individual serve not merely as a G500 director but as an *interlocker*, helping to connect the directors of the world's largest corporations into a corporate community. On this count, billionaires are relatively more active in the corporate elite than other G500 directors. Across the decade, 2,045 directors served at some point on multiple G500 boards. Of these 2.6 per cent (53) were *Forbes* billionaires and .7 per cent (14) were family members, a total of 3.3 per cent. Among billionaire directors, fully 22.6 per cent of *Forbes* billionaires and 14.7 per cent of family members were interlockers at some point, compared to 10.2 per cent of other

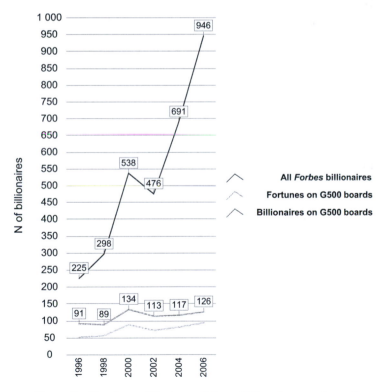

Figure 6.1 Numbers of *Forbes* and G500 billionaires, 1996–2006

G500 directors. Although they comprise a tiny minority of G500 directors, as a group billionaires are more likely than other directors to serve on multiple boards.

The spatial distribution of billionaires

In Chapters 2, 4 and 5, we noted that the global corporate elite is spatially organized in a distinctive configuration. Despite minor overtures towards the participation of directors from the global South, the network is centred in the North Atlantic heartland, and increasingly tilted towards Europe. Figures 6.2 and 6.3 show the spatial distribution of billionaires as of 1996 and 2006, comparing the *Forbes* lists with the complement of billionaires (including family members) who direct G500 corporations (hereafter, G500 billionaires). Only countries with at least ten billionaires on the *Forbes* list of either 1997 or 2007 are shown; the others are aggregated into larger regions.[12] The charts are calibrated with the USA (the world's leading locus of billionaires) as the reference category, defining the ceiling for each distribution. This allows us to compare across countries/regions, assessing whether billionaires resident in a given locale tend to participate on G500 boards more or less than their counterparts in the USA.

In 1996 (Figure 6.2) the USA dominated the scene. At the other extreme,

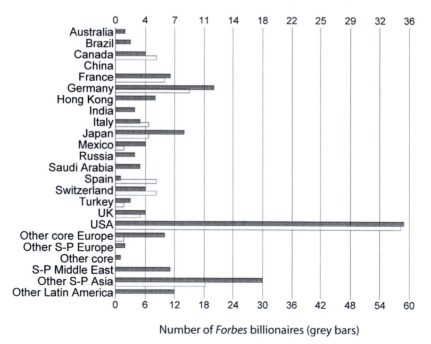

Figure 6.2 Distribution of *Forbes* and G500 billionaires, 1996

Africa was virtually shut out. A not inconsiderable number of the world's billionaires, however, resided in various semi-peripheral locations. Brazil, Hong Kong, India, Mexico, Russia, Saudi Arabia, Turkey and other semi-peripheral states of the Middle East, East Asia and Latin America all supplied billionaires to the *Forbes* list. But among these, only Mexico, Turkey and some East Asian states contributed billionaires to corporate boardrooms in 1996.

Most striking is the concentration of billionaires, including billionaire directors, resident in semi-peripheral East Asia. Our data refer to year-end 1996 and early 1997, a few months before the Asian financial crisis. At this conjuncture enormous fortunes had been amassed, many through speculation, as the East Asian region was a magnet for over-accumulation. Extreme class inequality in countries like Malaysia and South Korea is the subtext for the thirty billionaires based in the East Asian semi-periphery – more than double that of Japan, the world's second-largest economy.[13]

Among the core states, we also find great unevenness in participation on leading corporate boards. Billionaires based in smaller states such as Australia (also the Netherlands, Belgium, Austria and Israel – not shown in the chart) did not direct G500 companies in 1996, but those living in Spain, Switzerland, Canada and Italy tended to hold directorships. Among other triad states, few of

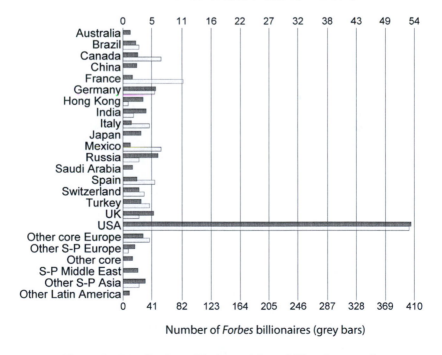

Number of G500 directors (white bars)

Number of *Forbes* billionaires (grey bars)

Figure 6.3 Distribution of *Forbes* and G500 billionaires, 2006

Japan's fourteen billionaires participated on G500 boards (the main exception being the Toyoda clan), which was also the case to a lesser extent for Germany's nineteen billionaires.

By 2006 (Figure 6.3), some interesting shifts are evident. The most dramatic growth is in the US-based complement, which increments at a rate of 588 per cent, compared to 225 per cent for the rest of the world. By the beginning of 2007, billionaires resident in the USA had jumped from 26 per cent to 43 per cent of the global total. The subset of US-based billionaires directing G500 firms had also grown faster than elsewhere, so that the proportion of G500 billionaire directors based in the USA had expanded from 38.5 per cent to 42.1 per cent. Notwithstanding the hypermobility of the super-rich as a social category, US capitalism, with its giant home market, political stability and low-tax regime, is the centre of gravity for the world's billionaires.

We also see in Figure 6.3 how the Asian financial crisis of 1997 took its toll: the number of billionaires based in semi-peripheral East Asia stays flat and the complement of G500 billionaires shrinks from eleven to three. Meanwhile, billionaires from Brazil, India and Russia join the ranks of G500 directors, and billionaires resident in Mexico and Turkey increase their boardroom presence. Yet despite the emergence of nineteen Chinese billionaires, none directs a G500 firm. Finally, among core states, Canada, France and Spain stand out as places where billionaires inhabit the corporate boardrooms, especially when compared with Japan, which has no billionaire G500 directors.

Gendering the global corporate elite

Recalling the results of previous studies of the super-affluent, it is not surprising that participation in the elite circle of billionaire directors, and in the even more exclusive circle of billionaire networkers, is highly skewed by gender. In 1996, only 8.2 per cent (i.e. thirteen) of G500 billionaires were women; a decade later, the proportion had increased modestly to 11.1 per cent, representing eighteen women. A sizeable proportion of women were (unlisted) relatives of billionaires on the *Forbes* list. In 1996, 46.2 per cent of the thirteen women were relatives of *Forbes* billionaires; by 2006, the proportion remained essentially unchanged, at 44.4 per cent. Conversely, men generally found their way into our population of G500 billionaires by virtue of their listing in *Forbes*, indicating that they either actively manage an inherited family fortune, or amassed the fortune themselves. Nearly three-quarters of G500 billionaire men were listed by *Forbes* in 1996 (73.8 per cent) and in 2006 (72.9 per cent). The few billionaire women on G500 boards did not differ sharply from the overall pattern of national residences in Figures 6.2 and 6.3, although Europe and two semi-peripheral countries became more prominent locations. In 1996, six resided in the USA, six in Europe and one in Turkey; in 2006, five resided in the USA, ten in Europe, two in Turkey and one in Mexico. Finally, women rarely engaged with the corporate network, beyond their directorship in the family firm. In 1996, only one billionaire networker was a woman; by 2006 two were. In both years, two women had a kinship tie to a G500 networker (compared to thirteen men in 1996 and ten men in 2006 with such ties).

In short, among the G500 billionaires, the historical marginalization of women from economic power continued into the twenty-first century, with barely discernible signs of greater equity.

Kinship and policy-group affiliations

Consideration of gender evokes the question of kinship, a central issue in the study of great fortunes. Our analysis so far has focused on individuals and their positioning vis-à-vis regional and gendered dimensions of inequality, largely bracketing the phenomenon of kinship. Yet super-affluent families tend to participate in 'kinecon groups' (Zeitlin et al. 1974), each one built around a family fortune and the strategic provisions for reproducing it on an expanding scale. The seminal study of these clusters of familial wealth and corporate power examined the thirty-seven largest corporations of Chile, circa 1964, and documented the control of these firms by wealthy families and individuals, via minority control and pyramiding inter-corporate ownership. Maurice Zeitlin and his colleagues provided a clear refutation of Berle and Means's (1932) claim that with the dilution of share control blocks, large corporations would achieve a separation of ownership and control, through which salaried managers gain effective power. Although by conventional Berle and Means methodology (which does not sufficiently consider kinship ties) fifteen of the thirty-seven companies were found to be ultimately under management control, a close look at kinecon structures, including pyramiding and the alignments of multiple families, reclassified fourteen of them as family controlled. Zeitlin and his co-authors commented that

> [...] the word 'family' may be [...] inadequate to encompass the intricate kinship network that unites a number of related officers, directors, and principal share-holders into a cohesive control group. The 'effective kinship unit' may include close relatives (secondary and tertiary) and other kin outside the immediate family who are nevertheless essential members of the extended and tightly organized network that controls a given corporation. (1974: 108)

Ordinarily, however, 'the kinecon group consists of the primary, secondary, and other relatives among the officers, directors, and principal shareholders whose combined individual and indirect (institutions) shareholdings constitute the dominant proprietary interest in the corporation' (ibid.: 110).

The implications of kinecon groups for the transnational capitalist class are important. William Canak, referring to Zeitlin's and others' research, avers that '[...] the emergence of large corporations has not undermined the cohesion of the dominant class. Through intertwined family and corporate structures (kin-econ networks), the dominant class reproduces itself across time, space, and place' (1991: 152). The kinecon group gives us a framework for understanding how billionaires might be embedded within the global corporate elite. That in 1996 eighteen billionaire families were represented by multiple members on G500 boards, and that the number grew to twenty-two families by 2006, suggests that such groups do play a role in the network.

One way to explore that role is through a network analysis that focuses ex-plicitly on the G500 billionaires and the organizations they direct, while also keeping track of kinship relations. We compiled all the organizational affiliations of G500 billionaires at two points in time – 1996 and 2006 – including corporate directorships as well as policy-group directorships in transnational organizations like the World Economic Forum (WEF) and the Trilateral Commission (TC). These data afford a two-mode network analysis, in which both individuals and organizations appear as nodes, with board memberships (connecting individuals to organizations) as the lines in the network.

Unlike the transnationalists of Chapter 5, who by 2006 formed a single con-nected component, arcing across the North Atlantic, in both years *most G500 billionaires kept to their own companies*: the network of billionaires and their organizational affiliations remained for the most part a collection of discon-nected fragments. Component analysis revealed many small components which resembled kinecon groups. In 1996, thirty-five components had four or fewer members (individual and organizational). Most of these small components con-sist of billionaires who, as directors of single G500 firms, tap into the global corporate elite through their contact with fellow board members. The larger components are of more analytic interest. In 1996 there were three components of five and one of seven, typically composed, in classic kinecon style, of individu-als affiliated with a single firm, as in the Chung-Mong family's directorships with Hyundai.[14]

The larger groupings of eight or more members merit further examination. Figure 6.4 plots them in a two-dimensional space. Persons are circles; organ-izations are squares (policy groups are marked with a leading 'P' in the label; leading characters for firms indicate the country of domicile). In the sociogram's lower right quadrant, a component of eight is recognizable as Warren Buffett's empire. It includes the patriarch as well as wife Susan and son Howard. All three sit on the family holding company, which in 1996 owned large stakes in Coca-Cola Bottling, Coca-Cola Enterprises and Gillette. Warren Buffett's directorship with the investment bank Salomon rounds out the affiliations. The lower left quadrant gives us another example of a kinecon group, involving five members of the Spanish Botins and their directorships in four financial institutions, including the flagship Santander Bank, the Royal Bank of Scotland and two Italian financials.

The space's upper left quadrant contains a larger and more diverse collection of billionaires, spanning the triad. Its eleven members include Shoichiro Toyoda, past president of Toyota and patriarch of the Toyoda family; Stephan Schmidheiny, heir to a fortune based in asbestos manufacture and active on multiple boards in his native Switzerland; Samuel Curtis Johnson, fourth-generation owner of Wisconsin-based S. C. Johnson & Sons Inc. (a non-G500 firm); and Anthony J. F. O'Reilly, chair and CEO of US-based H. J. Heinz, until 1998. In contrast to the kinecon structure of the Buffett and Botin groups, *what connects this otherwise disjoint trans-triadic assemblage is the participation of three billionaires on the World Business Council for Sustainable Development* (WBCSD), a major global policy group that Schmidheiny founded in the mid-1990s.

Similarly, with the largest component of 35 (shown in the top half of the sociogram, consisting of 17 organizations and 18 people), transnational policy groups play a major role in connecting otherwise discrete kinecon groups into a formation that traverses the triad. Here we find other members of the Toyoda clan, who in 1996 were still active on the board of Toyota, one of whom also served on the Trilateral Commission (TC) – a major point of articulation. Five billionaire families from each region of the triad are represented on the TC, including Riley Bechtel, head of Bechtel Corporation (which, however, does not clear the bar for G500 membership). Besides the Toyodas, families from North America and Europe contribute multiple members to the network:

- from the USA the Greenbergs (major shareholders in insurance company American International Group – UAMI);
- from Canada, the Bronfmans, heirs to the Seagram fortune, and the Desmaraises (owners of Power Corporation, aligned through jointly owned Pargesa Holding with Albert and Gerald Frère of Belgium, who did not qualify for the *Forbes* list in 1997); and
- from Italy the Agnellis, heirs to the Fiat fortune.

Other billionaires participate in the dominant component as individuals. These include Michel David-Weill, a director of the French firm Groupe Danone (although his fortune resided in New York-based investment bank Lazard Frères), and Jerome Seydoux, heir to the Schlumberger fortune.

Ten years later, the network continues to be largely disjointed. In the interim, there has been a proliferation of small components of the simple kinecon variety. Apart from the fifty-eight clusters with four or fewer members, there are two slightly larger groups,[15] and two more substantial ones which are mapped in Figure 6.5. The Buffett empire persists in a lesser component of eight persons and five organizations, with an emergent connection between Warren Buffett and Bill Gates, whose foundation received a considerable piece of Buffett's fortune in 2006. Gates sits on the Berkshire board, which by 2006 had the distinction of having more billionaire members than any other G500 directorate. Gates's

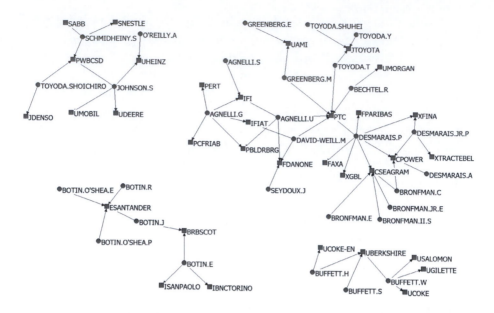

Figure 6.4 Main groupings of billionaires and their organizational affiliations, 1996

partner at Microsoft, Steve Ballmer, belongs to the TransAtlantic Business Dialogue (discussed in Chapter 8), as does Frederick W. Smith, owner of FedEx.

By 2006 the dominant component has grown in size and national diversity to comprise a configuration of thirty-eight individuals and twenty-five organizations. It takes in Lee Kun-Hee of South Korea (owner of Samsung Electronics), and several semi-peripheral billionaires – the Zambranos of CEMEX, Lakshmi Mittal (Indo-British owner of Arcelor Mittal Steel) and two associates of Mittal, Turkish-based Rahmi Koç and family, and the Ambanis of Reliance Industries (India). In contrast to their predominance in the league table of billionaires, American billionaires play a relatively muted role in this configuration. Private-equity player Henry Kravis attends the Bilderberg Conference; Wilbur Ross, another private equity player, directs Arcelor Mittal with French financier Romain Zaleski, whose 8 per cent stake in Arcelor was crucial to Mittal's takeover of it in 2006. Kravis and Ross are the only American billionaires who participate in the dominant component, and their positions are not particularly central. In contrast, the Montreal-based Desmaraises are firmly ensconced, even more so than in 1996, via holding companies Power Corporation on the Montreal side and Groupe Bruxelles Lambert (XGBL) on the European side, with their Belgian partners the Frère brothers also directing the latter. The Frère–Desmarais partnership is relatively unusual, both in the intermingling of vast assets and in its trans-Atlantic span; in fact, it is the only case of a transnational kinecon group. On the political side, Paul Desmarais Jr attends at Bilderberg and his brother André serves on the TC, continuing the earlier political activism of Paul Sr.

Figure 6.5 Main groupings of billionaires and their organizational affiliations, 2006

Their policy-group affiliations are critical to the network, as are Mustafa Koç's attendance at Bilderberg and Lorenzo Zambrano's service on both the TC and the WBCSD. In organizational terms, it is billionaires' participation on the TC and at Bilderberg which pulls what would otherwise be six disjointed pieces into a single network. Among the major European billionaires, the Botins (owners of Santander Bank) hook into the network through Ana Patricia's position on the TC and the Mohns sit with André Desmarais as shareholders of Bertelsmann, while German media magnate Hubert Burda attends at Bilderberg and directs France-based Lagardère Group. There is also, by 2006, a clutch of French billionaires including the Pinault, Arnault, Bellon, and Bouygues families.

This analysis highlights the billionaires as a distinct stratum within the global corporate elite, owning enormous assets and connecting into the corporate power structure primarily in terms of proprietary control over some of the world's largest firms. The tendency is towards discrete, kinecon groups, many of which remain detached from the larger elite social formation. The logic of these groups is that of *closure* in an introverted pattern of corporate directorships associated with strategic control of particular firms rather than *brokerage* and 'social capital'. Political activism, however, creates an extensive and expanding set of bridges across distinct family interests, putting to rest the idea that these billionaires confine themselves to the world of business and leisure. Still, only a small minority of billionaires reach in their organizational affiliations beyond the introverted kinecon structures of single families controlling large corporations.

Notwithstanding this dominant tendency, it is worthwhile considering how the super-affluent are embedded in the broader corporate interlock network. In focusing exclusively on interlocks among billionaires, we have not yet considered the ties that link billionaires with other members of the global corporate elite. In Table 6.1, we list the billionaire families that participate most extensively in the interlock network. The table features families whose members direct multiple G500 firms, thus showing an extraverted pattern of corporate affiliations that extends beyond the control of one corporation. It excludes families that participate in the network purely through affiliations with a single firm.[16] Five of the eleven families show increasing involvement in the network – the Frères of Belgium and their partners, the Desmaraises of Canada, the Bellons and Bouygues of France, and the Slims of Mexico. Families that come to participate less include the three US-based clans, the Botins of Spain and the Agnellis (whose presence on the Fiat board was diminished in 2003/04 with the deaths of Umberto and Giovanni).

TABLE 6.1 Leading billionaire families in the global corporate elite, 1996 and 2006

Family name	Principal residence	Main firm	1996*	2006*
Agnelli	Italy	Fiat	3 | 2	1 | 0
Bellon	France	Sodexo Alliance		4 | 1
Botin	Spain	Santander Bank	5 | 2	3 | 1
Bouygues	France	Bouygues SA	3 | 0	3 | 1
Buffett	USA	Berkshire Hathaway, etc.	3 | 2	2 | 0
Desmarais	Canada	Power Corporation, etc.	3 | 2	3 | 3
Fentener	Netherlands	SHV Holdings	3 | 1	2 | 1
Frère	Belgium	GBL, etc.	1 | 1	2 | 2
Ingram	USA	Ingram Micro	3 | 1	2 | 1
Slim	Mexico	Carso Global Telecom	1 | 1	3 | 1
Tisch	USA	Loews, etc.	4 | 1	3 | 0

Notes: * The first entry indicates the number of family members with one G500 directorship; the second indicates the number of family members with two or more G500 directorships.
   Criteria for inclusion in the list: in either year, at least three family members with a G500 directorship – one of whom is a networker, or at least two family members who are networkers.

Generalizing this analysis to all billionaire networkers and their kin, we can get a clearer sense of how the super-affluent are positioned in the global corporate elite. We begin with the twenty-one billionaires who sit on multiple G500 boards, as of either 1996 or 2006. As billionaires, they are key players on the personal-proprietary side of corporate power; as networkers they participate in corporate power's more social aspect. To one side of them are any kin who direct G500 firms; to the other are the corporate networkers with whom they serve on one or another board. Together, these social types constitute each billionaire networker's social circle, i.e. those kin and networkers with whom (s)he has immediate contact via service on the same board. Combining these social circles, we obtain the network segment that ties the billionaire networkers and their families into the larger corporate elite. Figure 6.6 shows the network of billionaires' social circles[17] as of 1996. In this one-mode network, nodes represent people, who are linked if they sit together on a corporate board. Thick lines indicate that two people sit together on multiple G500 boards. Nodes have been placed into the space according to a spring embedded algorithm; hence, the proximity of nodes to each other in the sociogram tells us roughly how close directors are to each other in the social space of the network (Freeman 2005: 251). Black nodes represent *Forbes* billionaires; dark grey nodes represent billionaire family members; grey nodes represent non-billionaire networkers who belong to one or more billionaire social circles. Shapes show the domicile of each person's corporate affiliations, with transnationalists depicted as diamonds. The twenty-one billionaire networkers and their kin are highlighted with name labels and slightly larger nodes.

The network is spatially clustered in two significant ways. Most obviously, members of each billionaire family are quite proximate to each other, confirming that within the social space of the network kinship exerts a strong gravitational attraction. Equally important is the clustering of the formation into European (circles) and American (squares) zones, with Canadian billionaires (the Desmaraises, Bronfmans and Westons) mainly aligned with continental Europe. The one exception to this clustering is the Spain-based Botins. The Botins' two directorships at the Royal Bank of Scotland (a partner to Santander Bank at the time) link the family to British capital via fellow RBS director Lord Vallance of Tummel, who in 1996 was chair of BT, a firm whose board contained seven other mainly British networkers. The Botins also hooked into the American zone, however, by virtue of John Creedon's directorship at Santander. Creedon, retired CEO of New York-based Metropolitan Life, was also a director at weapons manufacturer Rockwell International, whose board included seven other US networkers. The one semi-peripheral billionaire – Lee Kun-Hee, of Samsung – appears in the sociogram as an isolate from the larger network. Otherwise, however, the billionaire networkers, their kin, and the networkers that the former meet in the boardrooms form a single, connected network.

Figure 6.7 shows the network of overlapping social circles as of year-end 2006. Again, clustering by region and kinship is evident. American billionaires now claim more of the social space, with nine fortunes represented in the network, compared to six in 1996. Within Europe, the social circles of three French families – Bellon, Bouygues and Pinault – overlap extensively. Through the mediation of numerous non-billionaire networkers, these groups link to the

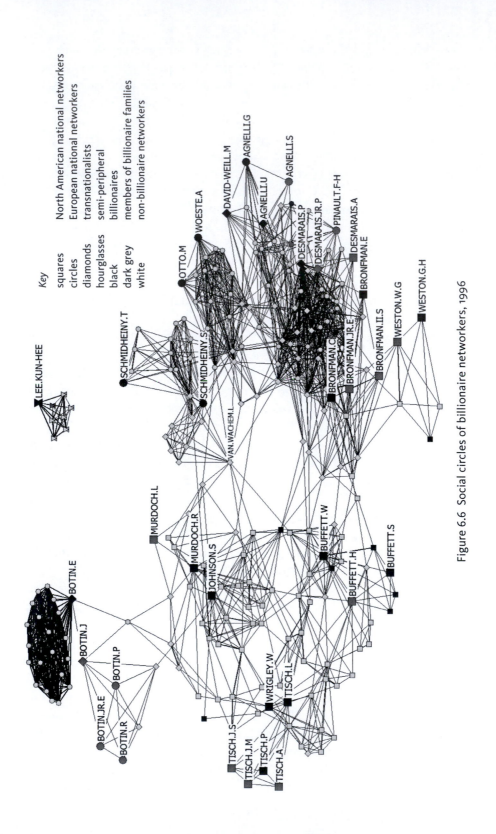

Figure 6.6 Social circles of billionaire networkers, 1996

Key

squares	North American national networkers
circles	European national networkers
diamonds	transnationalists
hourglasses	semi-peripheral
black	billionaires
dark grey	members of billionaire families
white	non-billionaire networkers

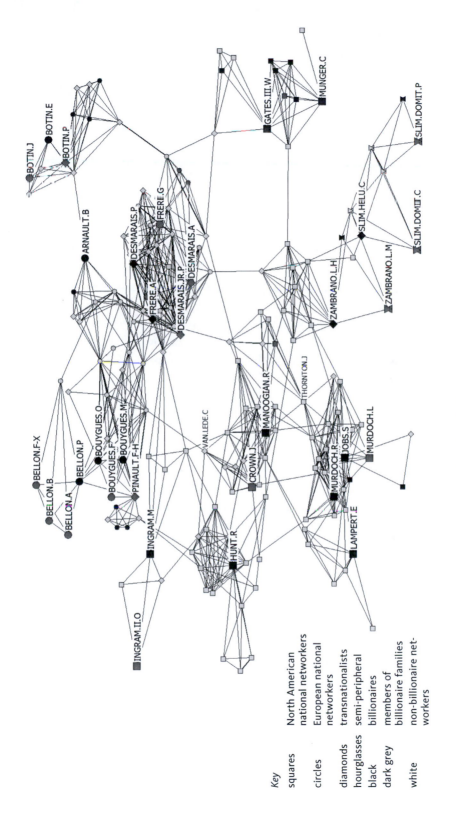

Figure 6.7 Social circles of billionaire networkers, 2006

Key

squares	North American national networkers
circles	European national networkers
diamonds	transnationalists
hourglasses	semi-peripheral billionaires
black	members of billionaire families
dark grey	non-billionaire networkers
white	

trans-Atlantic Desmarais–Frère alliance, which remains the network's densest segment. On the American side, Bill Gates of Microsoft and Steve Jobs of Apple Computers both participate as networkers, as does Richard Manoogian (owner of Masco Corp – not a G500 firm), who directs Morgan Chase and Ford Motor Company. The 2006 configuration of social circles includes the Zambrano and Slim fortunes, based in Mexico, by virtue of Lorenzo H. Zambrano's seat on the IBM board, which puts him in direct contact with eight American networkers. Fellow IBM director Cathleen Black (president of Hearst Communications) serves on the Coca-Cola board with Donald Keough (retired president of Coke), who in turn sits with Bill Gates on the board of Berkshire Hathaway. In effect, Keough mediates a relation, at one remove, between Bill Gates and a director of his one-time employer, IBM.

In fact, at both points in time, key non-billionaire networkers serve as *brokers*, connecting billionaire social circles that would otherwise remain disjointed. *Such brokerage weaves the social circles of the billionaires, built as they are around kinecon groups, into a single connected network which is entirely based in the North Atlantic zone.* By 2006, this zone has been extended to Mexico, with the participation of the Slims and Zambranos. The networkers who play key brokerage roles – bridging across social circles – tend to be outside directors of various large firms – often retired executives, or as Stokman and his colleagues would have it, *éminences grises* (Stokman et al. 1985). A leading example from 1996, marked in Figure 6.6 in small font, is Lodewijk Christiaan van Wachem, retired CEO of Shell, who sat with Stephan Schmidheiny on the board of Swiss-based ABB. Van Wachem's outside directorships with six other G500 firms, including Shell, US-based IBM and German-based BMW, linked Schmidheiny at one remove to a trans-Atlantic array of corporate interests. Two examples are marked in the 2006 sociogram. Cees van Lede, director and retired CEO of Akzo Nobel, also directs two other Dutch firms, Air France-KLM and US-based Sara Lee, where his contacts include US billionaire James Crown. Van Lede's fellow director on the Air France-KLM board, Patricia Barbizet, manages the Pinault family fortune and directs Bouygues; hence, Van Lede's affiliations mediate between French and American billionaires. Another social broker, John Thornton (former president of Goldman Sachs), is a professor at Tsinghua University, Beijing, chair of the Brookings Institution, and director of Ford, NewsCorp, Intel and the Industrial and Commercial Bank of China. Thornton's directorship at NewsCorp puts him in the social circle of the Murdochs; his directorship at Ford puts him in the circle of Richard Manoogian. He is not a billionaire – Thornton's net worth has been estimated at $300 million, pointing again to the fact that our focus on billionaires presents only the top layer of super-affluence within the global corporate elite.

Transnational billionaires?

The brokerage relations pulling kinecon groups into a single, global network direct us towards the final issue on this chapter's agenda: billionaires' participation in transnational corporate-elite relations. The super-affluent might participate in transnational practices in several ways. Earlier, we saw that global policy boards such as the Trilateral Commission, explored in depth in Chapters 2 and 8, integrate some billionaires into the political projects of the transnational capitalist class. In all, seventeen G500 billionaires sat on transnational policy boards in 1996 and twenty-one did so in 2006. Six served on policy boards in both years, making the total thirty two in either or both years, or roughly one in ten G500 billionaires. Like networkers, billionaires tend to serve on the Trilateral Commission (eleven billionaires), or the World Business Council for Sustainable Development (seven) or to attend the Bilderberg Conference (nine) – putting them in touch with other members of the corporate elite and with influential figures from other domains. Certain families and individuals have been especially active in this regard – the Desmaraises, the Agnellis, Marco Provera and Lorenzo H. Zambrano – providing leadership in crafting global corporate agendas.

Besides service on policy groups, a billionaire may connect into the transnational aspect of the global elite by being a transnationalist or by having transnationalists within his or her social circle. Among G500 billionaires, the ranks of transnationalists are rather thin, and in contrast to non-billionaire networkers, did not grow appreciably in the decade spanning the turn of the twenty-first century. In 1996, seven billionaire transnationalists (marked as diamonds in Figure 6.6) included two Botins and two Desmaraises. The ties carried by these seven served to integrate corporate Europe, or, in the case of the Desmaraises, to link European business with Canadian business. By 2006, four of eight billionaire transnationalists were principals in the Desmarais-Frère group, and two (L. H. Zambrano and Helu C. Slim) linked corporations across national borders within North America. Not surprisingly, billionaire transnationalists tend to have other transnationalists among their immediate contacts, a pattern we observed in our general analysis of transnationalists in Chapter 5. In 2006, except for Pinault and Zambrano, billionaire transnationalists had social circles in which a majority of contacts were other transnationalists.

As for the vast majority of G500 billionaires who are not networkers, let alone transnationalists, we find a shift, from social circles comprised almost exclusively of national networkers, to a fairly broad inclusion of transnationalists. In 1996, 61.6 per cent of billionaires with single G500 directorships had no transnationalists as contacts, indicating a predominantly introverted board composition. By 2006, the proportion whose social circles lacked transnationalists had fallen to 39.3 per cent, and the median proportion of transnationalists in their social circles, at 20.0 per cent, was comparable to the median for non-billionaire G500 networkers (23.8 per cent). In fact, if we think of a cosmopolitan social circle as comprised of a majority of transnationalists, by 2006 a greater proportion of single-directorship billionaires had cosmopolitan social circles (26.4 per cent) than did non-billionaire networkers (21.9 per cent). Within the global corporate elite, billionaires have followed the general trend towards more transnationalized contacts, and since they were especially parochial in the mid-1990s, the shift appears to have been especially big.

Conclusion

Our focus in this chapter on billionaires has had the virtue of concision; it also limits our gaze to the 'top layer' of kinecon groups, however – the tip of the iceberg. If we had full data on fortunes of less than one billion dollars, we could go much farther in identifying the confluence of personal ownership and corporate directorships that partially shapes the elite network. Still, this very conservative approach reveals the persistence of capitalist property ownership as a central element in the structure of global corporate power. The managerial revolution – the claim that the ownership of capital has been divorced from its control, leaving salaried managers in charge – was first intimated in the 1930s (Berle and Means 1932). During the post-war boom years, it was celebrated as integral to the decomposition of capital and labour, and thus of capitalism itself (Dahrendorf 1959; Bell 1961). Still later, academics fretted over the 'agency problem' that purportedly stems from the latitude that top managers have in corporate decision-making (DiDonato et al. 1988; Becht et al. 2003). In fact, even in the USA, where share dispersal went the farthest, this 'revolution' was never more than a sideshow to the reproduction of personal and family empires. Recent American research confirms the persistence of personal ownership at the heart of corporate power (Holderness 2009).

Among the outstanding findings from our analysis of personal wealth and corporate power is the sharp over-representation of Euro-North American men amid the billionaires who direct the world's largest companies. Traditional patriarchal and Eurocentric elements of closure operate strongly, with only a hint of diminution, in inducting individuals into the stratum of super-rich corporate capitalists. Embedded in the global corporate interlock network are some of the world's most opulent family fortunes, socially organized as kinecon groups. In the elite structure, policy-planning boards and outside directors (many of them *éminences grises*) serve as social brokers, bridging between billionaire kinecon groups. At the heart of global corporate power, we find a combination of super-affluent owners, top managers and organic intellectuals, constituent elements of a transnational capitalist class that is irrevocably grounded on the *terra firma* of property ownership.

PART THREE

A transnational historic bloc?

7 | Constituting corporate Europe

Now the world's largest single market, yet composed of twenty-seven loosely federated member states varying in their locations within global capitalism, the economic zone delimited by the European Union is the focus of this chapter. As we saw in Chapters 3–5, there is evidence, in the inter-urban network, in the inter-corporate network, and in the interpersonal network, of an increasing European prominence within the global corporate power structure. Although the EU is a relatively recent development, the idea of an economically and politically integrated Europe goes back nearly two centuries, to an 1814 treatise written by Claude Henri Saint-Simon and Augustin Thierry. In their technocratic vision, Europe was to be led by *la classe industrielle*, including manufacturers, farmers, craftsmen and scientists. Yet within the industrial class, the stratum they considered the most outstanding was, ironically, the bankers (Saint-Simon and Thierry 1975 [1814]). It is sometimes argued that European unification was a product of US intervention (see Fennema and Rhijnsburger 2007) and even of an American Plan for Europe (van der Pijl 1984). Whatever the initial motives, by the late 1990s Europe had been formed into an economic zone, governed by its own institutional norms and structures, and relatively free of political barriers to the accumulation of capital across national borders.

The leading role that Europe's corporate capitalists played in shaping this zone has been well documented (Balanyá et al. 2000). Contrary to Saint-Simon, but understandably (given the fixity of productive capital compared to the mobility of money capital, particularly in an era of globalizing financial markets), European industrialists, not bankers, have been the most active advocates of integration. Since 1983, much of their activism has issued from the European Round Table of Industrialists (ERT), a group that, according to van Apeldoorn (2002), produced among other influential initiatives the first draft of the European Constitution. Founded by Volvo CEO Pehr Gyllenhammar, the ERT consisted initially of the presidents of seventeen European transnationals. It formed in response to the challenge of the Japanese firms that had penetrated the European market so successfully that the automobile and electronic equipment producers were severely hit. Yet the strategy of the ERT was not to demand protection or engage in other defensive strategies. On the contrary, the ERT argued that Europe should constitute itself as an economic space by strengthening European governance and setting up private–public ventures to create a better European infrastructure (Holman and van der Pijl 1996: 71).

Van Apeldoorn (2000, 2002) emphasizes the distinct phases of that integrative project, from the early 'neo-mercantilist' emphasis on infrastructure and a single market until the late 1980s towards a consensus on what he calls 'embedded neoliberalism', beginning in the early 1990s.

Historical narratives such as Balanyá et al.'s and van Apeldoorn's have shed light on the formation of a pan-European capitalist class, based in Europe's largest corporations and politically mobilized through the ERT. Other research (e.g. Eising 2007) shows that large corporations and pan-European business associations tend to have regular contact with the EU's key governance bodies, in particular the European Commission (EC) – so much so that in constructing a European universalism, 'the heavenly chorus' has sung 'with a strong upper class accent' (Hueglin 1999: 260). In effect, 'the public–private partnership between the EC and the ERT can be seen as a self-organizing, interorganizational network which is not (directly) accountable to any government (supranational or national), or any democratically legitimated legislature for that matter' (Kennett 2004: 67). The *topography* of corporate Europe, however – the social organization of corporate power – has yet to be charted.

Despite more than fifty years of European integration, studies of corporate networks in Europe have restricted themselves to single countries, or have compared across national networks without mapping the trans-European network: cf. Stokman et al. (1985); Scott (1997); Windolf (2002); Aguilera and Jackson (2003); Aguilera (2005); Maclean et al. (2006). Staples (2006, 2007) and Nollert (2005), however, have pointed to the increasingly international composition of corporate boards in Europe and to an emerging European network of board interlocks. Earlier chapters in this volume have suggested that, with its growing regional cohesiveness, corporate Europe has gained prominence within the North Atlantic heartland that forms the centre of gravity for the transnational capitalist class. Yet these analyses, focused as they have been on the global corporate network, tell us little about the actual topography of corporate Europe.

The question that inspires this chapter is: *What is the emerging shape and form of Europe's corporate community, and what are the implications for capitalist class formation in Europe?*

Corporate Europe as a community

If corporate communities entail bonds that foster some degree of solidarity among members, such bonds are deepened to the extent that corporate directors participate in a collective political project. Indeed, since the 1970s, corporate communities in core capitalist states have mobilized politically by extending their reach into the political field, through neoliberal policy-planning groups whose boards interlock with leading corporate directorates (cf. Carroll and Shaw 2001; Domhoff 2006 [1967; 1998]; Maman 1997; Useem 1984). As we saw in Chapter 2, complementing such national corporate activism has been the formation of a transnational network of global corporations and policy groups, focused around the Trilateral Commission, the World Economic Forum and the World Business Council for Sustainable Development. If the trajectory in capitalist class formation, at both national and transnational levels, has been towards greater collective agency – towards a 'class-for-itself' (Robinson 2004: 48), the social solidarities afforded by corporate communities, articulated as they are with policy-planning groups, have provided organizational and cultural bases for this movement.

Below, we investigate the topography of corporate Europe by examining the network of interlocking corporate directorates and its ties to the ERT, the key policy-planning vehicle for the capitalist class's collective agency in the project of European integration.

Research questions

The conception of corporate Europe as a *community* is rich in implications for analysing transnational capitalist class formation. It points to four substantive issues and corresponding research questions.

First, *communities require closure* to cement collective identity and to ground generalized trust (Coleman 1988), and closure always creates an inside and an outside (Walker 1993). The EU itself has formed according to an inside/outside dynamic, with membership expanding beyond the initial core six countries (1952) via several 'accessions' to a total of twenty-seven member states by 2008. As a community, corporate Europe has taken shape through processes of inclusion and exclusion. Most obvious have been national and regional differences associated with uneven development – the affluence of the north-west, the historically semi-peripheral status of the south, the exclusion of the east until the collapse of state socialism, after which it joined the European semi-periphery.[1] The resulting spatial division of labour has tended to concentrate the major banks among the wealthier European nations (Heartfield 2007: 38). These political economic differences mean that certain European places have been favoured as centres for corporate command, and thus for the corporate community, while others have been selected out, setting up an unequal structure of representation (see Mahon 1977), whose vertical motif of inclusion/exclusion can conflict with the 'horizontal' logic of community development. Such inequity can be tempered through a conscious policy aimed at balancing interests. In striving for a semblance of equanimity, the ERT recruits its members so that various countries are represented. Unevenness in the accumulation of capital, however, will tend to skew membership towards Europe's affluent north-west, where the largest corporations are domiciled. A first question is whether representation is becoming less unequal, or perhaps more so. *Is the process of class formation tending towards a pan-European corporate community or an enclosed club for only the leading corporations of a few rich nations?* Over the decade, has the representation of national business segments become less unequal in the corporate network and on the ERT, implying a broadening of the corporate community?

Second, *communities are sustained by networks of association among members* – an established feature of capitalist class formation within each advanced country (Bottomore and Brym 1989). In an era of pan-European state formation the question for corporate Europe is how path dependencies stemming from pre-existing *national* corporate communities condition the formation of a *transnational* corporate community. Key here is the extent to which the 'social capital' of the corporate community accumulates mainly through *bonding* within countries – persistence of national networks – or through *bridging* across them (Burt 2005; Coleman 1988). In Chapter 1 we established that in the late twentieth century transnational networks, within Europe or beyond, did not herald the disappearance of national networks, but arose 'on top' of them. Still, nationalist path dependencies can be eroded by the increasing volume of transnational business transactions within Europe and by policies and normative frameworks, including the preference for multinational representation on corporate boards (Heijltjes et al. 2003). Our second question asks how national and transnational aspects of corporate Europe coexist within the corporate community. *Is there, over time, less national bonding and more transnational bridging?* Or do national corporate communities persist even as a transnational community emerges?

Third, *communities are strengthened to the extent that they are institutionally complete*. In his classic analysis of ethnic communities, Breton (1964) noted that institutional completeness furnishes the capacity to reproduce community itself. For an ethnic community, such completeness includes educational, religious and other cultural institutions; for a transnational corporate community, it requires that the institutional means for capital accumulation – an integrated circuit of production, finance and distribution (G. Thompson 1977) – are accessible within the community on a *transnational*, not simply a national, level. This implies, among other things, a European Central Bank, a European stock market and Europe-wide regulatory agencies, which are now in place.[2] Such institutions enable pan-European accumulation, but do not speak directly to the process of capitalist class formation.[3]

For the corporate community, institutional completeness implies the development of pan-European *finance capital* – 'the integration of the circuits of money capital, productive capital and commodity capital under the conditions of monopolization and internationalization of capital by a series of links and relationships between individual capitals' (Overbeek 1980: 102). In Rudolf Hilferding's (1981 [1910]) original analysis of finance capital, bankers provided industrial firms with money capital (often in exchange for blocks of shares), but in turn expected a seat on the board of the industrial firm, putting bankers in a dominant position within an 'oligarchic' form of capital integration (Scott

1997). Subsequent studies of national corporate communities showed the German system to be one variant in a common move towards financial–industrial integration within corporate communities (ibid.). In this generic sense, the concept of finance capital 'locates the importance of banks and insurance companies in their domination of capital flows and not in discrete spheres of influence' (Mintz and Schwartz 1985: 866). Directors of financial firms, many of them primarily affiliated with large industrial firms, collectively wield allocative power over capital flows, and 'set the parameters of the corporate environment within which all large enterprises must act' (Scott 1991: 188).

Financial–industrial integration of this sort bundles business interests into a nationally integrated network, within which 'the corporate community is capable of coordinated economic decision making and united political action' (Mintz and Schwartz 1985: 866). But at the global level, despite Andreff's (1984) intimations of an emerging regime of internationalized finance capital, in Chapter 4 we did not find evidence of a tendency for financial institutions to serve as the hubs of a transnational network, although our analysis did suggest a very recent tendency towards capital integration on the European continent. Concomitantly, however, neoliberal financialization, the decoupling of finance from the 'real economy', has attenuated but not eliminated the financial–industrial nexus within national corporate communities while paradoxically embedding financial logics more deeply within the management of giant firms as they seek 'shareholder value' (Montgomerie 2008: 243). These considerations lead us to a dual research question on the issue of institutional completeness within contemporary corporate Europe. There is first the question *whether pan-European financial–industrial integration is discernible in the most recent development of the corporate network*. If so, there is the question *whether Europe's transnational finance capitalists* – the directors whose corporate affiliations link financial and industrial firms across borders – *tend to be bankers* (as in the classic German model, and in Saint-Simon's ruminations) *or perhaps industrialists* (as in the American system of loosely structured financial hegemony; Mintz and Schwartz 1985).

Fourth, communities are typically embedded within larger formations that shape community identity itself. Any consolidation of a European corporate community has occurred within broader processes of *globalization* – increasing volumes of international investment and trade, the transnationalization of production and the development of a global financial market. In this larger context, the development of a European network could simply be a local instance of an emergent and fully 'global' transnational capitalist class, disembedded from regional particularities (as in Robinson 2004), *or* it could herald a specific intensification of elite relations among European businesses. Only the latter implies an actual process of corporate community development within Europe. Our final question, which revisits our earlier discussion of closure, asks *how the European corporate community articulates with business interests elsewhere.* Is the trend more towards consolidation of the regional, pan-European network, or does corporate Europe reach out to other segments of the global corporate network? If the latter, is the pattern mainly a reproduction of the 'Atlantic ruling class' (van der Pijl 1984), or are there indications of more multilateral global reach? If the former, do we envisage in the fragmented network at the global level the expression of capitalist rivalry that may in the present crisis lead to economic warfare between the USA, Europe and the emerging corporate economies in Asia?

To summarize, a robust process of European capitalist class formation should be discernible in four aspects of corporate community development:

1 broadening, pan-European representation of capitalist interests;
2 increasingly transnational, bridging interlocks relative to national, bonding interlocks;
3 financial–industrial interlocking that crosses national borders; and
4 increasingly pan-European relations relative to ties linking corporate Europe to the rest of the world.

Below, we take up each of these issues as they pertain both to the network of corporate interlocks and to the position of the European Round Table of Industrialists within the corporate community.

Empirics

Data for membership on the ERT were obtained from the organization's official website (www.ert.be/), which provides a complete membership archive. Data for the European corporate board memberships and for the attributes of firms were taken from same database of G500 companies used in Chapters 4–6 of this book. In addressing our first three research questions, we focus exclusively on the subset of G500 corporations domiciled in Europe; in addressing our fourth question, we include all G500 corporations, distinguishing them by domicile.

Our designation of corporate Europe as a subset of the Global 500 enables an assessment of the extent to which European capitalists improved their competitive standing in capital's global league table between 1996 and 2006. As we saw earlier, G500 firms based in Europe increased from 170 to 193, enlarging the basis, among the world's largest companies, for a European corporate community. In contrast, corporate USA (dropping from 166 to 154 firms) and Japan (dropping from 124 to 69) lost position. With the increased complement of companies, the number of directors of European G500 firms also increased from 2,687 to 2,803. The total number of directors with multiple directorships in G500 European firms, however, actually fell from 330 to 311, and the number of European board interlocks fell from 621 to 548. As the number of firms grew while the number of interlocks fell, the density of the European corporate network dropped (from

0.0432 to 0.0296). Even so, the size of the dominant component of mutually reachable European corporations increased from 143 to 159, indicating *a larger but sparser European corporate network of interlocking directorates.*

I The unequal structure of national representation

The composition of corporate Europe How are the national constituents 'represented' in the European corporate community? We take Europe's population distribution as an intuitive baseline for assessing representation. If corporate capital had accumulated on a relatively even basis, the regional distribution of G500 head offices would match the distribution of population (and thus of available labour power). The extent and pattern in which the distributions diverge give us a sense of spatial unevenness in the command of corporate capital. Figures 7.1 and 7.2 compare several percentage distributions of national corporate domicile, with the baseline population distribution shown as a line.[4] The grey bars in the figures show the percentage of European G500 corporations domiciled in each country, indicating how well countries are represented in corporate Europe. *Relative to population size*, in 1996 France, Germany, the Netherlands, Belgium, the UK and Switzerland were over-represented as domiciles for G500 firms. Of these, the first four were core to the European Economic Community from inception; the last two have long held central positions as sites for internationalized accumulation within and beyond the North Atlantic. Spain, Italy, Austria, Denmark, Ireland and especially the European semi-periphery were under-represented. By year-end 2006 France, the UK, the Netherlands, Switzerland and Germany continue to be over-represented, but are joined by Swedish and Irish companies. Italy, Spain and especially the European semi-periphery remain under-represented. In both years, corporate Europe's composition is highly skewed towards the affluent countries of the north-west.

Europeanized corporate boards The representation of national constituencies becomes even more uneven when we restrict ourselves to those corporations whose boards maintain at least two transnational interlocks with other G500 European firms. Through their *Europeanized* boards of directors, these firms participate extensively in the European corporate community. The total number of such corporate boards expands over the decade, from 55 of 170 in 1996 to 79 of 193 in 2006, indicating that within Europe transnational interlocking has become a more common practice. But again we find a highly skewed distribution (see the white bars in Figures 7.1 and 7.2). In 1996, Germany and France accounted for over half of all Europeanized boards. The Netherlands, Belgium and Switzerland also figured prominently, but corporate Britain, despite its large complement of G500 firms, was conspicuous in its marginal participation in the network. In the ensuing decade, however, Franco-German predominance weakened, especially on the German side, and although companies based in the

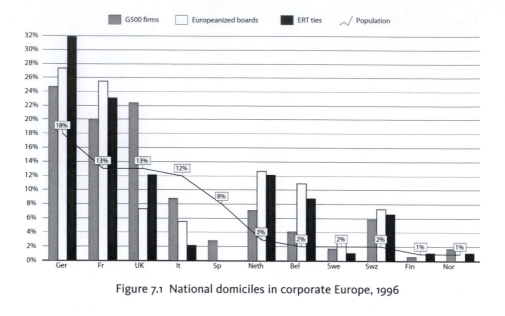

Figure 7.1 National domiciles in corporate Europe, 1996

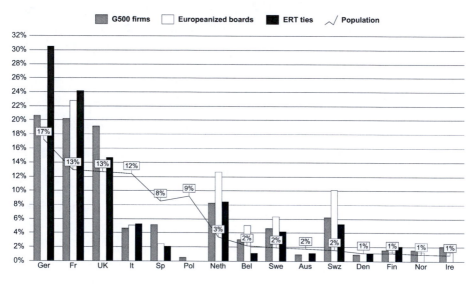

Figure 7.2 National domiciles in corporate Europe, 2006

Netherlands and Switzerland continued to be heavily over-represented (see also Heemskerk and Schnyder 2008), *the network came to include a greater diversity of domiciles*, reaching farther south to Spain and north to Sweden, though not east. British-based firms became more involved, so that by 2006 the proportion of population living in Britain matched the proportion of Europeanized boards domiciled there.

Overall, the same countries that provide domiciles for Europe's leading corporations predominate in the interlock network: the composition of the network has been shaped by corporate Europe's accumulation base. But some countries 'punch above their weights' in serving as hosts for a disproportionately large complement of Europeanized boards. Switzerland, the Netherlands, France and Sweden together account for 20 per cent of Europe's population, yet in 2006 fully 52 per cent of Europeanized boards were based in these four countries.

How are national domiciles 'represented' at the European Round Table? In 1996, sixty-seven top European firms were represented by their directors sitting on the ERT. Nineteen corporations had multiple directors on the ERT, generating a total of ninety-one interlocking memberships between G500 corporate boards and the ERT. The comparable figures in 2006 were sixty-eight firms and ninety-five interlocks. Some companies had as many as four directors on the ERT, indicating a very close articulation with the policy-planning process. Considering the black bars in Figures 7.1 and 7.2, we find that, overwhelmingly, German and French companies have predominated on the ERT, further sharpening the unequal structure of representation that is already built into the corporate community's accumulation base. In both years, approximately 55 per cent of all the interlocks with ERT involve firms headquartered in these two countries. Yet within this pattern of Franco-German predominance, there is also increased representation of firms based in Italy, Spain, Britain and Scandinavia.[5]

Clearly, the heartland of corporate Europe remains in the north-west of the continent, while the outer margins have been barely integrated into the corporate network. The spatial distributions of G500 firms, of transnational boards and of boards interlocked with ERT all point to a corporate community strongly centred in Germany, France, the Netherlands and Switzerland, with capital based in Britain and Sweden gaining position over the decade and capital based in Belgium losing out. There is only a weak tendency towards greater inclusiveness, as a few firms based in other western European countries take up positions in the corporate network or gain representation in the ERT.

2 The social organization of corporate Europe

Bonding and bridging Our second research question distinguishes between corporate interlocks that bridge national domiciles, creating a pan-European network, and those that bond companies within national networks. Before considering the entire complement of G500 firms based in Europe, we focus on Europe's 'Top Dogs': companies ranking among the G500 across the entire decade (i.e. in 1996, 1998, 2000, 2002, 2004 and 2006). These number ninety-six. Their size and growth over time (accomplished in part through taking over other firms) have placed them in a secure location within corporate Europe's accumulation base, affording the community a measure of institutional stability in a turbulent environment. Most of the Top Dogs (85.4 per cent of them) are domiciled in Germany, France, Britain, the Netherlands and Switzerland. The accumulation base for corporate Europe's most institutionally stable component is located primarily in the same few countries that host the lion's share of participants in the pan-European network and in the ERT.

This institutionally stable segment plays a central role in the European corporate community. Top Dogs are far more central in the network than are firms whose standing in global capital's league table has been less secure (see Table 7.1). In 2006, the former were interlocked on average with 7.4 other G500 European firms, while the latter averaged a degree of barely 4. Across the decade, the general incidence of interlocking drops, and although most interlocks continue to be of the bonding type (contained within a single country) *the overall decline is wholly attributable to the thinning of national networks*. Indeed, the tendency for interlocking to decrease over the decade *applies specifically to bonding ties, and particularly to firms whose status in the G500 is more episodic*. The Top Dogs at the heart of corporate Europe gain prominence in the network. Bucking the overall trend towards decreased interlocking, *the consistently dominant firms actually increase their transnational interlocking, while among other firms transnational interlocking falls slightly*.

TABLE 7.1 Mean degree for Top Dogs and other G500 European firms, 1996 and 2006

	Bonding		Bridging		Total	
	1996	2006	1996	2006	1996	2006
Mean degree, Top Dogs	6.14	4.86	2.27	2.53	8.41	7.40
Mean degree, other firms	4.53	2.79	1.35	1.19	5.88	3.98
Mean degree, all firms	5.44	3.82	1.87	1.85	7.31	5.68
Eta-squared	.021	.058	.025	.080	.034	.104

As national networks have thinned, the pan-European network has become more focused around a number of giant firms that have been the most consistently successful in accumulating capital. By 2006, the network, both in its bonding and bridging aspects, is predominantly carried by these firms, most of which are domiciled in a few countries of the north-west.

A systematic means of assessing the contributions of bonding and bridging interlocking to the European corporate community is provided by the 'External minus Internal (E-I) Index' (Krackhardt and Stern 1988). For a given network segment (for present purposes, country), the index subtracts the proportion of all the bonding ties from the proportion of all the bridging ties. It ranges from −1, indicating that the segment is completely 'introverted', to 1, indicating that the segment is completely 'extraverted'. In 1996, 74.4 per cent of all interlocks stayed within national boundaries; by 2006 that proportion had fallen to 67.3 per cent, reflecting both a decline in bonding interlocks and an increase in bridging interlocks. The shift was uneven across countries, however (see Table 7.2). The German network, which in 2006 remained the most integrated, actually became slightly more introverted; the Swedish network gained many trans-European ties but became even more internally integrated. But in four countries national interlocks disappeared as trans-European interlocks proliferated – most spectacularly in Italy (whose national network was eclipsed by burgeoning transnational interlocks) but also in Britain, France and Switzerland.

TABLE 7.2 Bonding and bridging analysis, 1996 and 2006

	N of bonding interlocks		N of bridging interlocks		E–I Index	
	1996	2006	1996	2006	1996	2006
Germany	430	368	73	56	−0.710	−0.736
France	260	184	74	94	−0.557	−0.324
UK	128	88	22	47	−0.707	−0.304
Italy	32	10	16	23	−0.333	0.394
Spain	4	8	3	9	−0.143	0.059
Netherlands	34	34	52	47	0.209	0.160
Belgium	18	4	50	20	0.471	0.667
Sweden	2	22	5	20	0.429	−0.048
Austria	–	0	–	1	–	1.0
Switzerland	16	18	23	28	0.179	0.217
Finland	–	0	–	8	–	1.0
Norway	–	0	–	2	–	1.0
Ireland	–	2	–	3	–	0.200

As a final assessment of trends in Europeanization, we chart in Figure 7.3 the mean degree of transnational interlocks for each European domicile. This controls for the size of each county's complement of G500 companies, indicating the extent to which corporations based in a country interlock with other large European companies based in other countries. Over the decade, the grand mean degree stays constant, just below 2. What is striking in the inter-country comparisons is the decrease in differences in degree of participation in the pan-European network, as individual countries move towards the grand mean, some dramatically so. Across the decade, the proportion of variance in transnational degree that is attributable to inter-country differences (Eta squared) drops sharply, from 0.265 to 0.098. This convergence in degree of transnational interlocking suggests that, *despite the unevenness we have noted, the network is tending towards equity in participation*, a structural feature of community.

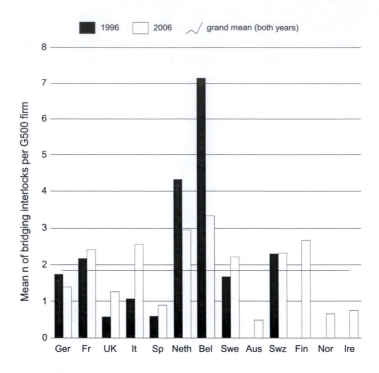

1996   2006   grand mean (both years)

Figure 7.3 Degree of transnational interlocking within Europe, 1996 and 2006

The integrative function of the European Round Table of Industrialists In constituting corporate Europe, the ERT has brought together disparate national and industrial sections of the European capitalist class, with the objective of finding a united way forward. Not surprisingly, when we include the ERT as a node in the European network, it stands out, in both years, as *the broker*, connecting, at one remove, pairs of firms that are not themselves interlocked. Moreover, true to its project, the vast bulk of its brokerage occurs across countries; the ERT adds very little to the cohesion of the existing *national* networks. Clearly, the ERT functions, as intended, to draw the European corporate community together.[6]

This integrative function gains significance as national networks thin (Heemskerk 2007). The ERT offers a meeting place that shrinks the social space of corporate Europe: its brokerage has the effect of shortening the distances between firms in the network. Considering only the European corporate network (excluding the ERT), in 1996 143 of the 170 G500 firms based in Europe formed a connected component, wherein the mean distance between firms was 3.234. By 2006, with 159 of 193 European companies in the dominant component, the mean distance had increased to 3.379. Yet when we calculate inter-corporate distances with ERT-mediated ties included, the mean distance among the same firms falls to 2.962 and remains constant across the decade.

What interests us particularly, however, is the contribution that the ERT makes to the reduction of *transnational* distances in the corporate community. In Table 7.3 we see that, without the mediating effect of the ERT, mean distances increase, especially in Europe's domestic networks. Including the ERT-mediated ties, the increase in transnational distances is more modest, and partly reflects the expansion of the network, as 'Rising Stars' with less-established elite connections join the G500. In 1996, the ERT played a modest role in reducing inter-corporate distances. By 2006, however, ERT affiliations play a stronger role in reducing both intra-national and transnational distances, but especially the latter. The result is that, despite reductions in overall interlock density and the ascension to the G500 of some new firms that lack historical linkages to the European corporate elite, mean transnational distances actually fall slightly between 1996 and 2006, when ERT affiliations are included in the analysis.

TABLE 7.3 Mean inter-corporate distances, with and without ERT mediation

Basis of calculation	1996		2006	
	Intra-national	Trans-national	Intra-national	Trans-national
A. Without ERT	2.012	3.688	2.909	3.904
B. With ERT	1.970	3.313	2.536	3.263
A–B	0.0421	0.375	0.373	0.641

From this analysis of bonding and bridging, our picture of European capitalist class formation gains definition. Corporate Europe's most institutionally stable segment, principally domiciled in a few countries of the north-west, increasingly forms the backbone of the community. Although national networks persist in weakened form, the tendency is towards Europeanization of interlocks, particularly in the most institutionally stable segment. Despite unevenness across countries, participation in the corporate community becomes somewhat more inclusive, at least among firms based in western Europe. Finally, the ERT plays an increasingly important role as a meeting place that shrinks the social space of corporate Europe by extensively brokering elite inter-corporate relations.

3 The issue of institutional completeness: towards European finance capital?

To what extent does the tendency towards Europeanization entail an integration of financial and industrial capital across borders? It is useful to recall at the outset that, as a group, G500 financial institutions based in Europe grew sharply over the decade. In 1996, 45 of the world's 100 largest financial institutions were based in Europe; a decade later, 56 were (see Figure 4.2, above). As a proportion of total assets, Europe's share of the top global 100 financials stood

TABLE 7.4 Financial institutions in the European corporate network, 2006

Domicile	Name	Bonding interlocks	Bridging interlocks	Total interlocks
Germany	Allianz	18	6	24
	Munich Re	10	5	15
	Commerzbank	14	1	15
	Deutsche Bank	12	2	14
	KFW Bankengruppe	7	0	7
France	BNP Paribas	14	13	27
	CNP Assurances Vie	6	1	7
	AXA	5	1	6
	Société Générale de France	2	3	5
UK	Lloyds TSB Group	4	2	6
	Standard Chartered Group	6	0	6
	Barclays Bank	3	2	5
Italy	Unicredito Italiani	1	9	10
	Assicurazioni Generali	2	7	9
Spain	Banco Santander	0	5	5
Netherlands	Aegon	3	3	6
	ING Groep	4	2	6
	ABN Amro Holding	1	4	5
Belgium	Dexia	0	6	6
Sweden	Skandinaviska Enskilda Banken	2	4	6

at 61 per cent, the result of a frenetic accumulation of paper assets, associated with what has been called financialization (Dore 2002; Krippner 2005).

There is no doubt that Europe is a major centre for global finance; the question is whether financial institutions, the traditional 'hubs' of national configurations, have come to occupy central locations in transnational European interlocking. Already in 1996, banks and insurance companies had a strong presence at the centre of the pan-European network. Seven of them placed among the twenty-nine firms with five or more transnational interlocks.[7] A similar situation held in 2006, as seven financial institutions ranked among the twenty-one corporations with five or more transnational interlocks. Considering in Table 7.4 the twenty financial institutions that each had five or more interlocks of any kind in 2006, we find that some of the most central financial institutions (notably BNP Paribas) combine extensive bonding and bridging interlocking, rendering them central both within their national networks and across Europe. Major German financials are ensconced within a national network, in which they occupy central locations. The same holds for two of the French financials. The Italian, Spanish, Belgian and Swedish financials attain centrality largely through transnational interlocking. The pattern suggests both the reproduction of national financial–industrial axes (particularly in Germany) *and* a pan-European capital integration, but it also points up the relatively weak participation of London-based financial capital in Europe's corporate community. Only three of the thirteen British financials maintain five or more interlocks, and their ties tend to be with other British firms.

We can get a clearer picture of these relations by mapping the network of companies that participate extensively in bridging across Europe's borders. In this analysis, we include the eleven financial institutions in Table 7.4 that maintained at least three bridging interlocks in 2006, and add the twenty-five industrials that maintained at least four bridging interlocks in the same year. Although they comprise barely 19 per cent of Europe's G500 firms, these thirty-six companies account for 59 per cent of all bridging interlocks (and 25 per cent of bonding interlocks). They also account for forty-two of the ninety-five interlocks that linked Europe's major corporations to the ERT in 2006.[8]

In Figure 7.4 we cluster the firms by their national domicile, and display the financials as black circles and the industrials as white boxes, as of year-end 2006. The thickness of lines indicates the number of shared board members, which ranges from one to four. We have given the ERT a ghostly presence at the centre of the network, linking directly with 25 of the 36 companies, including 6 financial institutions. Twelve corporations share multiple directors with the ERT.

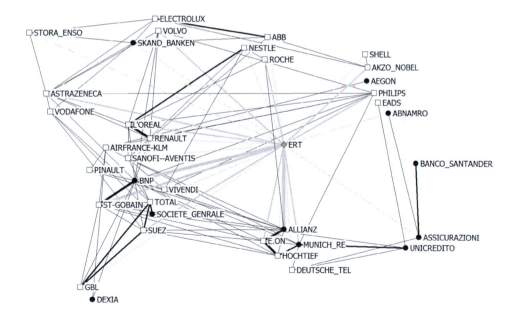

Figure 7.4 Ties among thirty-six European firms most involved in pan-European interlocking, 2006 (with ERT shown in the background)

Ironically, the thickest ties to the Round Table are claimed by giant financial institutions BNP Paribas and Allianz – each with four ERT members on board (predominantly created, as we will show, not by bankers). Bearing in mind that these thirty-six companies have been selected by virtue of their extensive transnational interlocking, it is striking how densely the French companies are interlocked with each other, in several instances via financial–industrial ties (e.g. BNP's strong tie to St Gobain, Société Générale's strong tie to Total). The same holds for German companies (consider Munich Re's strong tie to Hochtief and Allianz's strong tie to GE.ON), but not for the six Dutch firms, which are notably extraverted in their corporate affiliations. Looking across borders, we find various instances of financial–industrial interlocking, typically involving one shared director. Skandinaviska Enskilda Banken, for instance, interlocks with British-based AstraZeneca and Vodafone, with Norway-based Stora Enso Oyi and with Swiss-based ABB. BNP Paribas interlocks with British, Belgian, Dutch, Swedish and German industrials.

Finance capitalists in Europe For the European corporate community, financial–industrial integration occurs not only at the corporate level, but also through the various board affiliations of individual capitalists. Here we take the analysis to the level of individuals, categorizing them, following Soref (1980), as finance capitalists if they serve simultaneously on the board of one or more financial institution and one or more non-financial corporation. Such capitalists 'connect financial corporations with production corporations and thus create the institutional links that are typical of finance capital' (Fennema 1982: 207).

If corporate Europe is attaining institutional completeness, we should find finance capitalists in structurally prominent positions. In Figure 7.5, we categorize the interlocking directors of G500 European firms according to (1) status in the European network – whether engaged only in bonding (I), or in at least one bridging interlock (E) – and (2) status in directing industrials, financials or both (with finance capitalists abbreviated as 'finan-indus'). Given the increasing presence and centrality of major financial institutions in the trans-European network, we might expect to find finance capitalists playing a major role in the network, particularly in its transnational aspect, and this is indeed the case. In 1996, the largest category of European interlockers was *national finance capitalists* – directors of both industrial and financial companies domiciled within a single country. Although national finance capitalists lose prominence in the ensuing decade, there is a sizeable increase in the complement of *transnational finance capitalists*. Moreover, as the lines in Figure 7.5 show, finance capitalists tend to hold more corporate directorships than others. *As the network becomes more pan-European, transnational finance capitalists proliferate.* Concomitantly, the number of national 'pure' financiers shrinks as financial institutions domiciled in the same country largely sever their mutual ties. Transnational industrialists also gain ground, but more modestly, while national industrialists remain a quite substantial grouping, underlining the continued importance of national networks in the European corporate community. At year-end 2006, *seven out of ten European corporate interlockers participated only in national networks.*

The evidence suggests a shift in elite structure, from nationally focused regimes of capital integration to a more pan-European configuration. How does the ERT, ostensibly a vehicle of *industrialists*, figure in this? Strikingly, when we apply our classification of corporate interlockers to this question, we find that in 1996 15 of the 25 interlockers on the ERT were finance capitalists (7 of them trans-European) while in 2006 15 of 26 (7 of them trans-European) were. This is evidence in favour of van Apeldoorn's thesis that some ERT members 'should be regarded not as industrialists proper but as *finance capitalists*' (van Apeldoorn 2002: 100). Yet, as discussed earlier, finance capitalists should not be equated with bankers. Not surprisingly, 13 of the 15 finance capitalists on the ERT in 1996 and 14 of 15 in 2006 were primarily affiliated with industrial corporations. More revealingly, across the decade, among European transnationalists holding inside positions in a G500 corporation, the complement of bankers actually fell from 17 to 12[9] while the number of industrialists grew from 18 to 34. In this sense, bankers have become relatively less dominant in the European corporate community. Rather than bankers, who in the Saint-Simonian perspective are the

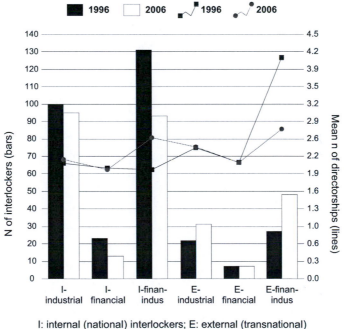

I: internal (national) interlockers; E: external (transnational) interlockers

Figure 7.5 Types of interlockers in corporate Europe, 1996 and 2006

most far sighted and focused on international business, it is *industrialists with financial connections* which form the core of the European corporate community.

This conclusion is further strengthened by an examination of the position of the European Financial Services Round Table (EFR), formed in 2001, within the elite network. The EFR's project is to encourage national governments and the EU institutions 'to commit to creating a truly single market for wholesale and retail financial services in Europe' while also working to 'promote free and open markets throughout the world' (European Financial Services Round Table 2007: 60). Its nineteen members comprise the leaders of Europe's major banks and insurers, yet in 2006 only seven had multiple directorships in G500 European corporations. Five of the seven were finance capitalists, linking the EFR to the boards of a dozen industrial corporations, although only one of them had transnational directorships.[10] In structural terms, the EFR makes a relatively modest contribution to the European corporate community, in comparison with the ERT, whose deeper roots and privileged access to European institutions have made it a uniquely influential policy planning group (Kennett 2004: 62).

4 Corporate Europe and the rest of the world

Given the trends we have found towards consolidation of a European corporate community, how does this community relate to the rest of the world, in an era in which the virtues of a borderless world, of unfettered capitalism, have been heralded if not hyped? Are firms central within corporate Europe detached from the wider global network; are some European firms marginal to the European network yet well connected beyond it? In what ways is the ERT itself embedded in the global corporate network? To deal with the last question first, when we widen our lens to include the entire G500, *we find very few extra-European corporate affiliations of ERT members.* In 1996, the ERT had overlapping memberships with a total of 73 G500 boards, 67 of which were domiciled in Europe. By 2006, the respective numbers were 73 and 68, giving no evidence of the ERT incorporating economic interests beyond Europe. Within Europe, the ERT acts as a *bridge* across national corporate communities, but

TABLE 7.5 Elite linkages between corporate Europe and the rest of the world

Pairs of interlocked G500 corporations	1996		2006	
	N	%	N	%
Within Europe	1242	40.5	1096	53.0
Between Europe and rest of world	135	4.4	131	6.3
Within rest of world	1692	55.1	840	40.7
Total	3069	100.0	2067	100.0
E-I Index for European corporations	−0.804		−0.786	

vis-à-vis the rest of the world its role is clearly to *bind* European capital into a self-standing community.

Leaving aside the ERT, in the European corporate community we again find no tendency towards extraversion at the expense of internal cohesion. If we differentiate the set of firms domiciled in Europe from all other G500 firms, we can assess whether the apparent consolidation of corporate Europe is simply a local instance of a global trend towards the formation of a transnational cap-italist class. Worldwide, the number of interlocked pairs of G500 companies actually declined by nearly one third in the decade under study (see Table 7 5) This was partly due to corporate governance reforms favouring 'leaner' boards and more focused commitments from directors, and partly due to the collapse of the Japanese corporate network in the 1990s (see Chapters 4 and 5, above). Within Europe, however, the decrease in total interlocking was mod-est, as the corporate community maintained internal cohesion in a thinning global network. *By 2006, corporate Europe forms the most integrated segment of the global corporate network*, accounting for a remarkable 53.0 per cent of all G500 interlocks worldwide. In comparison, the North American zone (the USA plus Canada) accounts for 35.0 per cent of worldwide interlocking (down from 44.2 per cent a decade earlier). At the level of individual firms, this shift in the global network's centre of gravity is mirrored in the fact that *the most central corporations globally are based in Europe*. In 2006, all 30 of the G500 corpora-tions with the highest degree of interlocks globally were European (19 German, 6 French, 2 British, 1 Dutch, 1 Belgian).

On the other side of the coin, only a few European firms have many external interlocks: the E-I Index shows that in 1996 and in 2006 the number of external interlocks was vastly overshadowed by the number of internal interlocks. Table 7.5 shows that in 2006 there were 131 elite linkages between corporate Europe and the rest of the world. Most European firms (121 of 193) had no interlocks beyond Europe. The twenty-eight companies with multiple extra-European ties account for two-thirds of all the external links between corporate Europe and the rest of the world, but they themselves vary in the extent of external linkage. At one extreme, London-based BP and Paris-based Alcatel were interlocked with seven non-European firms each; at the other, ten companies were each tied to two non-European firms. The twenty-eight also vary in their extent of integra-tion into the European corporate community, with the Swiss and British firms showing the least integration.[11] In line with what has been said earlier about the decreasing role of the bankers in the European network, only four of the twenty-eight 'world connectors' are financial institutions. Significantly, most of the European firms with multiple interlocks outside Europe are well ensconced in the European corporate community. The number of external links exceeds the number of internal links in only three cases (Zurich Financial, Alcatel and Telecom Italia), and, for eleven of the twenty-eight, links with Europe outnumber external links by a ratio of 3:1 or more. Still, there is some evidence that the most externally connected companies of Europe are recruited from its more internationalized zones – Britain and Switzerland in particular.

What also stands out when we place corporate Europe in a global context is the rarity of ties leading beyond the North Atlantic. At year-end 2006, only nine of 135 G500 firms domiciled outside the North Atlantic had any interlocks with European firms, and only four were interlocked with multiple European firms.[12] Even ties spanning the Atlantic are sparse compared to corporate Europe's internal cohesion. In 2006, two North American firms were 6.75 times more likely to be interlocked than were a European and a North American firm, while two European firms were nine times more likely to be interlocked than a European and a North American firm. *The trans-Atlantic corporate network lacks much of the integrative capacity we have documented in the case of Europe*, including the state institutions of the EU, which provide a strategic focal point for ERT initiatives.

Conclusion

Emerging as an economic community in the latter half of the twentieth century, corporate Europe underwent further consolidation in the late 1990s, through to early 2007, so that on the threshold of the current global economic crisis Europe's corporate community had achieved unprecedented unity as a key component of a transnational capitalist class in the making. This chapter has focused on how the community has been stitched together into a loose but serviceable social fabric. Our investigation was inspired by four lines of questioning, and on each count we have noted tendencies towards corporate community development.

- Although the structure of representation remains heavily skewed towards the affluent north-west, and towards the most institutionally stable segment of capital, the network came to include a greater number of firms and a diversity of domiciles, reaching farther south to Spain and north to Sweden, though not eastward. This suggests that within European integration, the process of 'state formation' and corporate community-building are two separate strands, where the latter is first and foremost geared to connect the current centres of capital accumulation. The political process of European integration at the level of states aims rather to include new hinterlands (eastern Europe, Balkans) which are not yet part of the affluent, 'networked' heartland. This practice enables the corporate community to accumulate capital in a larger, integrated field that includes markets in labour, products and services and thus to strengthen its power base vis-à-vis other regions in the world such as Japan and North America, while reproducing an uneven geography of capitalism within Europe.
- When we considered the dynamics of (continuing) national corporate com-

munities and the (emerging) European corporate community, we found that the overall decline in interlocking within Europe is wholly attributable to the thinning of national networks. Although national networks persist, particularly in Germany and France, the tendency is towards interlocking at the transnational European level. Again, it is consistently dominant firms domiciled in a few countries in the north-west which participate most heavily in transnational bridging. The measured inclusion of corporations from Europe's north and south into the European corporate network, however, coincides with a convergence in the degree of transnational interlocking per country, suggesting a tendency towards equity in participation. The ERT notably contributes to the European corporate network by brokering relations between companies based in different countries, thereby reducing distances in the network. Its integrative role grew over the decade, shrinking the social space of corporate Europe despite an overall thinning of the network.

- In the pattern of interlocking directorships we found both the reproduction of national financial–industrial axes (particularly in Germany) and the emergence of more pan-European capital integration. By 2006, with the notable exception of the City, major European financial institutions showed a clear pattern of bridging between countries – sometimes combined with and sometimes in preference to bonding within the national network. At the individual level the ranks of transnational finance capitalists grew, but a closer look revealed that bankers have become less dominant. It is industrialists with financial connections, many of them active at the ERT, who form the core of the European corporate community. The evidence suggests a partial shift from nationally focused regimes of capital integration centred around banks to a looser, more pan-European configuration. Of course, institutional supports such as the euro and the European Central Bank are major aspects of this capital integration. As the circuit of capital becomes more integrated, capital accumulates less within segmented nation-states and more in an integrated Eurozone. Europe's corporate community is indeed organized around a financial–industrial axis, but the era of bank dominance is over. The vision Saint-Simon held of bankers as the most far-sighted and engaged members of the corporate elite seems no longer applicable. The contrast is telling between the European Round Table of Industrialists, a centre of business activism, heavily networked with both the corporate community and the European Commission, at the cutting edge of European integration since the early 1980s, and the European Financial Services Round Table, which formed only recently and networks only modestly. It is the ERT which has defined and pursued a hegemonic project for European corporate capital; in comparison, the EFR represents little more than a sectional interest in improving conditions for the circulation of money capital in and beyond the EU.

- As for the embeddedness of corporate Europe in the global corporate network, by 2006 Europe hosted the most integrated segment of the global corporate elite, and this internal capitalist solidarity far outweighed the comparatively few interlocks linking Europe to the rest of the world. The nearly complete absence of ties leading beyond the North Atlantic, and the relative sparseness of ties spanning the North Atlantic, underscores both the robustness of corporate Europe and the comparative lack of integrative capacity between North America and Europe.

These findings raise three key issues for capitalist class formation in Europe. In the first place, they underline the relative success of the process. The consolidation of corporate Europe has been a conscious project, centred in organizations like the ERT and the European Commission and in emergent norms favouring multinational representation on corporate boards. But within that institutional framework, community formation has also proceeded molecularly, as the by-product of an increasing volume of pan-European practices among Europe's major corporations. Coexisting as it does with the persistence of attenuated national corporate networks, consolidation of a European corporate community, integrated in no small measure by the ERT, is an important aspect of class hegemony. Even as it reproduces patterns of unequal representation, this consolidation enables the leading segment of the capitalist class, the inner circle, to speak with one voice. Indeed, most of the transnational corporate interlocking that has been taken as evidence for the formation of a transnational capitalist class (Robinson 2004) has occurred *within* Europe.

Second, the formation of trans-European finance capital needs to be set in the context of a post-2006 global financial meltdown that has not spared corporate Europe. What meaning does 'finance capital' have in such ruinous circumstances? Harvey (2006: 283) has helpfully distinguished between a 'process view of finance capital' and a 'power bloc view', the latter of which we have taken here. In this latter perspective, the 'symbiotic relation' of industrial and financial capital implies a working unity, which dominates the accumulation process from the top (ibid.: 319). This unity, however, internalizes antagonism and contradiction, and presages 'perpetual shifts in the power relation' between financial and industrial capital (ibid.: 320). These shifts, articulated as they are with the rhythm of accumulation, oblige us to view finance capital as a *process* that 'reveals the underlying unity and antagonism between financial and surplus value-producing operations' (ibid.: 319). If industrial capital is dominant in the upswing, during the later boom phases of the accumulation cycle

industrial and financial interests unite to promote a credit-based expansion of commodity values. In the crisis, money is everything and the banks appear to hold the fates of industrial capitalists entirely in their hands because excess commodities cannot be converted into money. But banks themselves may also go under as the demand for high-quality money [...] far exceeds supply. In the depths of the crisis, power resides with those who hold money of last resort. (Ibid.: 319)

Applying this narrative to the recent developments, the consolidation of corporate Europe, to early 2007, was a phenomenon of the upswing that followed the Reagan recession of 1981/82 and of the credit-based, prolonged expansion that followed the 1997 crisis in East Asia and gained momentum after the dotcom bubble burst in 2000/01. The decade we have examined was precisely one of credit-based expansion, during which massive volumes of fictitious capital accumulated in the financial sector. Beginning in summer 2007, but most visibly in the autumn of 2008, the credit bubble burst, triggering 'a powerful global economic slowdown' (McNally 2009: 46).

We have indeed found that in the period of credit-based expansion, before the crash, industrial and financial interests were brought together in a pan-European network of interlocking directorates. The relatively marginal position of Europe's bankers in the network accords with Mügge's (2008: 234) observation that bankers were largely uninvolved in the emergence of supranational governance in EU capital markets and did not see the need for a European market for financial services. According to Mügge, their reticence reflected worries about losing advantageous positions in their national financial systems. But in addition to that parochial concern, financialization had weakened the role of bankers in financial–industrial integration. Following the US lead (Davis and Mizruchi 1999), European banks de-emphasized relationship-based finance and turned towards more speculative, transaction-based finance in the closing decade of the twentieth century (Heemskerk and Schnyder 2008). The cross-border financial–industrial interlocks we observed have been carried for the most part by finance capitalists aligned primarily with industrial corporations. And, to return to the quote from Harvey, since the crash of 2008 the state has emerged as the holder of money of last resort, as major banks have gone to the wall. State capitalism is back on the agenda. The likely result of the return to regulation and even public ownership of financial institutions is a resurgence of industrialists' power and influence. The change in the power balance may have consequences for the policies of European governments and the European Commission. They may be forced by the credit crisis as well as by public opinion to move away from neoliberal policies towards state support for ailing industries. This also moves the balance of power towards the industrial elite. Whether this process will strengthen pan-European class formation remains unclear. If public support for private firms is generated primarily at the national level it is likely to create national rivalry between the members of the EU. Alternatively, if political and business leaders succeed in creating new forms of 'state capitalism' at the European level, the shifting power balance will strengthen rather than weaken European capitalist class formation.

Finally, our findings carry implications for the geography of uneven development in Europe (Agnew 2001). Despite overtures towards greater inclusiveness, the corporate community remains strongly centred in the consistently dominant corporations of the north-west. For the most part, it has been constituted as an expression of the dominance of a regional capitalist fraction. The absence from the corporate community of bourgeois leadership from the eastern hinterland, or from such southern states as Greece, exposes a fault line whose implications for Europe's own future may be telling. As Harvey (2006: 321) has astutely observed, elite configurations such as the one we have mapped here often appear to be futile attempts to establish unity in the face of a contradictory process. Yet the shifting patterns of inter-corporate relations 'have also to be seen as part of a perpetual process of probing for an organizational form that will enhance the capacity of capitalism to survive in the face of its own internal contradictions'. The social bases we have discerned for a pan-European capitalist class, however tentative and contradictory, will provide Europe's bourgeoisie, or the dominant fraction thereof, with cultural and political resources in the struggle for Europe's future, but no outcome is preordained.

8 | Consolidating the transnational corporate-policy network, 1996–2006

Introduction

Transnational policy-planning bodies like the European Round Table of Industrialists have come to play important roles in constructing the consensus within business communities that enables corporate capital to project influence in political and cultural domains that transect national borders. As we saw in Chapter 2, such groups comprise a multi-organizational field, within what has been called global civil society, from which have emanated visions and policy proposals of a broadly neoliberal character. Indeed, our findings from Chapter 2 accord with Gill's (1995a) claim that in a context of rapid globalization of capital, global policy groups have become crucial elements in a transnational historic bloc: an assemblage of elite policy-planning organizations, transnational corporations and global-governance institutions that has promoted and consolidated a hegemonic project of neoliberal globalization.

This chapter takes the state of play in 1996 as its starting point and extends the analysis to year-end 2006, while enlarging the population of corporations from 350 to 500 and expanding the policy-planning bodies from five to eleven. Whereas our preliminary research in Chapter 2 considered policy boards with 'global' mandates, here we include four transnational business councils, including the European Round Table of Industrialists (ERT), with more regionally focused political agendas. The latter may promote regional solidarities among business leaders that fall well short of, and could even conflict with, the 'global' project that has been ascribed to an emergent transnational capitalist class by writers such as Robinson (2007).

Two sets of questions orient this chapter:

1 How does the most recent trajectory of the transnational corporate-policy network speak to claims about the formation of a transnational capitalist class? Does the evolution of the network indicate a process of *structural consolidation*, with policy boards becoming more integrative nodes in the global corporate power structure?

2 How does *regionalism* figure in the structure of the global corporate-policy network? Does the pattern of interlocks support hypotheses about the end of American hegemony (Went 2002; Go 2007), the continued dominance of an Atlantic ruling class (van der Pijl 1984), the rise of corporate Europe (Balanyá et al. 2000), or some other scenario?

To answer these questions, we will explore the ways in which policy boards furnish sites for integrating diverse corporate interests into a consensus while potentially differentiating those interests in ways that could promote regional rivalries.

Eleven transnational policy boards

All eleven transnational policy boards satisfy three selection criteria:

- they are transnational in their projects – they deal with international political-economic issues immediately relevant to the interests of corporate business;
- they are transnational and corporate in their make-up – they are composed primarily or very extensively of directors and executives from large corporations domiciled in a variety of countries;
- they were active in either or both 1996 and 2006.

The eleven comprise a judgement sample that includes two strata: (1) *global policy groups* and (2) *transnational business councils*.

The seven global policy groups pursue wide, 'global' political agendas and seek to incorporate social forces beyond the capitalist class per se. Within this category, we can recall, from Chapter 2, a historical stratification, ranging from the International Chamber of Commerce (ICC) – created by investment bankers who claimed the identity of 'merchants of peace' after the First World War – to the UN Global Compact (UNGC) – formed in 2000, with strong input from the ICC. The other five groups were formed in the intervening years, with the pace of group formation quickening over the twentieth century. The annual Bilderberg Conference was first convened in 1952; the Trilateral Commission (TC) was established two decades later; the World Economic Forum (WEF) emerged in 1987 out of a western European forum of business leaders; the International Advisory Board to the Council on Foreign Relations (CFRIAB) and the World Business Council for Sustainable Development (WBCSD) were both created in 1995.

As Table 8.1A shows, the global policy groups differ sharply in size. The Trilateral Commission (TC) is a large senate, while the board of the UN Global Compact (UNGC) is more seminar sized. Here, group size refers to the set of individuals on which we have based our network analysis of overlapping memberships. These sets vary by organizational form. For the Bilderberg Conference, an annual meeting with no fixed membership, we include those who attended the Conference in spring 1997 or 2007. For the TC, the International Advisory Board to the Council on Foreign Relations (CFRIAB) and the World Business Council for Sustainable Development (WBCSD), each composed of individual members, we include all members. For the International Chamber of Commerce (ICC), World Economic Forum (WEF) and UNGC, whose members are organizations, not individuals, we include the top directorate, which is comprised exclusively or (in the case of the UNGC primarily) of business leaders.[1]

	N of directors	
	1996	2006
A: Global policy groups		
International Chamber of Commerce Est. 1919, Paris headquarters	27	25
Bilderberg Conferences Est. 1952, Office in Leiden (Netherlands)	112	135
Trilateral Commission Est. 1972, Washington, Paris & Tokyo headquarters	304	413
World Economic Forum Est. 1971 (1987), Geneva headquarters	55	47
International Advisory Board of the Council on Foreign Relations Est. 1995, New York headquarters (CFR)	35	33
World Business Council for Sustainable Development Est. 1995, Geneva headquarters	116	185
UN Global Compact (Board) Est. 2000, New York headquarters (UN)	n/a	19
B: Transnational business councils		
Europe		
European Round Table of Industrialists Est. 1983, Brussels headquarters	56	57
Europe and Asia		
EU–Japan Business Round Table Est. 1995, Brussels & Tokyo headquarters	26	50
North Atlantic		
TransAtlantic Business Dialogue Est. 1995, Washington headquarters	68	33
North America		
North American Competitiveness Council Est. 2006	n/a	33

These seven groups also vary in the geopolitical reach of their constituencies. While five of them serve self-consciously 'global' constituencies, the Bilderberg, formed in the era of the Cold War (Wilford 2003), is based in the North Atlantic heartland of 'the West', although its project has always been broadly one of global governance within an Atlanticist frame. The TC is certainly global in its political vision, but from the start its constituency, encoded in its very name, has been the triad – the affluent countries of North America, western Europe and Japan (although since 2000 the third leg of the triad has been extended to include an array of Pacific Asian developing countries, alongside Japan, Australia and New Zealand).

All seven global policy groups seek to incorporate interests other than corporate capital into their projects. This is particularly evident in forum-type groups such as the Bilderberg, TC and WEF, whose meetings bring business leaders into dialogue with political leaders and intellectuals (Gill 1990; Graz 2003; Pigman 2007). Much the same process occurs at the CFRIAB and on the board of the UNGC, as political leaders (in the first case) and labour and NGO leaders (in the second) rub shoulders with the corporate leaders who comprise most of the membership. The ICC, the most free-market-oriented policy group (see Chapter 2), restricts membership to capitalists but incorporates other interests through joint ventures with United Nations agencies, including the Global Compact (Hocking and Kelly 2002). Similarly, although the WBCSD is structured as a business council – the CEOs of major corporations interested in sustainable development – its project to green global capitalism by facilitating firms to become 'eco-efficient' (Rowe 2005) seeks to persuade publics concerned about the growing ecological crisis worldwide (see Livesey 2002).

The seven global policy groups differ in priorities and practices, and in the policy and media networks they access. They thus bring a division of labour to the task of global policy formation. The WEF, WBCSD, ICC and TC are large and complex organizations that address not only their constituents but transnational publics, via publications, press releases and websites. Bilderberg Conferences, in contrast, are held *in camera* to encourage frank discussion, and no public statement is issued at their close. These five groups (including Bilderberg) have pursued wide agendas for global neoliberal governance. The CFRIAB's project is more focused. It advises the Council on Foreign Relations about US foreign policy issues; hence its global vision is US-centred and its voice carries only within the CFR, a major American think tank with extensive ties both to US corporate capital and to Washington's policy elite (Dye 1978; Paretsky 2004). Finally, the UNGC's project is one of moral reform. A 'public–private partnership' between the UN and corporations, it promotes ten ethical principles concerning human rights, labour standards, environmentalism and anti-corruption. The least neoliberal of the seven, the UNGC represents a tendency, since the mid-1990s, for global policy groups to incorporate 'civil society' into their processes and visions (Soederberg 2007).

The four transnational business councils are, with the exception of the ERT, quite recent inventions (see Table 8.1B). These organizations transpose, on to a transnational field, the highly successful model of national business councils, which in the 1970s and 1980s spearheaded neoliberal transformation in the Anglo-American countries (Useem 1984; Langille 1987). Each is composed of a few dozen CEOs or chairs of leading corporations domiciled in the given zone. Two of the councils promote the economic integration of Europe (ERT) and North America (the North American Competitiveness Council, NACC), res- pectively. The other two promote the trans-regional integration of the North Atlantic (the TransAtlantic Business Dialogue, TABD), and of Europe and Japan (EU–Japan Business Round Table, EJBRT).[2] As with nationally based business councils, these boards are less involved in reaching out to 'civil society' and more strategically focused on specific state agencies and policies that directly affect the interests of corporations. They pursue an agenda of 'free trade' that presses for deregulated markets and investor rights, but add to this a focal concern with transnational policy harmonization as a means of reducing fric-tions in the circulation of commodities and capital (Beder 2006).

Not only are the transnational business councils more instrumentally focused, they also differ from the global policy groups in promoting the conditions for robust accumulation *within regional political spaces*. The regional character of each transnational business council identifies it with a complex of affiliated states, and with the political partitioning of global economic space. All four business councils were founded with close involvement of the interested states[3] and maintain intimate advisory relationships with state agencies mandated to advance the project of regional economic integration. Indeed, each business council advises the relevant intergovernmental initiatives, typically by holding its annual summit shortly before the annual summit of political leaders, and forwarding recommendations to the latter.[4] These strong regional inflections may carry implications for the process of transnational capitalist class formation. As others have noted (Bieling 2006a; Ruigrok and Van Tulder 1995), the dynamic of regional integration – seeking competitive advantages within regional blocs – may be at odds with scenarios that attribute a homogeneously 'global' project to the transnational capitalist class (as in Robinson 2004).

Together, the eleven policy boards make up a complex organizational ecology (Hunt and Aldrich 1998) that divides the labour of policy formation among interdependent types and specializations, and which makes innovative use of new organizational forms. Over the latter decades of the twentieth century, each group came to occupy a distinct niche in an emerging organizational ecology that has amounted to a political mobilization of transnational capitalists.

Consolidating a global corporate-policy elite

Like other networks of overlapping memberships, the corporate-policy net-work has a dual structure: it exists as both an inter-organizational network of interlocked boards and as an interpersonal network of individuals who meet each other on boards. We map the network at each of these levels, focusing first on the individuals who comprise a global corporate-policy elite. This elite includes members of the global corporate elite – individuals who direct two or more G500 corporations – as well as individuals who belong to multiple policy boards or who sit on one G500 corporate and one policy board.[5] These are the people whose organizational affiliations create the corporate-policy network. In this section, we show how these affiliations became more transnational and more focused on the policy boards in the decade after 1996.

Individuals vary greatly in the number of corporate and policy-board affiliations they maintain. Over the decade, the total number of individuals with one or more board memberships fell by 27.3 per cent, to 6,785 in 2006 (see Table 8.2). The drop was particularly sharp among those directing only one G500 firm, reflecting a decrease in the average size of G500 corporate boards since the mid-1990s, associated with corporate governance reforms (see Chapters 4 and 5). Given the increasing number of organizations in the transnational policy field (and the increasing size of the TC and WBCSD), it is not surprising that the number of individuals sitting only on one policy board increased by over 50 per cent, to 650.

TABLE 8.2 Policy-board memberships and corporate directorships, 1996 and 2006

Patterns of affiliation	A 1996	B 2006	(B–A)/A % change
a 1 corporate board	7,921	5,248	−33.7
b 1 policy board	419	650	+55.1
c 2+ corporate boards	757	611	−19.3
d 2+ policy boards	26	32	+23.1
e 1 corporate board and 1 policy board	109	138	+26.6
f 1 corporate board and 2+ policy boards	9	22	+144.4
g 2+ corporate boards and 1 policy board	72	57	−20.8
h 2+ corporate boards and 2+ policy boards	27	27	0
Total: members of the corporate-policy elite	1,000	887	−11.3
Grand total	9,330	6,785	−27.3

Our interest, however, is in the board members who, in serving on multiple boards, create the inter-organizational network that constitutes the corporate-policy elite. This elite (represented by the shaded area of Table 8.2), which shrank by 11.3 per cent to 887, can be divided into several social types. The largest stratum – the pure corporate interlockers (category *c* in the table), who direct only companies – decreased by approximately one fifth, as did corporate interlockers who sit on one policy board (category *g*). The ranks of other members of the elite who sit on policy boards, however, expanded. These include, in 2006, thirty-two 'pure policy wonks' (category *d*) – members of multiple policy boards who do not direct any G500 firms[6] – as well as the 138 individuals who belong to one corporate and one policy board (category *e*). The most well-positioned players in the network, numbering twenty-seven in each year, are those who sit on multiple corporate *and* multiple policy boards (category *h*). The elite network, then, is composed of several kinds of interlockers, from pure corporate types to pure policy wonks. Although its membership is heavily weighted in the direction of corporate interlockers (reflecting the vastly greater number of corporations compared to policy boards in the global corporate power structure), the composition of the network is shifting. In the most recent decade, the complement of pure corporate interlockers has diminished (from 75.7 per cent to 68.9 per cent) as the complement of individuals affiliated with policy boards has grown (from 24.3 per cent to 31.1 per cent).

As shown in Chapter 5, the global corporate elite is itself composed of national and transnational segments, the latter of which grew while the former declined after 1996. Concomitantly, the composition of the corporate-policy network shifted. As the ranks of national networkers sitting on policy boards thinned from 58 to 43, the contingent of corporate transnationalists with positions on policy boards grew from 31 to 38. By 2006, nearly half of the corporate interlockers with policy-board affiliations were transnationalists. In effect, *the corporate-policy board elite has become more cosmopolitan*, in two respects:

1 among corporate interlockers, policy-board membership has shifted towards the transnationalists, who come to comprise a larger segment of the global corporate elite; and
2 a growing elite segment is made up of individuals with one or more transnational policy-board affiliations.

As national corporate networks become sparser, transnational corporate networkers and members of transnational policy boards (including pure policy wonks) play a more prominent role in elite integration.

Still, in 2006, corporate networkers continue to comprise four-fifths of the elite, and thus merit further investigation. Our distinction between national networkers and transnationalists reveals a shift in composition towards the latter, but it does not indicate how the elite is distributed spatially across the world system. In light of our findings from Chapter 5 that the vast majority of global corporate networkers are affiliated with corporations based in Europe or North America, and that most transnational interlocking occurs either within Europe or across the North Atlantic, it is instructive to categorize the corporate networkers according to the domicile of the firms they direct. The lines in Figure 8.1, which show the number of corporate networkers in each category of Chapter 5's typology, reflect this predominance of North Atlanticists in the global corporate elite.

The key question for this chapter is, to what extent do these regional categories of corporate networkers participate on policy boards? The bars in Figure 8.1 show participation rates for different types of corporate networkers. Overall, the participation rate increases slightly (from 11.6 per cent to 12.1 per cent), but

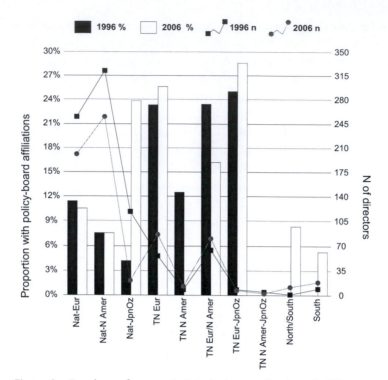

Figure 8.1 Typology of corporate interlockers: policy-board affiliations

varies greatly across the types. Among the numerically large categories (directors of firms based in Europe or North America), *it is transnationalists based in Europe or spanning the North Atlantic who participate extensively on policy boards.* European transnationalists, whose ranks grow during the decade, stand out as the most heavily engaged stratum: one in four of them serves on a transnational policy board. For North Atlantic transnationalists (another growing segment of the global corporate elite) the rate of participation on the policy boards trends downward, from 23 per cent to 16 per cent. As their ranks thin, national corporate networkers do not participate heavily on the policy boards, with the exception of those based in Japan/Australia.[7] Finally, there is some modest evidence of elites active in the global South becoming integrated into the network. In 1996, only a handful of G500 corporate directors were affiliated with firms domiciled outside the triad, and not a single one participated on a transnational policy board. By 2006, the global corporate elite includes a small contingent with North–South corporate affiliations or with affiliations only in the South, and a few of these corporate directors sit on policy boards.

Mapping the inner circle

Up to now, we have identified a corporate-policy elite that is becoming more cosmopolitan but which tends to be based either in corporate Europe or in the space that spans the North Atlantic. We now consider the individuals at the centre of the corporate-policy network: the twenty-seven directors who sit on multiple corporate *and* policy boards. A good deal of the entire network is carried by this inner circle.[8] Two-mode sociograms in Figures 8.2 and 8.3 show a predominance of Europeans and of European firms. The American-based firms and directors cluster at the left margin of each sociogram. They tend to belong to the Trilateral Commission and to attend the Bilderberg Conferences.

In either year, there are only a few non-North Atlanticists in this inner circle. In 2006, two of them were based on the North Atlantic's doorstep, in Mexico; the third was based in Japan.

- Ernesto Zedillo, credited with leading the neoliberalization of Mexico, sat on two US-based corporate boards and on three policy boards, including the CFRIAB;
- Lorenzo Zambrano, chair of Cemex, also served on the board of IBM and was North American deputy chairman of the TC and a member of the WBCSD;
- Yotaro Kobayashi, former chair and current director of Sony Corp, also directed Japan Telephone and Telegraph and was Pacific Asia chair of the TC, a member of the CFRIAB and a member of the EJBRT.

Several directors in this inner circle show trans-Atlantic affiliations of one kind or another, but most of them are based in Europe. At year-end 2006,

- Klaus Kleinfeld, CEO of Siemens until his ouster in a corruption scandal in April 2007 (Sims 2007), also directed Bayer and US-based Alcoa at year-end 2006 and belonged to the TC, TABD and ERT;
- Bertrand Collomb, chair of Lafarge until his retirement in May 2007 and a director of British-Dutch Unilever, was also in 2006 chair of the WBCSD, a member of TABD, the TC, the ERT, the EJBRT, and a Bilderberg attendee;
- Sir Mark Moody-Stuart, former CEO of Shell, chair of Anglo-American Corp and director of British-based HSBC and US-based Accenture, sat on the UNGC, TC and WBCSD;
- Gerhard Cromme, chair of ThyssenKrupp and a director of a quiverful of French and German firms, served on both the ERT and the CFRIAB;
- Jorma Ollila, chair of Nokia and Royal Dutch Shell and a director of US-based Ford Motor Company until his resignation in October 2008, sat on both the ERT and the EJBRT;
- Andrew Liveris, CEO of Dow Chemical Company and one of the few US-based directors in the inner circle, also directed Citigroup and served on the WBCSD and the TABD;
- Paul Desmarais Jr, CEO of Montreal-based Power Corporation, directed several European corporations in which his family held major stakes, sat on the NACC and attended the Bilderberg Conference.

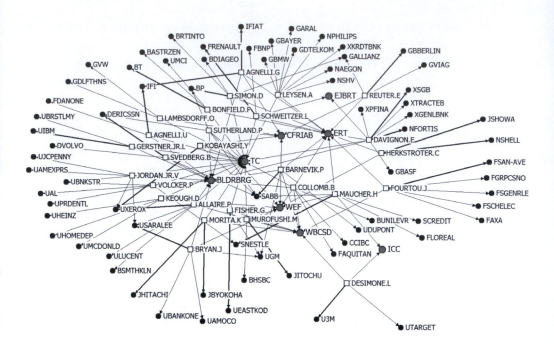

Figure 8.2 The corporate-policy elite's inner circle, 1996

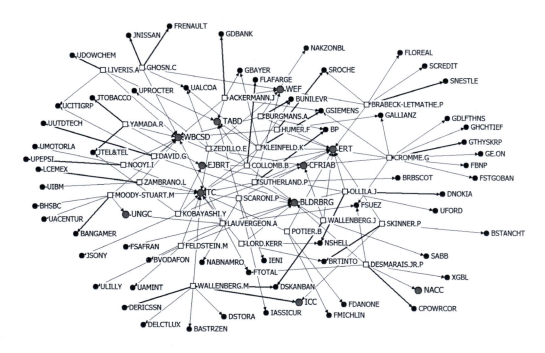

Figure 8.3 The corporate-policy elite's inner circle, 2006

Other interesting cases in Figure 8.3 with a more singularly European portfolio include:

- Peter Sutherland, chair of BP, former director-general of the WTO, a director of the Royal Bank of Scotland, European chairman of the TC, member of the ERT and the WEF Foundation Board, a Bilderberg attendee;
- Marcus Wallenberg, chair of Skandinaviska Enskilda Banken and a director of Ericsson, Electrolux (all three of which his family controls), AstraZeneca and Stora Enso Oy; he was until 2008 chairman of the ICC and a member of the TC;
- Anne Lauvergeon, CEO of the French nuclear energy firm Areva (not large enough for the G500), a director of Suez, Total and UK-based Vodafone, a member of the TC and WBCSD, a director of the UNGC, and a Bilderberg attendee.

These examples reveal a tightly interwoven inner circle of corporate and policy-board affiliations, consisting predominantly of male European business leaders. At year-end 2006, twenty-five members of the inner circle were men, and fourteen had exclusively European G500 corporate affiliations, compared to five whose G500 affiliations were exclusively North American and four who had affiliations on both sides of the Atlantic.[9] Moreover, of 60 corporations represented within the inner circle, 42 were based in Europe, 13 were based in North America, 4 were based in Japan and 1 was based in Mexico. Our sociograms leave out the 32 policy wonks who serve on multiple policy boards but do not direct G500 corporations. In this sense, we underestimate the extent to which the network of individuals is integrated at its core, through the affiliations of the global corporate elite's organic intellectuals.

The individual-level analysis presented above suggests that the network of high-level capitalists is indeed transnationalizing as its members become more actively involved in policy-planning groups. A tightly connected inner circle of multiple interlockers active on policy boards carries the bulk of the network. As we will now see, analysis of inter-organizational relations suggests similar conclusions, and at the same time sheds light on the regional structure of the network.

Regionalism in the inter-organizational network Our second research question highlights the spatial organization of the corporate-policy network. By geo-coding the organizations by their domiciles, we can map the network in space. A key issue is how the policy boards are embedded in the network of corporate interlocks. Figure 8.4 shows a spring-embedded solution for 2006, which iteratively determines the optimal location of points in a two-dimensional space, such that distances between points in the space approximate distances between points in the network (Freeman 2005: 251). Five major sectors of the

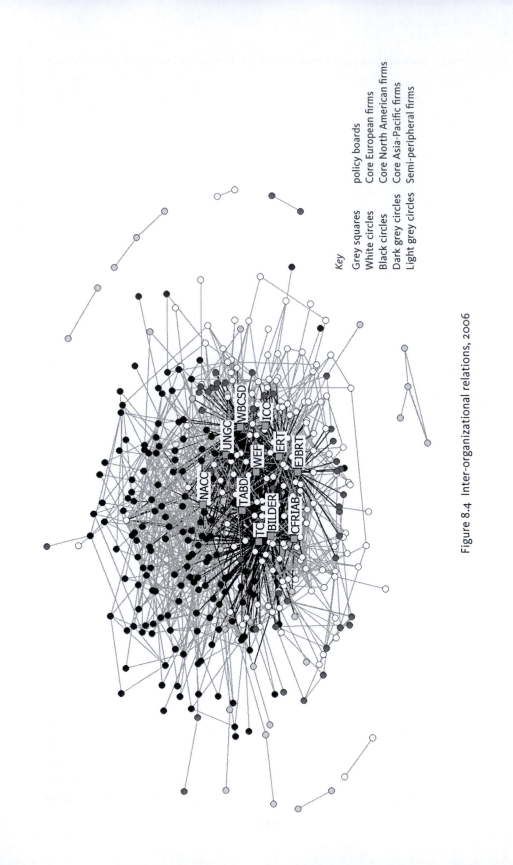

Key

Grey squares	policy boards
White circles	Core European firms
Black circles	Core North American firms
Dark grey circles	Core Asia-Pacific firms
Light grey circles	Semi-peripheral firms

Figure 8.4 Inter-organizational relations, 2006

corporate-policy network are distinguished: 1) the policy boards, 2) corporations based in Europe, 3) corporations based in North America (the USA and Canada), 4) corporations based in the core Asia-Pacific countries (Japan and Australia) and 5) corporations based in the semi-periphery (rest of world).[10] Given their profuse ties to each other, and to many corporations, it is not surprising that the policy boards are at the centre of the network. What is more interesting is that

1   the algorithm clusters the network into its two main geopolitical regions – Europe and North America, which occupy adjoining territories in the space, indicating both the coherence of each regional network and the many inter-locks that span across them;
2   even at year-end 2006, companies based in the global South had little to no involvement in the network; and
3   *the policy boards tend to cluster on the European side of the social space*, with the exception of NACC, which understandably lies in the North American zone.

Firms based in Japan hook into the network largely through their directors' participation on three policy boards: the TC (8 firms), WBCSD (14 firms) and EJBRT (16 firms). The 45 interlocks between Japanese corporate boards and the policy boards compare with only 11 interlocks between the former and all other G500 firms, confirming that the policy boards continue to play a crucial role in integrating Japanese business leaders into the global elite. The tendency by 2006 for policy boards to gravitate towards Europe is consistent with our finding in Chapter 7 of a 'shift towards Europe' in elite organization, partly in consequence of that region's increasing transnational integration.

Let's pursue this line of analysis one step farther. In Figures 8.5 and 8.6 Europe's relative prominence is evident in the pattern of weighted densities (the mean number of interlocks per pair of organizations) between and within segments of the network.[11] In addition to the four regionally defined segments (the three regions of the triad plus the semi-periphery), we consider the set of policy boards as a distinct network segment. As a segment, the policy boards are more tied to corporate Europe than to other regions, in both years. The weighted density linking North American firms to the policy boards is less than half that of European firms in 2006. Corporate Europe is also the most internally integrated region, followed by North America, and it is only between Europe and North America that we find any evidence of extensive trans-regional corporate interlocking. Even so, the Asia-Pacific core segment and the semi-periphery do show increased interlocks with the policy boards over the decade. What stands out, however, is a two-orders-of-magnitude gap between the integration of policy boards with each other and the integration of the most cohesive regional segment of corporate boards (Europe). In 2006, the eleven policy boards shared on average nearly 3.5 members; in the same

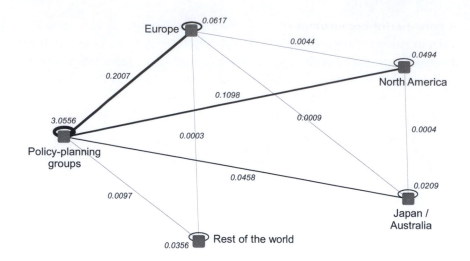

Figure 8.5 Weighted sectoral densities, 1996

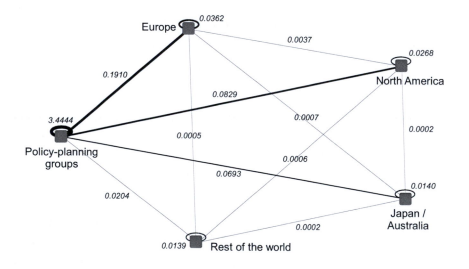

Figure 8.6 Weighted sectoral densities, 2006

year, European corporate boards shared a mean of 0.0362 members. In this sense, the policy-board network provides a politically active and socially co-hesive *hard core* to the global corporate elite. This hard core is primarily active within European corporate capitalism. When we consider the firms with more than five interlocks with policy boards, we find 76 per cent based in Europe in 1996, with the rest in North America. By 2006, 80 per cent were European, the other 20 per cent North American by domicile.

A core–periphery structure?

Our analysis of regionalism suggests that the network has a core–periphery structure, with the key policy boards constituting its core. We tested this hypothesis by fitting a continuous core–periphery model to the value matrix of board interlocks. This factor-analytic procedure identifies a single vector on which nodes in the network are assigned coreness scores, such that the product of the vector and its transpose comes as close as possible to reproducing the original value matrix (Borgatti and Everett 1999). The correlation between values generated by the model and the actual values (here, the number of interlocks) in the network gives a measure of fit. The increase in this correlation from 0.497 in 1996 to 0.596 in 2006 indicates that across the decade the corporate-policy network aligned increasingly along a core–periphery dimension. In Table 8.3 the core members of the network as of year-end 2006 are listed, including eleven policy-planning groups and thirty corporations. Together, the coreness scores of these 41 boards account for 58.6 per cent of the total coreness of the network of 511 organizations; the 11 policy boards alone account for 35.5 per cent.

Most of the policy-planning boards rank at the centre of the network, both in 2006 and in 1996, and the most central four retain the same rankings across the decade, providing the network with institutional stability. Among the global policy groups, the TC, Bilderberg and WBCSD stand out as especially central. Among the transnational business councils only the ERT is comparable to these most central policy groups. Three policy boards are somewhat removed from the network core – the ICC (ranked 15), the UNGC board (ranked 23) and NACC (ranked 31). In the first decade of its existence, the TABD moves from the periphery of the network to the core.

Among the corporations positioned in or near the network core, the predominance of European capital is palpable. Only 4 of the 30 firms are based in the USA, 1 (Accenture) is domiciled in Bermuda to avoid taxes (though it is effectively an American corporation), 1 (Sony) is based in Tokyo, and the rest are domiciled in Europe, including 8 based in Germany, 6 in France, 5 in Britain and 3 in the Netherlands. Also worth noting is the intermingling of large financial institutions (indicated with an F) and industrial enterprises at the core of the corporate-policy board network. Eight corporations remain among the most central thirty firms across the decade, signalling continuity in the presence of politically active directors on their boards. Seven of these are European (namely Allianz, BP, BNP Paribas, Unilever, Groupe Danone, Rio Tinto and Deutsche Bank); the eighth (the insurer American International Group) is based in the USA.

The coreness measure points again at the central position that European firms occupy in the corporate network, at the same time as it shows that policy-planning groups consitute the very heart of the network.

TABLE 8.3 Organizations ranking highest in coreness, 2006

Rank 06	96	Name	Coreness	City of head office	Country of domicile
1	1	Trilateral Commission	.681939	Wash-Paris-Tokyo	Triad
2	2	Bilderberg Conference (Spring 2007)	.419438	Leiden	Netherlands
3	3	European Round Table of Industrialists	.313872	Brussels	EU
4	4	World Business Council for Sustainable Development	.251819	Geneva	Switzerland
5	201	TransAtlantic Business Dialogue	.160462	Washington, DC	USA
6	8	EU–Japan Industrialists Round Table	.135937	Brussels/Tokyo	EU/Japan
7	6	CFR International Advisory Board	.132661	New York	USA
8	5	World Economic Forum	.096194	Geneva	Switzerland
9	23	Allianz Aktiengesellschaft Holding F	.084015	Munich	Germany
10	84	Suez SA	.077541	Paris	France
11	66	Siemens AG	.067988	Munich	Germany
12	96	TOTAL SA	.064875	Paris	France
13	46	Bayer AG	.061361	Cologne	Germany
14		Assicurazioni Generali F	.059956	Trieste	Italy
15	102	International Chamber of Commerce	.058925	Paris	France
16	348	Alcoa, Inc.	.056269	New York	USA
17		Lafarge SA	.055795	Paris	France
18	11	BP	.053166	London	UK
19	24	BNP Paribas F	.053113	Paris	France
20	289	ConocoPhillips	.050834	Houston	USA
21	18	American International Group F	.050280	New York	USA
22	14	Unilever Plc	.050171	London	UK

23		UN Global Compact	.049617	New York	USA
24		E.ON AG	.049593	Düsseldorf	Germany
25	52	Thyssen Krupp AG	.047361	Düsseldorf	Germany
26	81	Deutsche Lufthansa AG	.042881	Cologne	Germany
27	55	Citigroup F	.041932	New York	USA
28	62	Royal Dutch/Shell Group	.041710	The Hague	Netherlands
29	234	ABN AMRO Holding NV F	.041080	Amsterdam	Netherlands
30	170	British American Tobacco Plc [BAT]	.039699	London	UK
31		North American Competitiveness Council	.039689		
32		Hochtief AG	.037563	Düsseldorf	Germany
33		Vodafone Group plc	.036302	Berkshire	UK
34	129	Akzo Nobel	.035003	Arnhem	Netherlands
35	44	Commerzbank AG F	.034419	Frankfurt	Germany
36	219	Sony Corporation	.034157	Tokyo	Japan
37		Accenture Ltd	.034038	Bermuda	Bermuda
38	37	Groupe Danone	.031982	Paris	France
39	82	Saint-Gobain	.031722	Paris	France
40	32	Rio Tinto plc	.030847	London	UK
41	30	Deutsche Bank AG F	.030557	Frankfurt	Germany

Policy boards as brokers: the structure of mediations

Brokerage analysis can shed further light on the role policy boards play in pulling corporate directors on to common ground around shared political projects. Structurally, *a broker brings together parties who are not directly linked to each other*. In social structures where actors are divided into segmented groups, brokers occupy key mediatory positions (Gould 1989: 547). This is very much the case in the global corporate interlock network. As we saw in Chapters 1 and 4, it continues to be divided into (thinning) national corporate networks, spanned by a (growing) number of transnational interlocks. Brokerage analysis can assess the structural impact of policy boards as they mediate elite relations within and across macro-regions, thereby providing an additional layer of social and political organization for the global corporate elite.

The brokerage scores in Figure 8.7 show the total number of instances in which each policy board mediates between pairs of non-interlocked organizations in the network. There is a large variation among groups, but except for the TC and WEF, most groups register increases in brokerage, some of them spectacular (e.g. Bilderberg, WBCSD). The two inter-regional business councils, TABD and EJBRT, also show sharp increases. Although the TC remains the leading mediator, its total volume of brokerage shrinks by 34 per cent. This is due to a contraction, from 151 to 114, in the number of G500 firms whose

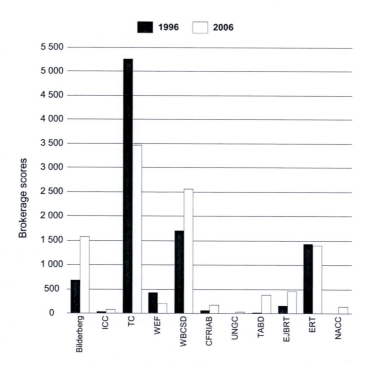

Figure 8.7 Total brokerage scores for transnational policy boards, 1996 and 2006

TABLE 8.4 Distribution of inter-corporate relations brokered by policy boards

Domicile of firms	1996	2006
Both in core North America	11.3	7.6
Both in core Europe	27.3	36.2
Both in core Asia-Pacific	3.1	2.3
One in core North America, one in core Europe	32.1	31.2
One in core North Atlantic, one in core Asia-Pacific	26.0	16.7
One in semi-periphery, one in core or semi-periphery	0.083	6.0
Total	100.0	100.0
N	9,590	9,838

directors are Trilateral Commissioners, which implies a 42 per cent decline in the number of inter-corporate relations that could be brokered by the TC.

Of particular interest is the pattern of mediation that ensues from the participation of G500 directors on the policy boards. Do liaisons mediated by policy boards cut across the major regions of the world system – fulfilling a function of global integration? To assess the extent of inter- and intra-regional brokerage we partitioned the corporate-policy network into the same five sectors as in Figures 8.4–8.6. Focusing purely on instances of inter-corporate brokerage by policy boards, we categorized each relation by the region of each firm's domicile. It is clear from Table 8.4 that the policy boards mainly broker two kinds of inter-corporate relations: 1) those between firms based in Europe[12] and 2) those between firms based on each side of the North Atlantic. Considering the three regions of the triad, the policy boards broker a growing proportion of relations between firms based in Europe, but a declining proportion of relations in core North America and in core Asia-Pacific. And although the proportion of mediations between the North Atlantic and the Asia-Pacific core drops substantially, companies domiciled on the semi-periphery become more linked into the global business community through the policy boards. By 2006, 6 per cent of all inter-corporate relations mediated by the policy boards include one or two firms based in the semi-periphery. As a structure of policy-board brokerage, the network has been gravitating towards Europe. Since the policy boards are themselves diverse, however, generalizations of this sort have to be tempered by examination of each board's location in the structure of mediations.

In Figure 8.8, we display the regional brokerage profiles for each of four key global policy groups. The graphs indicate the percentage distribution of inter-corporate brokerage relations across several regional categories. Three of the four groups are heavily engaged in trans-Atlantic liaisons. The WBCSD also brokers such relations but is even more extensively engaged in mediating relations between North Atlantic and core Asia-Pacific corporations. The 14

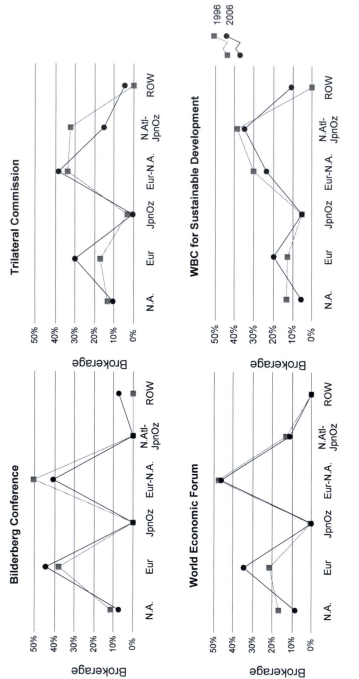

Figure 8.8 Inter-corporate brokerage within and between regions for four global policy groups

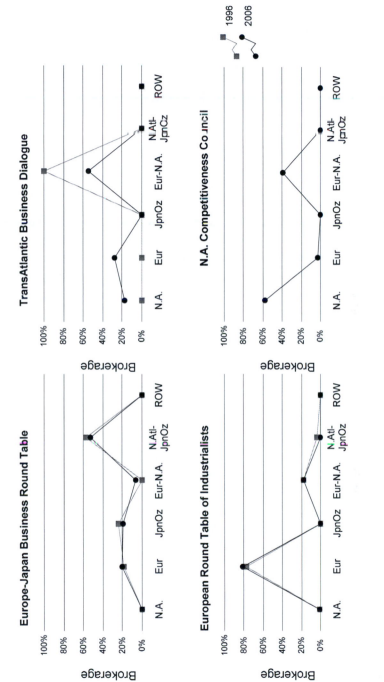

Figure 8.9 Inter-corporate brokerage within and between regions for four transnational business councils

Japan-based and 3 Australia-based firms whose boards interlock with the WBCSD in 2006 are thereby linked at one remove to the 37 European, 18 American and 4 Canadian corporate boards that also interlock with the WBCSD. In contrast, the TC plays a reduced role in brokering relations between companies based in the Asia-Pacific core and those based in the North Atlantic, as the number of Japanese G500 firms with directors on the TC falls from twenty to eight. All four groups broker more ties within Europe than within North America, and this tilt towards Europe increases over the decade. *Corporate Europe*, already the most cohesive region in terms of corporate interlocking, *is rendered even more integrated by virtue of policy-board brokerage*.

Finally, with the exception of the WEF, the key global policy groups have, since 1996, developed mediations to the global South (ROW), suggesting that a process of elite integration of the semi-periphery has been under way. In particular, the TC and the WBCSD pull together regionally diverse segments of the corporate elite.[13] By 2006 the WBCSD is the most diversified broker, as 11 per cent of its mediations involve semi-peripheral companies and 40 per cent involve firms based in the Asia-Pacific core.

The transnational business councils manifest quite diverse brokerage profiles, underlining the specificity of their regional political projects (see Figure 8.9). As one might expect, the two inter-regional business councils, both of which dramatically increased their volume of brokerage between 1996 and 2006 (see Figure 8.7), primarily mediate relations across the specific regions they strive to integrate; secondarily they broker relations between companies based in one or the other of the regions. The intra-regional business councils primarily integrate their respective regions, although both show a tendency collaterally to contribute to North Atlantic integration. Most of ERT's mediations occur within Europe, and most of NACC's occur within North America, but both councils also create liaisons between firms based in Europe and firms based in North America, precisely because some council members hold corporate directorships on both sides of the Atlantic. For instance, in 2006 39 per cent of the NACC's brokerage was between European and North American firms. In endeavouring to build a more competitive North America, a good deal of what NACC has brought to the table has been capitalists whose European contacts and knowledge of European capitalism are very likely integral to that regional project. At least within the Euro-North American heartland – the most integrated zone of global capitalism – the regional business councils appear to internalize the trans-regional character of corporate business: they are not vehicles for regional economic closure, but contribute to trans-regional integration of the global corporate network.

Conclusion

Returning to our research questions, in the first place network analysis reveals a process of structural consolidation after 1996 through which policy boards have become more integrative nodes in the global corporate power structure. The corporate-policy network, already well developed in the mid-1990s, has become denser and more extensive in its range of organizations.[14] As national corporate networks have thinned and transnational interlocks have proliferated, transnationalists have come to play enhanced roles in a network increasingly focused around the policy boards.

The corporate-policy network is highly centralized, at both the level of individuals and that of organizations. Its inner circle is a tightly interwoven ensemble of politically active business leaders; its organizational core includes the Trilateral Commission, the Bilderberg Conference, the European Round Table of Industrialists and the World Business Council for Sustainable Development, surrounded by other policy boards[15] and by the directorates of leading industrial corporations and financial institutions based in capitalism's core regions. While coreness is a major organizing dimension, specific groups, with their particular projects, occupy distinctive positions in the network. The global policy groups differ among themselves in their brokerage profiles, as do the more regionalized transnational business councils. Although in principle the latter could furnish a structural basis for cleavage and possibly rivalry, as in Europe versus North America, there is no clear evidence of this. Instead, as corporate interlocks span national borders, the capitalists that staff regional business councils tend towards cosmopolitan corporate affiliations. The different organizational forms, constituencies and network positions of the policy groups and business councils add up to a complex organizational ecology, unified by a neoliberal consensus yet differentiated by regional and other issues and interests. With Carroll and Shaw (2001: 211), we might infer that such an organizational ecology provides a rich discursive field and 'offers possibilities for nuanced debate and diverse action repertoires, all within the perimeters of permissible neoliberal discourse'. To the extent that the network embodies the leading edge of a transnational capitalist class, in concordance with Robinson's (2004) analysis, we can discern in this formation an increased capacity to act as a class-for-itself.

Turning to our second query – the regional question – our findings suggest a process of transnational capitalist class formation that is regionally uneven. Certainly, a North Atlantic ruling class remains at the centre of the process. The transnational corporate-policy network continues to be carried by an elite inner circle of well-connected persons and organizations, *centred in Euro-North America, but weighted increasingly towards Europe.*

The shift towards Europe takes a similar finding from Chapter 5, based purely on interlocking corporate directorships, one step farther. Partly it reflects a shift in corporate capital's locus of control, as the number of G500 firms based in western Europe expanded while the number of firms based in the USA and in Japan contracted. Partly it reflects sharpening differences in business systems, with (continental) Europe retaining, to some extent, a regime of organized capitalism, while the USA, already in the 1980s, embraced a 'shareholder capitalism' organized more around the stock market than around extra-market relations such as interlocking directorates (Davis and Mizruchi 1999). The upshot, as we saw in Chapter 7, has been corporate Europe's consolidation as the US corporate network lost its centre, while Japanese capitalism stagnated in the wake of the Asian financial crisis of 1997. Within the network of corporate and policy-board affiliations, the shift towards Europe is evident in several respects:

- policy boards are increasingly staffed by pan-European transnationalists, who predominate in the network's inner circle;
- the ERT – a major vehicle of European integration – is positioned at the core of the global network;
- with the exception of North-American-based NACC, the policy boards tend to be ensconced on the European side of the network's social space;
- corporate Europe, the most socially integrated segment of the global corporate network, is also the most densely tied to the policy boards;
- a large and increasing number of firms at the core of the network are based in Europe;
- the transnational policy boards broker a growing complement of relations between European firms, adding further to regional cohesion.

The tilt towards Europe, however, is not the whole story. We also find a modest increase in participation of corporate elites from the global South. This reflects the growing number of G500 firms based in the semi-periphery: the world outside the triad hosted twenty-three G500 firms in 1996, but fifty-eight in 2006. In light of this growth in Southern-based corporate capital, the increased participation by directors of these firms in the corporate-policy network is unspectacular.[16] Insofar as the network comprises a key component of a transnational historic bloc, that bloc remains, at its higher reaches, overwhelmingly centred upon the North Atlantic.[17]

9 | Hegemony and counter-hegemony in a global field

Global corporate power does not go unopposed; rather, its very practices and their human and ecological impacts provoke resistance, which can fuel a bottom-up counter-power – a globalization from below. Since the spectacular announcement of the new politics of global justice in the 1990s – in Chiapas (1994), Paris (1995) and Seattle (1999) – social scientists have begun to pay attention to the networks, discourses, communication technologies and non-governmental organizations that have enabled and shaped anti-corporate politics (e.g. Keck and Sikkink 1998; Olesen 2004; Smith 2001, 2002; Smith and Wiest 2005). In the same period, and in earlier chapters of this book, researchers have charted the formation of a neoliberal *transnational historic bloc*, an assemblage of elite policy-planning organizations, transnational corporations and global-governance organizations that has promoted, and to some extent consolidated, a hegemonic project of neoliberal globalization (Gill 1995a; Sklair 2001; Robinson 2004; Nollert 2005). On the premise that these phenomena are dialectically related, this chapter traces the war of position between hegemonic and counter-hegemonic forces in the current era; a struggle in which conflicting visions of justice clash within a global field.

Globalization-from-below is diverse in its conceptions of social justice, yet its minions agree that injustice is rooted in contemporary social arrangements and structures that can be transformed through collective action. As globalization accentuates both human interdependencies and the awareness of those interdependencies, this 'movement of movements' appears to be converging around a counter-hegemonic vision that integrates struggles against 'maldistribution, misrecognition and misrepresentation' within a dialogical framing of social justice in terms of parity of participation and the all-affected principle (Fraser 2005: 79, 82–4).[1] Such a holistic project is not easily posited, let alone pursued, yet it gains shape and form as 'activists create spaces, both physically and emotionally, that promote ideas of social justice in explicit opposition to the injustice enacted by the global institutions of neo-liberalism and global capital' (Lacey 2005: 405).

Globalization-from-above, as we have seen, has trumpeted unfettered capitalism as the harbinger of individual liberty and material abundance, creating optimal consumer choice in the marketplace and a rising tide of affluence that lifts all boats. The neoliberal doctrine informing this vision locates 'plain justice' in the market mechanism itself and denies that 'social justice' is any-thing but 'a dishonest insinuation that one ought to agree to a demand of some special interest which can give no real reason for it' (von Hayek 1976: 90). Notwithstanding von Hayek's faith in the plain justice of the marketplace, by now we are painfully familiar with the logic and consequences of neoliberalism. These include policies of fiscal retrenchment that degrade social programmes, the accumulation by dispossession (euphemized as privatization) and 'com-modification of everything' (Harvey 2005), the harmful impact of deregulated global market forces on workers and communities, as exchange value reasserts itself at the centre of life (Teeple 2000). This triumph of 'plain justice' over social justice has been a global phenomenon – hence the currency of the term *transnational neoliberalism*. If, as Jessop (2002: 113) holds, globalization is the complex and emergent product of various forces operating on many scales, in the economic field its most salient impact has been to strengthen the structural power of capital vis-à-vis agents enclosed within national states, as the circuitry of accumulation becomes more internationalized (Gill and Law 1989). Neo-liberalism is the political paradigm that converts that structural power from a contingent and contestable accomplishment to a seemingly permanent reality, within which market-driven politics holds sway (Leys 2001).

There can be little doubt that the power of neoliberal concepts 'goes hand in hand with the changed orientation of an increasingly internationalised business community – industrial TNCs [transnational corporations], big banks, financial conglomerates and other investment-related firms – or as some call it, of an "ex-panding transnational managerial class"' (Bieling 2006b: 211). United through the ideological practices of various international forums and policy groups which have become venues for promoting a consensus around the cosmopolitan vision of a borderless world of friction-free capitalism, this transnational bloc of social forces is more extensive than its strict class base might suggest (ibid.: 221). It encompasses public officials in international and national agencies of economic management, and a great range of specialists and experts who help maintain the global economy in which the TNCs thrive – 'from management consultants, to business educators, to organizational psychologists, to the electronic operators who assemble the information base for business decisions, and the lawyers who put together international business deals' (Cox 1987: 360; Sklair 2001).

As a hegemonic project, however, transnational neoliberalism poses great problems. Its basic mechanisms – market liberalization, accumulation by dis-possession, densification of capital circuits – do not allow for the wide-ranging material concessions that, at least in the global North, stabilized class relations during the national-Keynesian era (Carroll 2006). If hegemony is secured by constructing and maintaining a historic bloc whose constituent elements find their own interests and aspirations reflected in a shared project, neoliberalism's bloc – while thick among the global corporate elite – is thin on the ground, and made incrementally thinner by widening economic disparities worldwide and within national societies (Held and Kaya 2007). The pervasive social injustices that attend upon neoliberal policy have been well documented by Bourdieu and Accardo (1999) and Chossudovsky (2003), among others. Accompanying them are looming ecological issues, which neoliberalism seems incapable of seriously addressing, and a worrying record of economic instability, evident since the 1997/98 Asian financial crisis, and provoking crisis interventions against the neoliberal doctrine itself in the aftermath of the 2008 financial meltdown. Neoliberal hegemony, to say the least, has been far from secure. It is subverted not only by its own contradictions, which have inspired a movement for global justice, but by the territorial logic of states – most stridently expressed in the US-centred imperialism of the G. W. Bush years (Amin 2005; Harvey 2005; Stokes 2005). It is in this context that we can understand the *challenges* facing neo-liberalism's organic intellectuals as they advance the project in an incipiently global civil society.

Global civil society as an emergent field

We saw in earlier chapters that organized policy planning behind the scenes has long been 'a form of the socialisation of the conduct of class struggle on the part of the bourgeoisie' since the late seventeenth century (van der Pijl 1998: 108). In the late nineteenth century, as inter-imperialist rivalry and revolution threatened transnational bourgeois solidarity, the Rhodes-Milner Round Table Group emerged as a British Empire-centred network of elite planning, to be joined in 1919 by the International Chamber of Commerce. Since the founding of the Mont Pèlerin Society in 1947, but especially since the corporate offensive of the 1970s, strategized in the Trilateral Commission's report on *The Crisis of Democracy* (Crozier et al. 1975), neoliberal policy-planning groups have played a signal role in building, consolidating and bolstering this bloc, along with its norm of plain justice. They have conducted a war of position to shift 'the balance of cultural and social forces' (Femia 1981: 53), and thereby win new political space in a global field.

If initially the bourgeoisie held sway in global civil society, from the late nineteenth century onwards international labour organizations and left-party organizations entered the field. Since the 1990s, a wide range of subaltern groups opposed to neoliberal capitalism has begun to mount a concerted struggle for position, constituting a potentially counter-hegemonic bloc of aligned social forces. Certainly, the thousands of international NGOs that now have 'consultative status' with the United Nations' Economic and Social Council confirm the arrival of global civil society, and indeed of a global civil society–state complex. Civil society, however, is not a unified 'agent' (Olesen 2005b), nor is it a collection of politically progressive groups (as implied in Lipschutz 1996), but a field within which interests and identities take shape vis-à-vis each other (Urry

1981); and, furthermore, it is hardly a level playing field (Swift 1999). From the neo-Gramscian perspective taken here, global civil society appears as

> the terrain for both legitimizing and challenging global governance. [...] Further, global civil society is not just a sphere of activity, but a discursive space, which helps to reproduce global hegemony. [...] [S]ocial movements must recognize they are positioned within this hegemonic constellation, and [...] that there are structural and discursive forces at play, of which the very framework of global civil society is itself a part, and which social movements themselves may actually be actively reproducing, rather than challenging. (Ford 2003: 129)

Global civil society is profoundly tilted to the right by the dominance of capital in national politics, in international relations, in global governance and in mass communications. In these circumstances, movements for global justice must find openings that do not lead into co-optative capture, while building constituencies at the grass roots. But neoliberal groups, in spite of their greater resources and central locations within the ruling historic bloc, also face the challenge, mentioned earlier, of legitimizing their practices and positions in a crisis-ridden era in which social injustices sharpen while the margin for dispensing concessions narrows.

Finally, it is helpful to understand global civil society as a *multi-organizational field* wherein diverse groups championing (or challenging) globalization, from above or below, take up specific niches in an organizational ecology that is itself substantially networked (Carroll and Shaw 2001; Fisher et al. 2005). Global civil society comprises not only a terrain of struggle, not only a discursive space, but also a rich variety of organizations, with distinctive structures, projects and interrelationships, addressing transnational publics – whether privileged or subaltern (Olesen 2005b). In examining some of these organizations this chapter opens a window on the struggle for social justice in a global field.

Paired comparisons

Our focus here is on four key groups on each side of the complex relation between dominant class and subalterns. Groups struggling within global civil society are diverse in their organizational structures, constituencies and modi operandi, making the task of comparative analysis quite complicated. To facilitate the process, we will use a method of paired comparison across four aspects of the struggle for hegemony: 1) the relation between capitalism's 'fundamental classes' (Gramsci 1977: 5), 2) the exercise of intellectual/ideological leadership, 3) the looming ecological question, and 4) construction of public spheres for forming consensus. For each aspect, a key hegemonic organization is paired with its counter-hegemonic counterpart – for instance, the World Economic Forum and its antithesis, the World Social Forum. Some pairings might be arguable, and the analysis is hardly exhaustive. The point of the exercise is not to satisfy some sort of multifactorial research design but to highlight the role certain organizations have played and the niches they have taken up in global struggles for hegemony.

The four pairs of organizations are listed in Table 9.1, along with sketches of core membership, organizational form and action repertoire/strategy in Table 9.2. In this small, purposive sample we can glimpse some of the dynamics of hegemony and counter-hegemony in a global field. Comparing year of formation alone, it is clear that groups promoting neoliberalism attained positions of early influence in the global field, expressing the material, organizational and intellectual advantages that accrue to the dominant class, with defensive responses, on a global terrain, coming later, as in Polanyi's (1944) 'double movement' of capitalist disembedding and social re-embedding. On economic matters, intellectuals of the cosmopolitan bourgeoisie took the lead in the early decades of the twentieth century, promoting market liberalization as a philosophical principle – already inscribed in the International Chamber of Commerce's 1919 constitution, and given more rigorous definition in the work of the Mont Pèlerin Society following the Second World War. In both instances, liberalization received impetus from world wars, in the wake of which an open world economy – extending what van der Pijl (1998) has called the Lockean heartland, progressively dissolving Hobbesian regimes committed to statist developmental logics – was trumpeted as a premise for peaceful international relations. Yet despite the US Open Door policy, after the Second World War consolidation of a corporate-liberal paradigm pushed neoliberalism to the margins. The same paradigm limited prospects for global oppositional politics. The Keynesian class compromise marked the apogee of the Westphalian political imaginary: it cleaved 'domestic' from 'international' political space (Fraser 2005), and in particular contained labour politics within national, reformist frameworks whose

TABLE 9.1 A judgement sample of eight key organizations for paired comparisons

Paired comparison	Name	Est'd
Capital/labour struggle	International Chamber of Commerce (ICC)	1919
	International Trade Union Confederation (ITUC)	1949
Intellectual/ideological leadership	Mont Pèlerin Society (MPS)	1947
	Transnational Institute	1973
Ecological politics	World Business Council for Sustainable Development (WBCSD)	1995
	Friends of the Earth International (FoEI)	1971
Global public spheres	World Economic Forum (WEF)	1971 (1987)
	World Social Forum (WSF)	2001

TABLE 9.2 Eight key organizations: constituencies, organizational forms, action repertoires

Name	Core membership	Organizational form	Action repertoire/strategy
ICC	Corporations large and small, increasingly global membership	Federation, including companies and C of Cs from 130+ countries	Consensus formation, lobbying, services to members, engagement with UN, WEF, etc.
ITUC	170+ million, US dominated until 1960s, recent shift to Southern constituency	Confederation of national labour centrals	Elite diplomacy until recent shift to international labour solidarity and engagement with WSF
MPS	Economists, capitalists, think-tank directors, plus a few politicians and journalists from Europe and the USA	Annual retreat, with close links to neo-liberal advocacy think tanks worldwide	Constituting a global network of neoliberal knowledge production and dissemination
Trans-national Institute	Two dozen activist scholars, allied with many NGOs, including WSF	Vanguard of Fellows spearheads programmes and projects attuned to a multi-frontal war of position	Facilitation of/critical reflection on praxis, outreach to partners in a range of targeted priorities
WBCSD	180 global corporations (as represented by CEOs) committed to eco-efficiency, mainly based in the triad	Council of CEOs, subdivided into working groups chaired by CEOs and reaching farther via a regional network and 47 partners	Serves as a forum, educates its business constituency on the virtues of eco-efficiency, promotes its vision as ecologically sufficient
FoEI	1.5 million members, in national and local activist groups striving for environmentally sustainable and socially just societies	Decentralized network of autonomous organizations, coordinating collective action globally within six campaigns	Activist campaigns, popular education and communication, research
WEF	Initially European, increasingly global organization of 1,000 CEOs with other elite interests arrayed on the margins	Massive annual elite meeting, recent shift to more continuous engagement of members in task forces	Increasingly outcome-oriented, diffused into various regional activities, and interested in co-opting the opposition
WSF	Many thousands of liberal anti-globalization and radical anti-capitalist activists, facilitated by an International Council with delegates from 136 national and global non-party organizations	Annual meetings: 'open space' in which movements might converge without sacrificing autonomy, membership by organizational affiliation	Dialogical forum process, spreading from Pôrto Alegre to regional, national, local and thematic forums and various Days of Action throughout the year

counter-hegemonic potential was further drained by a trade union imperialism ideologically aligned with Cold War anti-communism (Munck 2002: 141–4).

Despite the more recent successes of Thatcherism and Reaganism and the triumph in the 1980s of the Washington Consensus, the struggle to neoliberalize the world has been far from straightforward. In the years surrounding the turn of the century, it met with major setbacks, including economic crises and the emergence of new forms of civil resistance to capitalist globalization.

International Chamber of Commerce, International Trade Union Confederation Let us proceed to the first of our paired comparisons by considering two global organizations that encompass large memberships on each side of the divide between capital and labour. The Paris-based *International Chamber of Commerce* (ICC), the oldest and largest global business policy group, has functioned as the most comprehensive business forum committed to the plain justice of liberal markets.

As stated in its constitution (available online), the ICC's fundamental objective is 'to further the development of an open world economy with the firm conviction that international commercial exchanges are conducive to both greater global prosperity and peace among nations'. This basic goal implies three aims – to promote 1) international trade, investment and services, 2) a market economy based on the competitive principle, and 3) global economic growth. The aims, in turn, are pursued via two principal means: 1) 'political advocacy and lobbying' directed at international organizations such as the WTO and UN and at national governments, and 2) 'provision of a range of practical services to business', such as the International Court of Arbitration (Kelly 2005: 259).

As a forum, the ICC integrates capitalists and their organic intellectuals into a common international policy framework. Since the mid-1990s its efforts to institutionalize an agenda of *corporate self-regulation* have fostered close working relationships with international institutions such as the WTO and the UN General Secretariat (ibid.: 166–74). Finally, the ICC's World Chambers Federation (WCF) knits the multitude of national chambers into a single global network that articulates transnational capitalist interests to national and local ones. As we noted in Chapter 2, this combination of a free market vision, a programmatic emphasis on institutionalizing transnational business practices, and an incorporation of local business into a global capitalist perspective has given the ICC a unique niche within transnational neoliberalism's organizational ecology. The Chamber reaches deeply into regional and national contexts, and mobilizes capitalists themselves as organic intellectuals engaged in business leadership. This organizational form lends impetus to a social bloc that extends from the global to the local.

Beyond its contribution to class formation per se, the Council reaches into global political processes.[2] Although its ties to the UN weakened during the years in which a Keynesian developmentalism held sway, by the 1990s, on the other side of the Reagan/Thatcher era, the ICC 'pushed to the forefront of international affairs'. In the process, it expanded its membership and overhauled its identity, rebranding itself in 1998 as the 'World Business Organization' (ibid.: 263). In its recent efforts, the ICC has targeted the UN, entering in 2000 into a Global Compact for peaceful development and poverty alleviation and taking active roles within a host of UN agencies (ibid.: 267–9) – all with the effect of securing legitimacy as an organization of both global governance and global business.

If the ICC has become the 'World Business Organization', perhaps what is most striking is the lack of any counter-hegemonic labour organization that could credibly make a parallel claim. Factionalized into social-democratic and communist centrals at the very time that the ICC emerged as a source of transnational capitalist unity, organized labour would become largely contained within national states in the middle decades of the twentieth century, striking up social accords under the aegis of the KWS or being absorbed into the party-state. Whatever its fate in that sense, labour showed little interest in international organization or action – at the very time that capital, under the hegemony of the US Open Door policy, was rapidly transnationalizing. This meant that labour's initial response to the neoliberal offensive would deploy largely within national (or sub-national) fields and would be tinged with nostalgia for restoration of the status quo.

The International Trade Union Confederation (ITUC) was formed (as the International Confederation of Free Trade Unions) in 1949. But not until the departure of the labour-imperialist AFL-CIO in 1969 (and arguably not until its 1996 World Congress, which recognized the need for transnational action in response to capitalist globalization; Munck 2002: 151, 13) could it be considered a candidate for counter-hegemonic leadership of any sort. In a post-Cold War context of neoliberal ascendance, the world's largest international labour central finally took up the call for a global Keynesian regime of social and environmental rights based on international regulation (ibid.: 156). In 2006, it merged with the much smaller, Christian-based World Confederation of Labour, to form the ITUC. The ITUC remains bureaucratic in structure, and skewed in its leadership towards a minority of unions from industrialized countries. Still, it is the world's largest, most representative trade union body, claiming 170 million members and 316 affiliated organizations in 158 countries.

Organizationally, the ITUC is structured as a confederation of national trade union centrals. Its professional staff are tasked with organizing and directing campaigns 'to better the conditions of work and life of working women and men and their families, and to strive for human rights, social justice, gender equality, peace, freedom and democracy'.[3] One can see in this list a basis for alliances with a wide range of contemporary social movements, and indeed, since its 2000 congress in Durban, the ITUC has been committed to building 'alliances with NGOs and civil society around shared values of human rights' (K. Davis 2004: 124). Yet in that very year, the ITUC signed up to the same Global Compact as endorsed by the ICC – a purely voluntary framework that brings business, labour and environmental representatives together under the auspices of the UN (Munck 2002: 169). We noted in Chapter 8 that the Global Compact's board is interlocked with other policy boards and with major corporate boards, but among its twenty members (fourteen of them representing business) are two labour representatives, including the general secretary of the International Trade Union Confederation.[4]

The ITUC's quest for global regulation has engendered a vicious circle – 'a lack of mobilizing capacity, modest objectives, equally modest achievements, limited recognition by and relevance for rank-and-file trade unionists on the ground' (Hyman 2005: 148). The elite and grassroots 'sides' of ITUC's action repertoire are potentially complementary strategic elements in a war of position, but only if the former does more than provide an ethical cover to the TNCs and if the latter helps mobilize workers in ways that build alliances with other democratic movements. With membership from the global South (half of its total in 1999) rapidly increasing, the challenge is 'to integrate the struggles and concerns of workers both North and South' (Jakobsen 2001: 370), to create a 'new internationalism' that moves beyond elite-level deals at the WTO within the logic of neoliberal global governance (Waterman 2005: 200).

Peter Waterman (2001: 313) has put his finger on the biggest task: to break free of 'the ideology, institutions and procedures of "social partnership" [which] have become hegemonic [...]' The ITUC continues to express the national, industrial, colonial capitalism that gave it initial shape and form. Two massive challenges reflect its disadvantageous position in the global field, both institutionally and culturally:

> One major challenge has to do with the role of a literally inter*national* confederation in times of globalisation. The ICFTU [now ITUC] [...] is at the peak of a pyramidal structure several removes [...] from any flesh-and-blood workers. It is also an institution heavily incorporated into a traditional world of the inter-state institutions, with much of its energy addressed to lobbying these. The second major challenge [...] is the virtual *invisibility* of the ICFTU. Here is an organisation with 155 million members and rising that has no presence at all in the global media or culture, whether dominant, popular or alternative. (Ibid.: 315)

In comparison with the ICC, whose aggressive drive for market liberalization has paid political dividends to its constituency, the ITUC has cautiously sought global accords, clauses and protections against the ravages of the market. Whether this key organization is capable of leading, or at least actively participating in, a new social unionism (ibid.: 316–17) is a central question in the future of counter-hegemony. If, as Hyman (2005) argues, the ITUC has served primarily a 'diplomatic' function for labour within the machinery of international institutions, its counter-hegemonic prospects hinge on going beyond that carefully circumscribed role, to participate in globalization from below. ITUC's involvement in the World Social Forum is a hopeful sign, to be placed alongside the major structural trend that favours a formative role for labour in any global counter-hegemonic bloc – the expanding size of the world's working class and the sharpening class contradictions associated with neoliberal accumulation.

The Mont Pèlerin Society, the Transnational Institute The struggle for hegemony involves production and dissemination of ideas. In this, the Mont Pèlerin Society (MPS) has been distinctively in the vanguard of neoliberalism, serving 'a more militant intellectual function than an adaptive/directive role in the background', as has been the case with elite groups like the Bilderberg Conference or the Trilateral Commission. For MPS, 'the neo-liberal intervention was of a much more "willed" than organically hegemonic nature' (van der Pijl 1998: 130). When the Society was founded in 1947, Keynesian corporate liberalism was becoming a hegemonic policy paradigm; hence the task was to create, under less than felicitous conditions, a hegemonic project that could ultimately inform a neoliberal counter-revolution. In his paper 'The intellectuals and socialism' (1949), which can be read as a founding document of MPS, Friedrich von Hayek drew two conclusions from his analysis of the influence of socialism in post-war policy and media circles. First, the right lacks such rising stars as Keynes, hence the need 'to rebuild anti-socialist science and expertise in order to develop anti-socialist intellectuals' (Plehwe and Walpen 2006: 33). Second, the socialist filter in the knowledge-dissemination institutions – universities, institutes, media – has to be attacked by establishing anti-socialist knowledge centres able to filter, process and disseminate neoliberal knowledge (ibid.: 33). The MPS addressed itself directly to the first task and indirectly to the second, with impressive results over the long haul.

Although the Society laboured in relative obscurity for more than two decades, as the post-war hegemonic bloc dissolved it emerged as a major centre for neoliberal propaganda and informal policy advice, whether to Pinochet's Chile or Thatcher's Britain (van der Pijl 1998: 129). Its membership, comprised mainly of intellectuals (particularly economists), with a relatively small contingent of capitalists, grew from an initial group of 38 to a total membership of 1,025 (48 women), with almost equal numbers from the USA (458) and Europe (438) and with a smattering of members in 27 non-Euro-North American states. Many members established or became active in 100 national-level right-wing think tanks, constituting a global network of neoliberal knowledge production and dissemination (Plehwe and Walpen 2006: 34–40). By periodically assembling 'scientists' (mainly economists) and 'practical men' (including corporate capitalists, politicians and journalists) committed to neoliberalism's core principles of the minimal state and the rule of law, by fostering a worldwide network of neoliberal advocacy think tanks, the MPS has not only provided neoliberalism with a durable anchor point within the space of economic doctrines (Denord 2002), it has managed to build capacity in global civil society for neoliberal culture, securing in the process the conditions for its own continued relevance.

Perhaps the closest left analogue to the MPS is the Transnational Institute (TNI), 'a worldwide fellowship of committed scholar-activists', as its website proclaims (www.tni.org).[5] Funded initially as a branch of the Washington, DC-based Institute for Policy Studies (with which it continues to have close relations), the TNI was one of the first research institutes to be established as a global organization – transnational in name, orientation, composition and focus. Founded in Amsterdam late in 1973, just as neoliberalism was beginning to find political traction, the TNI has been a consistent critic of the new right. Its first conference, 'The lessons from Chile', attended in 1974 by about fifty people including Ralph Miliband, André Gunder Frank, Herbert Marcuse and Johan Galtung, helped build a political response to the military coup that brought the first neoliberal regime to power. The conference established the TNI's presence on the European radical left, as did its first book-length publication, *World Hunger, Causes and Remedies* (1974).

According to its own website account, the TNI's mission is to provide 'intellectual support to those movements concerned to steer the world in a democratic, equitable and environmentally sustainable direction'. The Institute has assembled an international network of hundreds of scholar-activists, strategically mobilized to locate the most appropriate people to design and participate in study groups, international conferences and the production and dissemination of working and policy papers and accessible books, often translated into several languages. At the centre of the network are the Amsterdam-based staff and a couple of dozen Fellows, appointed to three-year renewable terms. They include journalists, independent researchers and senior scholars from similar institutes in Africa, Asia, Latin America, Europe and the USA. The Fellows meet annually in Amsterdam, in a small-scale answer to MPS's annual retreat. But many of them are also actively engaged in specific TNI programmes and projects, where we see a wide-ranging yet coherent framework for counter-hegemony, organized around the themes of new politics, environmental justice, alternative regionalisms, militarization and globalization, public services, crime and globalization, and drugs and democracy.[6] The knowledge that TNI produces is both critical of dominant institutions and proactively oriented to creating or strengthening democratic alternatives, as in New Politics' emphasis on participatory governance. Despite its meagre resources (a budget of US$1.1 million in 2003 and a staff of ten), the TNI engages in a multi-frontal war of position and gains energy from active collaboration with other NGOs, institutes and movements throughout the world. One TNI initiative worth highlighting is the 'Social Forum Process', which falls under the rubric of New Politics. An active participant in the WSF and the European Social Forum (ESF), the TNI has reflected critically on the process in play at these events – the innovative developments and the nagging problems. At the designated webpage, one can find varied analyses by TNI Fellows.[7]

At a certain level of abstraction, and despite vast differences in scale, the MPS and the TNI are kindred organizations. Both engage proactively in knowledge production and dissemination to inform effective political practice; both have strategically built global networks and have collaborated with like-minded groups. Yet while the MPS's hegemonic project places the market at the centre of human affairs, the TNI arises both as a critic of neoliberalism and an advocate for participatory democracy, social justice and ecology. The knowledge they create circulates, in the former case, among right-wing think tanks, academics, politicians and journalists mainly in the USA and Europe, and in the latter case among left-wing think tanks and NGOs, scholar-activists, social movements and alternative media, often in the global South. Concretely, the two projects are embedded in opposing historic blocs, as each group develops and deploys knowledge with the strategic intent to make its bloc more coherent and effective. This, however, entails quite different practices: the MPS, firmly committed to hierarchy as a principle of social and political organization, fits easily into existing elite structures: its messages need carry no farther than a relatively small circle. The TNI, on the other hand, as a collective intellectual of the left, faces the challenge of reaching a massive, diverse potential constituency and creating new political methodologies that go against the grain in giving shape to emergent oppositional practices.

World Business Council for Sustainable Development, Friends of the Earth International If on economic matters the global oppositional groups have been respondents to neoliberal initiatives, the reverse is the case on the ecological question. Capital is largely inured to ecological degradation (Kovel 2006), at least until it registers in value terms as a threat to profits. The ecological movement that was inspired in the 1960s by critical texts such as Rachel Carson's *Silent Spring* met largely with corporate stonewalling until the Rio Earth Summit of 1992. Yet already in the 1970s, ecological groups like Friends of the Earth International and Greenpeace International were organizing and acting globally, and developing wide-ranging critiques of the devastation of nature by industrial civilization, even if they lacked a critique of capital. On ecology, the transnational capitalist class fought a rearguard battle until its intellectuals developed an eco-capitalist response, to win back lost legitimacy.

On its information-rich website (www.foei.org), Amsterdam-based Friends of the Earth International (FoEI) describes itself as 'the world's largest *grassroots* environmental network', challenging the current model of corporate globalization and promoting solutions that will help to create environmentally sustainable and socially just societies. Our decentralized and democratic *structure* allows all member groups to participate in decision-making. We strive for gender equity in all of our campaigns and structures. Our *international positions* are informed and strengthened by our work with communities, and our alliances with indigenous peoples, farmers' movements, trade unions, human rights groups and others.[8]

In this framing we can see a project that transcends 1970s environmentalism. The description highlights the organization's global scope, the close connection it draws between ecological and social issues, the direct challenge it mounts to capitalist globalization, and its commitment to participatory democracy, gender equity and building alliances through grassroots organizing. FoEI's global social ecology has evolved from a project limited to specific concerns over whaling and nuclear power. The group's membership was at first entirely Euro-North American; only in the 1980s did its Southern membership expand. FoEI's global profile received a boost at the 1992 Earth Summit in Rio de Janeiro, 'where a vocal mosaic of FoE groups critiqued the business-as-usual approach of governments and corporations attending the meeting'.[9] Two years later, the AGM adopted an explicit 'agenda', which has been developed further in the form of the Sustainable Societies Programme, whose basic principles combine ecology with radical democracy:

> Our vision is of a peaceful and sustainable world based on societies living in harmony with nature. We envision a society of interdependent people living in dignity, wholeness and fulfilment in which equity and human and peoples' rights are realized. This will be a society built upon peoples' sovereignty and participation. It will be founded on social, economic, gender and environmental justice and free from all forms of domination and exploitation, such as neoliberalism, corporate globalization, neo-colonialism and militarism.

Structurally, FoEI is highly decentralized. It is composed of autonomous organizations that must agree to open, democratic and non-sexist practices, to the pursuit of environmental issues in their social and political context, and to campaigning, educating and researching while cooperating with other movement organizations. The International serves to coordinate collective action globally, within the framework provided by four designated programmes: climate justice and energy, food sovereignty, forest and biodiversity, and economic justice – resisting neoliberalism. What is noteworthy in this list, and in the website sketches of each programme's priorities, is the extent to which FoEI organizes its praxis in conscious opposition to neoliberalism and global capitalist domination. Even in matters such as climate change, where a technocratic discourse might easily prevail, the group frames its politics in opposition to powerful corporate interests and institutions such as the WTO and the WEF.

Not surprisingly, the group has participated actively in the World Social Forum, hosting sessions in 2005 on four of its campaign themes and participating with other NGOs in projects on forests and on the commodification of nature. At the 2009 WSF, FoEI was active in several events, including the climate justice assembly, whose declaration insisted that 'the struggles for climate justice and social justice are one and the same'.[10] The impressive global linkages that FoEI has forged since the 1980s and its social-ecological vision make it an important agency of counter-hegemony within global civil society.

If the 1992 UN Earth Summit helped catapult FoEI on to the global scene, it also catalysed the global corporate elite to enter the debate. The *World Business Council for Sustainable Development* (WBCSD), whose central position in the global corporate-policy network was noted in Chapters 2 and 8, instantly became the pre-eminent corporate voice on the environment upon its formation in 1995. Currently the membership is 180 corporations as represented by their CEOs, with members drawn from more than thirty-five countries, and with membership heavily skewed towards the developed capitalist core.[11] Council members co-chair WBCSD working groups, act as advocates for the WBCSD's policy positions, and oversee adoption of sustainable management practices within their own companies. These top-flight global capitalists are complemented by a regional network of close to sixty Business Councils for Sustainable Development (BCSDs) – an informal confederation of organizations that, following the ICC model, promote green capitalism in their respective countries or regions. Finally, and as a measure of the degree of its commitment to broadening the eco-capitalist bloc, the WBCSD has developed what its website describes as 'strong relationships' with sixty partners. These include international and intergovernmental organizations, eco-capitalist news and information organizations, research institutes, foundations, universities, business organizations (notably, the ICC and WEF) and NGOs (equally notably, World Wildlife Fund International and Earthwatch Institute).[12] Apart from the organization's successful co-optation of WWFI into the cause of green capitalism, the list of partners is remarkable for its location in the Euro-North American North: only four of the sixty groups reside outside of the triad, and only one partner is based in Japan.

As we observed in Chapter 2, the WBCSD reflects a maturing elite awareness that transnational corporate enterprise must be coupled with consensus over environmental regulation. WBCSD efforts to replace the 'business versus the environment' dualism with a vision of eco-efficiency that couples the health of nature with the 'health' of the global economy have been key. In this way, Gramsci's (1977) formula for ruling-class hegemony – that concessions granted in organizing consent must not touch the essential nucleus of economic relations – is satisfied.

As one might expect, WBCSD serves as a forum for its member corporations, whose CEOs meet annually, and carries out an elite lobbying function vis-à-vis institutions of global governance. But it directs much of its energy at educating its business constituency to adopt eco-efficient practices, a programme of moral reform that aims to pre-empt coercive state regulation. Its Chronos 'e-learning tutorial on the business case for sustainable development', developed in partnership with the University of Cambridge and published online in 2006,[13] is exemplary. It purports to move the user 'from personal values to corporate action' through an elaborate series of exercises. By working through dilemmas, case exercises, role-plays and quizzes, the executives, managers and engineers at whom the programme is aimed are taught how to appraise current performance and how to incorporate eco-efficient decisions into their business. As a hegemonic trope, eco-efficiency intends to reach well beyond the top tier of management, into 'the hearts and minds of employees. Demonstrating the value of an eco-efficient approach will help employees recognize why it is important to implement and motivate towards action [sic]' (WBCSD 2005: 5).

The WBCSD promotes, as an alternative to state regulation of capital, a global self-regulatory framework, emphasizing benchmarking and 'best practices' as voluntary means towards green capitalism. Its project incorporates what neo-liberal economics terms 'externalities' – not only ecological but also relating to labour relations, the health of consumers and the like – into a long-term perspective on sustainable accumulation. Already in the 1990s, individual corporations, some of them active in WBCSD, were adopting corporate environmentalism as an integral aspect of their globalizing capitalist ideology (Sklair 2001). The WBCSD has integrated these scattered corporate initiatives into a hegemonic project.

World Economic Forum, World Social Forum The *World Economic Forum* (WEF) was founded in 1971 to mark the twenty-fifth anniversary of the Centre d'Etudes Industrielles, a Geneva-based business school associated with Europe's post-war managerial revolution, and it was not until 1987 that the Forum changed its name to the *World* Economic Forum. Its inception as a truly global collective actor may be dated from that year. In the subsequent decade the number of participants grew from fewer than a thousand to over three thousand, about half of whom are invited as guests of the core membership. The guests – political leaders and officials, journalists, executive officers of research foundations and academic Forum Fellows – animate many of the panels and provide the Forum with reach into civil society and a strong media profile (Graz 2003: 330).

As we saw in Chapter 2, the WEF, like the WBCSD, is organized around a highly elite core of transnational capitalists and, like the ICC, actively extends its geopolitical reach and influence. In 2000 it established a distinct operating body called the Centre for Regional Strategies (CRS) to 'advance regional development and cooperation in the global economy'. Indeed, in recent years the WEF has sought to 'shift away from an event-oriented organisation towards a knowledge- and process-driven organization', as founder Klaus Schwab has remarked (quoted in ibid.: 334). In the months between the yearly extravaganza at Davos, its members and 'constituents' populate a hodgepodge of policy working groups and forums, including the InterAcademy Council, the Business Consultative Group and the Global Leaders of Tomorrow (ibid.: 334).

The move to a more outcome-oriented institutionalization has coincided with a broadening of ideological discourse, from a rather narrow, free market conservative agenda, closely aligned with the Washington Consensus, to the multifaceted vision of 'entrepreneurship in the public interest', as vigorous private–public partnerships build 'the networked society'.[14] With the WEF, as with the WBCSD, we see an organization adapting to challenges from below and to crises associated with global capitalism, retooling neoliberal hegemony for changing times.

If the WEF can be described as 'the most comprehensive transnational planning body operative today, [...] a true International of capital' (van der Pijl 1998: 132, 133), it nevertheless has faced major challenges in the form of responses from below that highlight a structural limitation of the elite club as a collective agent of global hegemony. Such organizations 'rely on a total cleavage between those sufficiently powerful to interact behind closed doors and those having no place in such exclusive arenas. The mobilization of creative forces takes place in a confined space cut off from the public sphere' (Graz 2003: 326). While exclusionary practices intensify elite unity, and even create a powerful social myth of capitalist consciousness, the retreat from the public sphere puts the WEF and other elite organizations at a strategic disadvantage. 'Divorced from society at large [...] paradoxically their influence emphasizes their lack of legitimacy and therefore their inability to compete in the public debate. Sooner or later this situation will foster the development of contending forces disputing their very existence' (ibid.: 337).

Enter the *World Social Forum* (WSF), a counter-hegemonic 'open space' that was first convened in January 2001, as the progressive-democratic antithesis to the WEF (Teivainen 2004: 123). Although both groups are sites for wide-ranging discussion on issues of globalization, its promise and its discontents, the contrast between the WSF and global elite institutions like the WEF is acute:

> While meetings at the World Economic Forum, UN, WTO and other global institutions are often closed and maintain top-down hierarchies, the WSF promotes a transparent organizing structure for its events. All workshops, seminars, round tables, panel discussions and testimonials are openly posted and participants are free to attend whichever event they want. There is no special entrance for different delegates, no excessive scrutiny as one enters a certain venue. (Byrd 2005: 156)

Although European activists were engaged from the planning phase forward, the WSF has local roots in the labour and other progressive movements of Brazil, and particularly Pôrto Alegre, whose municipal and state governments allocated substantial human and material resources to launch the Forum. After 2004, the Forum moved to a decentralized, radically democratic mode of organizing its annual meeting, with participating organizations setting the agenda. In this and other respects, the WSF is 'a new kind of political space created by and helping to consolidate a transnational subaltern counterpublic' (Conway 2004: 376) that in its diversity contains multiple public spheres. In contrast to the worldwide protest symbolized by 1968, which entailed parallel movements, each bound by national borders, the protest against neoliberalism that is at the core of the WSF is organized globally (Waterman 2004: 60–61).

A dilemma built into the Forum process is that between its mission as 'an open meeting place' (stated as the first clause in its Charter of Principles) and the aspiration of many activists to transform it into a global social justice movement. In the former conception, the WSF's 'open, free, horizontal structures' enable a process of prefiguration, bringing into being new forms of participatory democracy that incubate movements. To instrumentalize the Forum would be to sacrifice prefigurative potential for tactical gains in the immediate conjuncture (Whitaker 2004: 112–13). Yet the absence of a 'Final Document' at the conclusion of each Forum has led to criticisms that the WSF is little more than 'one huge talking shop' (Keraghel et al. 2004: 487). At the close of the 2005 Forum, nineteen high-profile thinkers, including Tariq Ali, Samir Amin, Walden Bello and Immanuel Wallerstein, issued a twelve-point 'Consensus Manifesto' that would pull the WSF in the direction of a meta-movement – foregrounding the ends to which the Forum should direct its energy and the (state-centred) means for reaching them.[15] In June 2006 the Forum took a step closer to an action orientation when it invited participating groups to indicate 'the actions, campaigns and struggles' in which each is engaged, as a basis for the 7th Forum, held in Nairobi in January 2007.[16] This shift, from organizing the Forum around themes for discussion to organizing it around actions and their interconnections, continued in subsequent years, as the WSF called for Global Days of Action, which by 2009 claimed thirty days of the calendar.[17] Whether the WSF can constitute itself as a *hybrid* of actor and arena, without devolving to either a tool for conventional political mobilization or a talking shop, remains unclear.

Notwithstanding this issue, and concerns as to whether the Forum is becoming neither arena nor actor but logo and world franchise (Sen 2004: 223; Huish 2006), the WSF comprises a signal development in global justice politics. It has struck directly at the level of meaning, countering the central premise of neoliberal hegemony since Thatcher – that 'there is no alternative' (Sen 2004: 213) – with 'there are many alternatives' (De Angelis 2004). This claim 'opens up a problematic of empowerment and defetishization of social relations, the two basic "ingredients" for the constitution of a social force that moves beyond capital'. The WSF is indeed a site for prefiguration, for welding the present to alternative futures. As De Angelis surmises, it is open to 'alternative ways of doing and articulating social cooperation, at whatever scale of social action'; and thus serves 'to recompose politically the many diverse struggles for commons that are already occurring' – suggesting alternative, decommodified ways to fulfil social needs (ibid.: 602–3).

The WSF's ongoing war of position within transnational civil society complements and extends the episodic wars of manoeuvre that have disrupted the summits of the WEF, WTO, G8 etc. The WSF and its regional and local offshoots 'offer the liberal anti-globalization and radical anti-capitalist movement a summit of their own, able to devise alternative strategies of globalization, [...] to make "another world possible"' (Farrer 2004: 169). In nurturing the convergence of movements, the WSF produces 'unprecedented coordinated action on a global scale' while embracing diversity – a paradoxical deepening of democracy (Conway 2004: 379).

As a springboard into an alternative discursive and organizational space, the WSF embodies the 'distinguishing mark' of the global justice movement: the commitment 'to build solidarity out of respect for diversity' (Patel and McMichael 2004: 250). Still, the WSF faces great challenges in maintaining and enlarging the space it has opened. If, as Graz (2003) claims, the WEF's growth has subverted its founding myth that the world's elite can be brought into one place for content-rich networking, the WSF's phenomenal growth may subvert its promise of open dialogue, if most participants become relegated to the role of spectators (Huish 2006: 4).

Conclusion

Our paired comparisons allow a few guarded inferences about the dynamics of hegemony and counter-hegemony in a global field, and their implications for corporate power and its antithesis. On both sides, groups have become *more institutionalized, complex and networked*. The MPS, WBCSD, WEF and WSF have moved from the simple and non-cumulative practice of holding periodic meetings to more continuous and cumulative knowledge production, campaigns and outreach; the ICC, ITUC, TNI and FoEI have extended their organizing activities to broader constituencies – reflecting a process of historic bloc formation. Within each historic bloc, groups take up complementary niches in an organizational ecology. The intellectual/ideological leadership that the MPS has exercised, for instance, is distinct from the contributions of the ICC, the WBCSD and WEF. It is their combination – ramifying through the multiplex networks of media, academe, business and states – which advances neoliberalism globally. Of course, there is much more to a transnational bloc than a few peak civil-society organizations. We have glimpsed only the 'tip of the iceberg'; indeed, a crucial component of the various groups' praxis is in the connections they foster with national and local organizations.

Moreover, although reference was made earlier to 'global governance', this chapter, indeed this book, has not directly considered the panoply of transnational quasi-state apparatuses (e.g. the World Bank), most of which articulate with, or form part of, neoliberalism's historic bloc (Cammack 2003). National states also matter, not only as complexes whose relations to transnational bodies and treaties can encourage citizens' participation in global politics (Smith and Wiest 2005), but as crucial agents in those politics. The Bolivarian Alternative for the Americas (ALBA), a transnational extension of the Venezuela-based Bolivarian project, presents a state-centred aspect of historic-bloc formation no less important than the activities of the groups examined here. ALBA poses a radical alternative to 'free trade', a 'direct assault on the money-based trading networks that have dominated the world since the emergence of capitalism' (Kellogg 2007: 206). From origins in a Venezuela–Cuba mutual-aid arrangement, ALBA has expanded to include Bolivia as a partner as of April 2006 and Nicaragua as of January 2007 (ibid.: 200). Our analysis has focused on global civil society, but agreements like ALBA and its hegemonic counterparts (the WTO, FTAA, etc.) are integral to the formation of transnational historic blocs.

In the conduct of a global war of position, the dominant class and its allies have several obvious advantages, which translate themselves into effective and distinct forms of organization. Neoliberal civil-society groups are resource rich, and they form on the sturdy basis provided by a transnational corporate elite – an organized minority that is already ideologically cohesive, politically active and extensively networked. Business activists are well positioned to influence policy and culture, via established political and mass communication channels. Their action repertoire – a combination of producing and disseminating knowledge via elite channels and corporate media, lobbying key institutions such as the UN and facilitating consensus formation among global and national elites – reflects this advantaged location. Understandably, dominant forces organized themselves in the global field early. The story of globalization-from-above recounts their successful construction of a transnational historic bloc, including civil-society groups as well as TNCs and institutions of global governance, around a vision of plain justice and possessive individualism (Neufeld 2001). This historic bloc, however, does not reach very deeply into the social infrastructure; for the most part, it is restricted to the higher circles of the organized minority that is its real constituency: a North Atlantic ruling class. Its lack of reach into the global South, as revealed by our paired comparisons, is striking.

For groups resisting corporate power and promoting global justice, the situation is exactly reversed. Constituencies are dispersed across many sites and networks, and issues of *translation* – from language to language, from culture to culture, from local to global – are central (Santos 2006). Groups have scant resources and occupy the margins of political and cultural life, although the information revolution has opened up opportunities for low-cost communications with distant places, and for the production of alternative media that now form key components of global counter-hegemony (Hackett and Carroll 2006). The action repertoire of these groups is unavoidably skewed towards mobilization at the grass roots through dialogue within and across counter-publics, consciousness-raising and building capacity to act collectively – using volunteer labour as the prime resource. Conjunctural wars of manoeuvre, such as the 1999 Battle in Seattle, are feasible only on this organizational and cultural basis. The *labour intensivity* of counter-hegemony is rooted in a basic difference between capital and its other:

> [...] the *atomized* form of living labor that stands in conflict with the *integrated*, or liquid, form of 'dead' labor causes a power relationship; the capital ('dead' labor) of each firm is always united from the beginning, whereas living labor is atomized and divided by competition. (Offe and Wiesenthal 1980: 74)

If this microeconomic reality underlies the structural power of TNCs, international financial markets and institutions such as the IMF, it also explains the resource richness of groups like the ICC and WEF. Subalterns can only compensate for the dominant bloc's inherent advantage in the control of vast pools of dead labour by building associations of living activists, armed with a willingness to act. Given the power differential, globalization-from-below occurs in response to the social and ecological dislocations and crises that follow in neoliberal capitalism's train. The bloc that is forming, however, as indicated by our four groups – all of which participate in the social forum process – penetrates much more extensively into humanity's manifold life-worlds, and increasingly includes the global South as a majority force.

Finally, from our paired comparisons we can distinguish between a logic of *replication* and a logic of *prefiguration*. The deeply structured relations that ground neoliberal hegemony – the market, the capital–labour relation, the liberal state – are already regnant in the global formation. The neoliberal project is primarily to rework, to repackage and to reform; to validate, to demonstrate global capitalism's continuing viability; to deflect calls for social justice by insisting on the plain justice of the market; to suggest pragmatic solutions that add up to a passive revolution – as in the WBCSD's notion of eco-efficiency and the WEF's call for entrepreneurship in the public interest. The groups comprising the neoliberal globalist bloc follow a logic of replication. For counter-hegemonic groups, the social relations that might sustain an alternative way of life are immanent, emergent or need to be invented. As history shows, this is no mean feat. Although abstract principles such as parity of participation or cosmopolitanism[18] can provide theoretical guideposts, the challenge is an eminently practical one. The prospects for moving beyond global corporate power hinge significantly on discovering political methodologies that activate democratic social learning as to how we might live differently, as in FoEI's social-ecological vision of a peaceful and sustainable world of 'interdependent people living in dignity, wholeness and fulfilment'. This involves a logic of prefiguration.

Conclusion

This book has mapped, in some detail, the social space of global corporate power in the late twentieth and early twenty-first centuries. What can we conclude from our examination of this topography? In particular, what do the continuities and discontinuities in network structure tell us about transnational capitalist class formation? To begin these reflections, it might be helpful to summarize some of our key findings under three thematic rubrics of geography, continuity and change, and hegemony.

The geography of global corporate power

- Overall, there has been no massive shift from nationally bound corporate elites to a transnational network detached from national moorings. Rather, as the recent wave of capitalist globalization gathered momentum and then reached a frenzy around the turn of the century, national corporate communities persisted, joined together by an accretion of transnational interlocks, and transnationalists. Especially since the mid-1990s, however, national networks have tended to become sparser while transnational interlocking has become a more common practice among directors of the world's largest firms, producing a relative shift towards transnational elite connections that form a kind of superstructure bridging national corporate communities.
- The global corporate network is overwhelmingly a Euro-North American configuration. This shows the enduring influence of a North Atlantic ruling class, which has long been at the centre of global corporate power. It is evident in the composition of the world's largest corporations, in the positions of cities and corporations in the interlock network, and at the level of individual directors. Most of the world's corporate networkers and billionaires are based in the North Atlantic zone.
- Within this zone, it is corporate Europe which has most recently undergone significant elite consolidation, and with the relative decline of corporate Japan, the centre of gravity of the configuration has been shifting towards Europe. The trends point to the declining predominance of US-based capitalists in the global corporate elite. The shift towards Europe registers the successes, from a business standpoint, of European integration, along with the decline of American hegemony. The sheer number of large US-based corporations, however, and the continuing coherence of the American network, ensures that an enormous portion of the entire global network is fixed

224

within the USA, enabling capitalist interests based there to retain a dominant position in the global network, despite trends in capital accumulation and even corporate interlocking that subvert that dominance.

- The global configuration is a networked hierarchy constituted through the selective participation of corporations and directors, but also of the cities and countries they call home. A relatively small inner circle of mainly European and North American men constitute the network; a relatively small number of countries hosts most of the interlocked corporations, and within those countries a few cities predominate as command centres for global corporate power. For the most part, the network strings together directors of corporations based in the major urban centres of north-west Europe and north-east North America, with London, Paris and New York enjoying pride of place.

- Corporate capital based in the global South has made inroads into this Northern-dominated class configuration, but the increasing numbers of Southern-based giant corporations are only very tentatively reflected in the elite network of corporate interlocks. Our findings underline a certain disjuncture between class formation as a sociocultural process and the economic process of capital accumulation. Giant corporations have achieved unprecedented global reach, and world financial markets are highly integrated, but the governance of corporations, and the life of the *haute bourgeoisie*, remains in important ways embedded in national and regional (including trans-Atlantic) structures and cultures. Owing to this cultural and organizational inertia, most transnational elite relations bridge across the countries and cities of world capitalism's centre, replicating the long-standing structure of imperialism.

Continuity and change in the power structure

- There are definite relations between accumulation and interlocking that shape the social space of the global corporate elite. Corporations transnationalized in their accumulation tend to participate in transnational interlocking. Successful capital accumulation and corporate interlocking are mutually reinforcing processes, particularly in Europe, whose continental network is focused upon giant companies that have been consistently successful in accumulating capital. Highly networked firms tend to remain near the top of the global corporate hierarchy, and the boards of firms that have managed to stay near the top tend to be well connected to other giant companies. In this way, the corporate network is reproduced as an elite within an elite: at any given time, it is the well-established firms which dominate the network, providing a basis for continuity.

- The persistence of family fortunes as power bases within the capitalist class is reflected in the participation of billionaires, often organized into discrete, male-dominated kinecon groups, in the global corporate elite. Such groups represent dense clusters of inter-corporate strategic control that contrast

225

with the diffuse interlocks that facilitate class-wide hegemony. For the most part, super-rich directors are nationally oriented in their corporate affiliations, although as a group they have followed the general trend towards more transnational contacts.

- Transnational interlocks tend to be thin, weak ties, carried by single outside directors. These ties contribute to a structure of community more than control; they facilitate business scan and the cultivation of solidarity, but not the construction of coherent transnational financial empires (the major exception being the Desmarais–Frères group that links Montreal and Brussels-based families).
- Over the most recent decade, as capital accumulation became more transnational, the locus of corporate command centres became more *dispersed* to include smaller states of Europe, more of the global South, and a greater range of global cities represented in the interlock network. In this sense, globalization contributed to a diffusion of corporate power.
- The same decade witnessed an overall weakening in financial–industrial elite relations, as corporate governance tended towards the Anglo-American exit-based system – favouring the disciplinary mechanisms of financial markets over the oversight of creditors. Europe, however, saw something of a counter-trend, as the consolidation of a European economic space increased trans-border financial–industrial interlocking.
- The tendency towards Anglo-American-style corporate governance has led corporations in many countries to slim board size and discourage directors from extensive interlocking. These emergent norms, promoted by groups such as the OECD, help account for an overall thinning of the global network, and particularly of its national components.
- At the level of individual directors, the shift from national to transnational interlocking has augmented the ranks of transnationalists, many of them Europeans, well connected to each other, but also to the various Northern-based national networkers who continue to form the backbone of the global network. At the level of corporations, the world's largest firms tend to bifurcate into a growing number of isolates from the interlock network, on the one hand, and a growing number of transnationally networked firms on the other.

The issue of class hegemony

- When we address the issue of class hegemony more directly, by considering the role of transnational policy boards, we find that these boards offer an additional layer of social organization, underwriting the elite cohesion behind what has been a hegemonic project of transnational neoliberalism. The corporate-policy network, however, is highly centralized. A few dozen extensively networked corporate directors serve as organic intellectuals for an incipient transnational capitalist class, with certain organizations, such as the Trilateral Commission and the WBCSD, playing especially integrative roles in shrinking the social space of the global elite and creating a unified voice.

- Again, however, the tendency is for the policy boards to reproduce unevenness in participation as they draw together North American and especially European corporate elites more closely than elites based elsewhere. The boards also differ among themselves in their specific political projects, forming an organizational ecology that generates a rich discursive field in which various transnational political initiatives can take root.

- Over time, the policy boards have proliferated and become more integrative nodes in the global corporate power structure, as national corporate networks have thinned, giving the TCC an increased capacity to act, through the policy boards, as a class-for-itself.

- Policy planning boards play distinctive roles in transnational brokerage relations. Among the transnational business councils, the ERT has pulled the dominant elites of Europe into a regional hegemonic project while the TABC helps integrate the North Atlantic business elite. In contrast, the NACC, tied to the North American Security and Prosperity Partnership (SPP), was left in limbo when the US government declared SPP to be 'no longer an active initiative' (Dobbin 2009). The differing fates of ERT and NACC point up the qualitative difference between projects of political–economic integration, and capitalist class formation, on the two sides of the North Atlantic. Overall, the development of elite transnational policy planning seems to have reinforced a drift in the global corporate elite's centre of gravity towards Europe; there has also been increased participation by a few Southern-based capitalists, however.

- Finally, paired comparison of organizations promoting the 'plain justice' of globalization from above with those promoting the social justice of globalization from below shows that collective actors on both sides have become more institutionalized, complex and networked – reflecting a dialectical process of historic bloc formation. Within each historic bloc, groups take up complementary niches in an organizational ecology that provides for the exercise of intellectual leadership across a range of global public spheres and issue areas. These comparisons bring the class character of corporate activism into sharp relief. The project of elite policy-planning boards and other collective agencies of the transnational capitalist class is one of building and maintaining a historic bloc in favour of *replicating* the global status quo, using superior material and communicative resources to forestall the *transformative* ambitions of the more radical agents on the globalization-from-below side.

Our analysis of the architecture of global corporate power offers support for a qualified version of the TCC thesis. Overall, there has been some decline in national corporate communities and a shift to transnational affiliations. Yet even in early 2007, most corporate networkers remained national, and most transnationalists participated primarily in one national network. Even the overall decline in national interlocking has been uneven, with France actually showing a resurgence of its national corporate network, and some other countries holding steady. Dramatic instances of decline in specific national networks (e.g. in Japan) reflect in part recent shifts towards Anglo-American corporate governance regimes.

The thinning of national corporate networks and the attenuation of financial–industrial relations suggest that interlocking directorates increasingly serve more of a hegemonic function of community development than an instrumental function associated with control of capital stocks and flows. Attenuation of the financial–industrial nexus, however, should not be mistaken for its disappearance. Financial–industrial axes have persisted in several countries, and such interlocks, on a transnational basis, have been an element in constituting corporate Europe. As I have argued elsewhere (Carroll 2004, 2008a), what seems to be in the offing is not the end of finance capital, but a new form of it. The financial–industrial axis becomes centred less upon banks, their long-term credit relations with big industry, and the interlocking directorships that enable monitoring, and more on other institutional concentrations of financial capital (institutional investors, mutual finds, private equity), whose relations with big industry are more ephemeral and do not necessarily entail interlocking directorates. Such relations may include one-on-one meetings between corporate CEOs and institutional investors (Beckmann 2006: 6), private equity workouts that extract value through corporate restructuring (Froud and Williams 2007), and the 'new American system of finance capitalism' in which ownership of many corporations is concentrated in a few mutual funds that exercise exit, not voice (G. F. Davis 2008). What has changed is the institutional structuring of allocative and strategic power. In the new regime, the symbiosis of financial and industrial capital is partially displaced, from the boardrooms into less durable and formalized venues (Carroll 2008a) – with corporate Europe registering as a partial exception.

Perhaps the strongest evidence for TCC formation lies in the further elaboration of an elite corporate-policy network, part of a transnational historic bloc of capitalists and organic intellectuals that builds consensus and exercises business leadership in the global arena. Despite this ideological solidarity, however, the TCC exists neither as a free-standing entity (it is deeply embedded in national business communities) nor as a homogeneous collectivity. Below, I discuss some bases for fractional division.

Unity and difference within the TCC

As we have consistently seen, global corporate power is substantially organized on a regional basis. This suggests a place-specific interpretation of TCC formation. Such a perspective accords with the analysis of Ruigrok and van Tulder, who point out that much of what passes for globalization is actually *regionalization*, including what they call 'Triadisation' (1995: 151). Indeed, at the level of TNCs, Rugman and Verbeke's 'regionalization hypothesis' of world business fits our findings. Compared to inter-regional expansion, intra-regional expansion offers firm-specific advantages of lower costs and more tractable managerial networks. In view of the fact that only nine of the world's top 500 firms have been able to achieve balanced sales across the three regions of the triad, Rugman and Verbeke argue that most transnational business is characterized by 'semi-globalization', and that many TNCs 'are organized at the regional level rather than the global level' (2007: 200–201). The global corporate elite seems to follow a similar logic in its organization: linked together by a single, connected network, it is nevertheless strongly clustered along regional and national lines.

Most significantly, the transnational corporate interlocks that have been proliferating are not abstractly global so much as they are pan-European. Michael Mann surely exaggerates when he claims that economic globalization under the sign of the Washington Consensus was 'not without nationality', but 'substantially American' (2002: 467). It would be less of a stretch to claim that the most recent movement towards transnational capitalist class formation has been substantially European. This consolidation of a European corporate community should not be read as a mere instance of TCC formation. Politically, the project of European unification is less about relinquishing national sovereignty than about consolidating monetary and financial integration and accelerating neoliberal restructuring to ratchet-up competitiveness (Bieling 2006a: 439). This process is fraught with internal contradiction, but it may also intensify trans-Atlantic rivalry over trade issues and exchange-rate policies, and possibly over US world leadership (ibid.: 441; van der Pijl 2006: 287–90). Instead of the seamless integration of global business interests into a unified TCC, William Tabb (2009: 49) submits that such conflicts are 'the dominant realities of the dynamics of the global political economy'.

At the Asia-Pacific corner of the triad, another regional aspect of restructuring over the most recent decade has been the weakening position of corporate Japan, particularly its financial sector, both in global capital's league table and within the global corporate elite. This decline reaches back to the 1985 G5 Plaza Accord, which in setting the yen on a path of appreciation against the US dollar led to massive but unsustainable growth in financial assets controlled by Japanese financial institutions. Despite the 1990 collapse of the bubble economy, Japanese financial institutions controlled a substantial share of global financial assets as late as 1996. But the 1997 East Asian financial crisis hit Japan-based financial capital hard, and contributed significantly to the 'debacle' that is evident in our findings (Ikeda 2004: 370–72). What financial institutions based in Japan have lost has been gained by their counterparts in Europe and North America. Meanwhile, the long-term erosion of the USA as a site for the command of capital continued into the early twenty-first century. Although in the most recent decade the number of giant non-financial corporations based in the USA dropped only slightly, the decline of US-based industry continued,[1] while US dollar hegemony seemed on the verge of unravelling (Fisk 2009).

The North–South disparities that have long characterized capitalism are strikingly evident in the global corporate network, despite the dramatic rise of China and a few other semi-peripheral states. Control over economic sectors central to financialized, hyper-consumptive capitalism still resides predominantly in the North, and the global corporate elite remains almost entirely contained within the triad. With some notable exceptions, capitalists of the semi-periphery have not joined the elite[2] – although each semi-peripheral country has its local elite network, not charted here.

On this issue, however, the disjuncture between the economic process of capital accumulation and the sociocultural process of class formation needs further interrogation. Although our mapping of elite relations shows a shift towards Europe, and only slight overtures towards inclusion of Southern-based capitalists, broader political-economic dynamics may favour not Europe but a select group of high-growth 'statist globalizers' that, according to Harris (2009: 6), now form part of the transnational capitalist class. What Harris points to is the emergence of transnational state capitalism on the semi-periphery as a new stage in globalization, unforeseen by neoliberal elites based in the North. The global economic crisis that morphed from a US-centred sub-prime mortgage crisis in 2007 to an international financial meltdown in 2008 and a global recession in 2009 exposed not only the problems of neoliberal deregulation and financialization, but the advantages of state capitalism in countries like China, which presents the most stunning example of this tendency. In its rapid rates of accumulation, massive trade surpluses and foreign currency holdings, burgeoning sovereign wealth fund and growing clutch of companies listed on the London Stock Exchange, Harris discerns a mixing of state and private capital that is key to 'the organic construction of the TCC' (ibid.: 20):

> The mixing of foreign institutional and private investors in government-owned banks, and in turn Chinese acquisitions of foreign assets, is an important path for TCC integration. It results in common entanglements in transnational investments through which the Western and statist TCC share profits and losses based on the competitive edge of Chinese state banks. (Ibid.: 19)

On this account, the TCC arises out of the intersecting circuits of transnationalized capital, which instil in the agents that subtend them 'a shared class consciousness based in a common economic existence and political interdependence' (ibid.: 30). Our analysis of directorate interlocks has operated at a different level – that of the global corporate elite – and although it has included major Chinese and other semi-peripheral firms, it may not fully represent the more statist elements that Harris has in mind. As we emphasized in the Introduction, corporate elites include only the top tier or leading edge of capitalist classes: 'the TCC is much wider than the composition of boards of directors' (Sprague 2009: 505, quoting Leslie Sklair).

Yet Harris may overstate the extent to which such state capitalists are 'on board' as members of a transnational capitalist class. Our approach here has been to stake out a middle ground between simple acceptance or rejection of the notion of a TCC. William Tabb, who has enunciated a similar position, points out that those who see the TCC in full flower tend to underestimate the continuing salience of national states, and of state-based divisions and rivalries. In summarizing his own middle-ground position, he asserts

> that there is an interpenetration of national capitals and greater interaction and cooperation among leaders of the capitalist class based in different states; that these interactions reflect the reorganization of thinking about the world economy from a predominantly inter-national competition for colonies and markets [...] to a globalization in which the home country is one market among others and profit maximization is globally organized; but finally, that state power over various aspects of national territorial integrity is not willingly surrendered. Territorial issues are negotiated within the confines of relative strength and alliance formations. (2009: 37)

Thus, for instance, although the economies of the USA and China are deeply entwined, this does not mean that their elites are joined together as part of a single TCC operating within a transnational space that escapes national control. Our findings show that this is not at all the case. Nor does the integration of individual countries into the global economy necessarily mean that 'national' political priorities are sacrificed to the greater good of the TCC (ibid.: 46), even if such priorities do come to be viewed through the lens of international competition for investment capital (McBride 2006).

The nuances that surround relations between Chinese and American capital, or Europe and the United States for that matter, highlight the need to acknowledge complexity in transnational class formation. In like measure, analyses in this field should resist abstract, polarized characterizations – as in *either* national *or* transnational capitalist class; *either* an American hegemon bent on world domination *or* a Washington that acts at the behest of the transnational capitalist class; *either* inter-imperialist rivalry *or* the united rule of global capital. Despite competition among capitals, interstate rivalry and uneven development, it is certainly the case that capitalism's globalization creates an objective basis for capitalist class unity (also for proletarian unity, though that is another story). If nearly a century ago Lenin's prognosis of inter-imperialist rivalry leading to war proved more accurate than Kautsky's notion of ultra-imperialism, since the end of the Second World War the latter has been the dominant tendency, without, however, eliminating rivalry. In the midst of the First World War Kautsky speculated that 'the striving of every great capitalist State to extend its own colonial empire in opposition to all the other empires of the same kind [...] represents only one among various modes of expansion of capitalism' (Kautsky 1970: 45). For Kautsky, the result of war between the great imperialist powers might be 'a holy alliance of the imperialists' that would usher in an era of *'ultra-imperialism'* (ibid.: 46): a 'shift from conflict between imperialist powers to maintenance of a world system of exploitation' (Brewer 1980: 124). The WTO, World Bank, IMF, OECD and the like are precisely vehicles for the sort of collective imperialism that Kautsky envisaged, which now runs under the banner of 'global governance' (Soederberg 2006).

Clearly, the transnational policy boards we have found at the centre of the global corporate power structure contribute significantly to this project. Proliferating since the 1970s, these boards have been agents of business activism, mobilizing corporate capitalists and various strata of intellectuals around visions and policies that enunciate the common interests of transnational capital, and which persuade state managers, journalists and others to see those interests as universal in scope. This process is one of the surest signs that a transnational capitalist class is indeed in the making. Its hegemony, as we have seen, faces challenges from below. Yet in the ongoing war of position, the TCC, operating in concert with statist bodies like the WTO and IMF, holds an ideological trump card. It is able to present its world view not simply as 'common sense', but as 'expert sense', claiming power through expertise in economic policy formation (Peet 2007: 15). Such technocratic hegemony aims to instil in workers and communities a disciplined passivity in political life, founded in a faith in economic experts.

But this transnational historic bloc, along with extensive cross-penetration of capitalist investment and global financial markets, does not eliminate rivalries based in the objective necessity of capitalist states to influence capital flows to their own territorial advantage (Harvey 2005; Lacher 2005); it only mutes and manages them. And the political-economic integration of Europe, which is where most of the action has been in TCC formation, does not break from the logic of the interstate system; it replicates it on a larger scale, even as it provides firmer conditions for the international investment flows that ultimately integrate the world economy.[3] The Lisbon agreement, initiated in 2000 and finally fully ratified in 2009, takes pan-European state formation to a new level, with 'an unmistakable thrust towards rivalry with the US' (van der Pijl

2006: 287), expressed in the objective of making Europe the most competitive economy in the world.[4] Even as 'the global partly inhabits and partly arises out of the national' (Sassen 2007: 1), tendencies towards TCC formation coexist and intersect with counter-tendencies, limiting the prospects of a TCC-for-itself, abstracted from state-based divisions that remain part of the terrain of global capitalism (Tabb 2009: 44). Conscious efforts to create such a class should not be confused with its arrival. As a class-for-itself, the transnational capitalist class is in the making, but not (yet) made.

Taking a page or two from van der Pijl (1984, 1998), we can say that this class continues for the most part to take the geographically specific form of an Atlantic ruling class. It remains centred in capitalism's Lockean heartland of self-regulating market relations and civil society – a unique state/society complex that originated in England and expanded initially by colonial settlement to North America and elsewhere (van der Pijl 1998: 7). In the twentieth century, contending, 'Hobbesian' formations such as the fascist-corporative Axis powers and the redistributive party-states of the Soviet bloc attempted to confront and catch up with the Lockean heartland by means of state-directed socio-economic mobilization (ibid.: 78–89).

If in hindsight imperialism has been about expanding the heartland and incorporating Hobbesian contending states, by peaceful means or otherwise, we have surely not reached the end of that story; nor have the bases for rivalries within the heartland been transcended. Alongside the return of a modest state capitalism to Europe, there are continuing grounds for state-mediated struggles over incorporation, and ex-corporation. One basis lies in a key finding from this study: the detachment of Southern bourgeoisies, including state-capitalist fractions, from the elite network of the North. Isolated for the most part from the global corporate elite and organized along more statist lines, the leading lights of semi-peripheral capitalism may be more open to new alignments that although transnational do not endorse neoliberalism's vision of a deregulated, borderless world for investment and trade. Such groupings as the BRIC countries (Brazil, Russia, India, China), the IBSA Dialogue Forum (India, Brazil, South Africa) and the Shanghai Cooperation Organization (which includes China, Russia, Kazakhstan, Kyrgyzstan, Tajikistan and Uzbekistan; Tabb 2009: 42–3) highlight the regional and fractional character of transnational capitalist class formation. Concomitantly, however, transnational practices centred upon the North are incorporating Southern economies, as exemplified in China's entry to the WTO and its opening of the door to foreign financial participation (and board representation) in its semi-privatized banks (Engardio 2007). Transnational capitalist class formation takes place not as the unfolding of a borderless world ruled by capital but in the context of an ongoing tug-of-war between Lockean liberalization and Hobbesian territorialization, with alter-globalization thrusts from below opposing both options.

The crisis of 2008–10 and beyond

What lies ahead for the transnational capitalist class and its inner circle of corporate transnationalists is inherently uncertain. Not only is the trajectory of corporate power and capitalist class formation in high-growth semi-peripheral states unclear; what appears to be a protracted global economic crisis has undercut some of the authority of financialized capitalism's deregulated marketplace, and placed American-style corporate governance in doubt. In contrast to the crises of the 1990s and early 2000s, which were contained either regionally (e.g. East Asia in 1997) or sectorally (the dotcom bust of 2000/01), the current crisis metastacized from a financial meltdown in the autumn of 2008 to a *'generalized global crisis'* by 2009 (McNally 2009: 41).

Crises of this magnitude necessarily redraw the corporate landscape, and with that, the global corporate elite. Bankruptcies, mergers and acquisitions transform the roster of the world's largest corporations; corporate directors are unseated and replaced as the constellations of interest in control of specific firms change. The partial nationalization of some of the world's top financial institutions, and the re-regulation of finance particularly in Europe (Hardie and Howarth 2009: 1031–4), could lead to governance changes affecting board composition and directorate interlocks, and possibly a shift away from American-style practices that have weakened financial–industrial relations and amplified the accumulation of paper assets. The very discourse that, since the 1980s, has sustained a transnational capitalist consensus has lost some of its lustre as the perils of deregulated capitalism become obscenely palpable. Leading capitalist states engineered a remarkable management of the crisis in 2008/09, temporarily suspending the neoliberal creed through select use of quasi-Keynesian – or perhaps what Robinson and Harris (2000) would term neoliberal regulationist measures. A prolonged downturn, however, uneven in its geography – what Gramsci called an 'organic crisis'[5] – could intensify conflict and weaken collective resolve among state managers and transnational capitalists alike.

As I write this, incessant chatter in the financial pages about 'green shoots' of recovery jostles for headlines with compelling symptoms of further economic collapse, to say nothing of impending ecocide. The substantive failure of the Copenhagen Conference on Climate Change in December 2009 not only exposed regional fault lines in global capitalism while confirming the vitality of a North–South imperialism that asked Africa 'to sign a suicide pact';[6] it posed a stark choice, eloquently framed by Bolivian president Evo Morales. Referring to the 'Western model and capitalist way of life' as a 'culture of death', Morales held that 'at this summit we must decide whether we are on the side of life or the side of death'. He stated categorically, 'We have to abolish the slavery of Mother Earth. It is unacceptable for her to be the slave of capitalist countries. If we don't end this, we can forget about life' (quoted in Pierri 2009).

For the TCC (well represented by the Copenhagen Climate Council, whose main partners include the WBCSD, WEF and UN Global Compact), the future is in this respect clear. It lies in the cumulative 'reinscription of the earth into capital' (Escobar 1996: 340) – as in carbon markets on which bundled carbon credits trade like derivatives (Reyes 2009) – in the hope of not only green shoots but sustainable accumulation. There is good reason to believe that, once it attains global scale, a way of life devoted to endless accumulation of capital is incompatible with the ecosphere's finite operating principles (Kovel 2006), and there can be little doubt that deepening class polarities and ecological degradations worldwide will provide increasing grounds for counter-hegemonic struggles.

In the contestations to come, the network of giant corporate and policy boards will offer to the transnational capitalist class and its organic intellectuals cultural and political resources in the struggle to protect what was won in the last three decades: investor rights, trade freedoms, debased social programmes, disorganized labour, low corporate taxation and other items in neoliberal globalization. In the midst of the financial meltdown of October 2008, French president Nicolas Sarkozy, at the time EU president, declared that 'a certain idea of globalisation is drawing to a close' and 'a new form of capitalism' is in the offing (Samuel 2008; S. Taylor 2008). If this is so, we can predict with confidence that the TCC and its inner circle of transnationalists will play an influential role in shaping the contours of the new regime.

Whether 'a new form of capitalism' is all that is on offer, however, is itself an open question, and on this point the practical value of resisting the notion of a transnational capitalist class that has already arrived as a hegemonic collective actor must be emphasized. If the TCC is not the product of a globalizing teleology but rather more of a tendency dialectically linked to counter-tendencies, if elite networking and the like produce solidarity without eliminating rivalry, and if the TCC now finds itself operating on a new terrain of struggle, arising within an organic crisis, that terrain offers openings for capital's critics. For them, also, nothing is guaranteed, and the challenges are many. As Rupert (2005: 472) observes, 'if progressive forces are unable creatively to confront the political problems of transnational solidarity, the abstract possibility of global transformative politics will be moot'.

It is in this spirit that we should revisit our opening quotation from Warren Buffett, the world's third-wealthiest capitalist according to *Forbes* (Kroll and Miller 2010). In a 2006 interview with the *New York Times*, Buffett made the acute observation that 'there's class warfare, all right, but it's my class, the rich class, that's making war, and we're winning'. In the era of neoliberal globalization that has framed this study, capitalists have held all the strategic advantages that stem from the structural power of transnational capital. Yet capital ultimately accumulates as the alienated product of those excluded from Buffett's class, and the formation of a transnational capitalist class implies the formation of its other. Capitalist globalization creates both the need and the conditions for such global justice initiatives as international Zapatismo (Olesen 2005a), the World Social Forum, the Bolivarian Alternative for the Americas (Kellogg 2007) and even the stirrings of a Fifth Socialist International,[7] which have developed in dialectical interaction with the making of a transnational capitalist class. The acuity of Buffett's remark lies not only in the frank acknowledgement of class struggle from an unimpeachable source, but in the recognition that capital's victory, to date, is no more than provisional.

Notes

Introduction

1 Namely, 'practices that cross state boundaries but do not necessarily originate with state agencies or actors' (Sklair and Robbins 2002: 82).

2 There is also a sceptical literature on globalization, preceding the work of Sklair and Robinson, that still has relevance. See especially Hu (1992) and Hirst and Thompson (1996).

3 The last of these, a capitalism in which workers control their own retirement savings, was trumpeted in 2003 by US president George W. Bush. See Soederberg's (2010) penetrating analysis.

4 As Gramsci observed, 'every social group, coming into existence on the original terrain of an essential economic function in the world of economic production, creates together with itself, organically, one or more strata of intellectuals which give it homogeneity and an awareness of its own function not only in the economic but in the social and political fields. The capitalist entrepreneur creates alongside himself the industrial technician, the specialist in political economy, the organisers of a new culture, of a new legal system, etc.' (1971: 5).

5 With a nod ultimately to E. P. Thompson's majestic *The Making of the English Working Class* (1991 [1963]).

6 Sources for cross-checking individual directorships (1996–2006) included the Lexis-Nexis database (www.lexisnexis.com/), *Forbes* People Tracker (www.forbes.com/cms/template/peopletracker/index.jhtml), *Business Week*'s Company Insight Centre (investing.businessweek.com/research/company/overview/overview.asp), as well as www.google.com.

1 Is there a transnational corporate community?

1 Our corporate sample, throughout this book, excludes wholly owned foreign subsidiaries, which typically function more as operating divisions of TNCs than as corporations in their own right, and which rarely share directors with companies other than their own parents (Fennema and Schijf 1985).

2 As noted earlier, a *line* between two firms may be *thin* (carried by a single-director primary or secondary interlock), or *thick* (carried by multiple-director interlocks). We call a multiple line that contains at least one primary interlock a thick primary line and a multiple line that contains only secondary interlocks a thick secondary line.

3 A detailed analysis of six countries (each with more than ten firms in the sample in both years) showed that in each country and in both years leading corporations interlocked much more with each other (i.e. nationally) than with firms sited beyond the national border (i.e. transnationally).

4 In this study, we employ semi-periphery descriptively, as a synonym for those regions lying outside the triad (western Europe, the USA and Canada, and Japan, Australia and New Zealand), but serving as domiciles for giant corporations. For a discussion that questions the theoretical value of the concept of semi-periphery, see Lee (2009).

2 Forging a new hegemony

1 See 'The transnational ruling class formation thesis: a symposium', *Science & Society*, 65(4): 464–9.

2 These include Mexico in 1995, East Asia in 1997, and Russia and Brazil in 1998.

3 Sklair (2001), quite similarly, sees 'proactive global corporate citizenship' as a cornerstone of contemporary processes of transnational capitalist class formation.

4 For instance, see the *Building Cooperation in Africa Report* (December 2001) and the *ICC Business Charter for Sustainable Development* (April 1991).

5 *The Spotlight*, Special Bilderberg Issue, 1995/96.

6 See 'Global Agenda Councils' at the WEF website: www.weforum.org/en/Communities/GlobalAgendaCouncils/AbouttheGlobalAgendaCouncils/index.htm, accessed 23 December 2009.

7 'Eco-efficiency' was first coined by the WBCSD in 1992. In its 1997 *Annual Review*, the WBCSD defined eco-efficiency as 'a management approach [...] that allows companies to improve their environmental performance while meeting the demands of the market [...] [by increasing] economic and ecological efficiency' (p. 8).

8 The sample of corporations was constructed on the basis of a number of sources, beginning with the Global 500 published in the June 1997 issue of *Fortune*, which ranks firms by sales or revenue. A drawback in the *Fortune* listing is that revenue is not a particularly good measure of the size of financial institutions, some of which have relatively small revenue streams (often equivalent to net income) compared to their asset size. The latter is a far more appropriate measure of the concentration of capital within financial institutions; thus we divided the sample into two strata and selected from the sources at our disposal all financial institutions with assets of $100 billion or higher and all non-financial corporations with revenues of $14 billion or higher. All values were taken for the time closest to year-end 1996 and denominated in US dollars. This yielded a sample of 300 corporations. To this initial sample we added fifty companies, in an attempt to represent domiciles and sectors that by the size criterion alone were thinly represented, in particular the semi-periphery (see Carroll and Carson 2003 for details). Our

sample, then, combines quantitative and qualitative considerations in representing the leading corporations worldwide, as of year-end 1996.

9 These directors are cosmopolitans much in the sense originally employed by Gouldner (1957): they are oriented not towards particular national firms and networks but towards a wider field of action.

10 Its 1996 executive board of 27 members and international officers included 12 corporate directors based on the semi-periphery, 11 based in Europe, 3 in the USA or Canada, and 1 in Japan.

11 Among our 350 corporations, the Pearson correlation between n of interlocks with policy groups and n of interlocks with other corporations is .434.

12 The distance between two points in a network is the length of the 'shortest path' between them: the minimum number of steps one must take to reach one point from the other. Corporate boards that are directly interlocked are connected at a distance of 1; corporate boards that are not interlocked but which both share directors with a third board are connected at distance 2, and so on.

13 Note that the thickest lines represent the shortest mean distances. Mean distances greater than 4 are represented as absent ties, although in fact all corporations in the component are, by definition, ultimately connected.

14 Note that the chair of the regulationist WBCSD is also an ex officio director of the ICC, owing to the ICC's founding sponsorship of the WBCSD.

3 Global cities in the global corporate network

1 Note that the transnational network includes 'national' interlocks carried by transnationalists. For instance, in 1996 Paul Allaire, CEO of Stamford-based Xerox, directed three other Global 350 firms: Newark-based Lucent Technologies, Chicago-based Sara Lee Corporation, and London-based SmithKline Beecham. Allaire thereby carried three transnational interlocks (linking SmithKline to the three

US-based firms) as well as three national, inter-urban interlocks (linking the US-based firms to each other).

2 The very nature of corporate inter-locking as an elite activity implies that even in a well-integrated interlock network the numbers of directors who actually carry most of the ties will be relatively small. Research on national corporate networks has shown that a scant few dozen well-connected directors typically carry most of the ties. Stokman et al.'s comparative studies of corporate networks in ten countries found, for instance, that just 50 'big linkers' (each holding four or more directorships) carried 75 per cent of all the interlocks in the Austrian national network of 250 firms (1985: 24).

3 Note that the manner in which the sample was assembled favoured British-based corporations to some extent (see Carroll and Carson (2003) for methodo-logical details). Half of the London-based corporations, though all of them were large industrial corporations, were slightly smaller than the quantitative floor cri-terion for inclusion in the Global 350. Most of the London-based participants in the transnational network (10 of 14), however, met the quantitative size criterion. Among the fifteen smaller London-based firms, only four participated in the transnational network, namely British Airways, Grand Metropolitan, SmithKline Beechham and the mining transnational RioTinto (RTZ-CRA Group). The complexities and pitfalls in assembling and delimiting the network of the world's largest corporations are discussed in Carroll and Fennema (2004).

4 Ornstein's (1984) longitudinal study of the Canadian corporate network found that, over three decades, primary inter-locks were far more likely than secondary interlocks to be reconstituted after the death or retirement of a director – a find-ing that supports our interpretation of primary interlocks as, typically, functional and instrumental relations. The most extensive study of primary and secondary interlocking in corporate networks is that of Stokman et al. (1985).

5 On the concepts of condensation and reduction in network analysis see Sprenger and Stokman (1989: 184–91, 399–414).

6 The two Anglo-Dutch transnationals in the Global 350 have head offices in both London and the Netherlands (Unilever in Rotterdam, Shell next door in The Hague). These cases of corporate binationality, the only two in our sample of 350, exemplify the difficulties in 'locating' highly trans-nationalized capital in one domicile. Our (arbitrary) categorization of both firms as based in The Hague/Rotterdam partly mitigates the over-representation of London-based firms in the Global 350. See note 3.

7 The lines shown are only interlocks carried by transnationalists. The smaller, London-centred archipelago is made up of 20 firms, 10 of them based in London, 2 in The Hague/Rotterdam, 6 in New York and 2 in Hong Kong. This configuration is much less integrated than the Continental one; at the corporate level, it is made up of three disconnected networks. Overall, the density of inter-corporate relations in the Paris archipelago is 0.218; in the London archipelago only 0.095.

8 The detachment of American cor-porate boards from this inter-urban 'core' of the European business community is remarkable. Of the ninety US-based firms in our sample, only four have any interlocks with the European companies in Figure 3.5.

9 In calculating these aggregated degrees, each interlocking directorship is given a value of 1. An interlock between firms based in the same city therefore contributes a value of 2 to that city's degree (one for each directorship). An interlock between firms based in different cities contributes a value of 1 to each city's degree.

10 A local corporate-interlock network comprised of fourteen ties did exist in Seoul in 1996, but there were no interlocks linking it to any of the other eighty-seven cities.

4 Transnational accumulation and global networking

1 Additional sources of data in identifying the largest firms were the Mergent and Corporate Affiliations databases on the world's largest firms, the *Forbes* Global 2000 (www.forbes.com/lists/), the *Financial Times* Global 500 (www.ft.com/reports/ft5002007) and lists of the largest companies published annually by the *Wall Street Journal* ('World's largest financial companies'), *Global Finance* ('The world's biggest banks') and *The Banker* ('Top 1000 world banks').

2 In a small number of cases, annual reports were not available. Alternative sources of board data were: a) official corporate websites listing contemporary directors – earlier versions of a company website were accessed through the Wayback Machine (www.archive.org) – and b) secondary sources including EDGAR, the website of the US Securities and Exchange Commission (www.sec.gov/edgar.shtml) and business databases listing members of the board of directors at different years (www.CorporateAffiliations.com and Standard and Poor's *Register of Corporations, Directors and Executives* – New York, published annually). In a few cases, where no directorship data were available, companies were dropped from the G500 and replaced with the next-biggest industrial or financial firm.

3 We include Canada, the USA and Bermuda (tax haven and super-affluent domicile to several G500 firms) as 'core North America' and consider Mexico to be part of the Latin American semi-periphery. Japan and Australia compose the 'core Asia-Pacific' category (New Zealand has no G500 firms); the other states of Asia, from India eastward, are categorized as Asian semi-periphery. We include all the states of western Europe, extending eastward to Finland, Germany, Austria and Italy, as 'core Europe', and states to the east as the European semi-periphery. To make the categorization fully inclusive, we have stretched the boundary of Europe's semi-periphery to include the Middle East

(domicile to a total of two G500 firms) and Africa (domicile to a single G500 firm, which relocated to Britain before 2006). With 14.2 per cent of the world's population, Africa is completely absent from the global corporate elite.

4 The three Chinese financial institutions enter the G500 as they adopt the form of capitalist-style corporations. Most significantly for this study, in 2000 the Bank of China established a board of directors as distinct from a supervisory council of state managers. CCB and ICBC followed suit in 2004 and 2005, respectively. The only other G100 financial based in the semi-periphery as of 2006 was Banco Itau, headquartered in São Paulo.

5 Capital based in the Asian semi-periphery does make modest inroads. By 2006, four such G500 firms were listed in the UNCTAD 100, up from one in 1996.

6 Namely, Mitsubishi UFJ Financial Group, Mizuho Financial Group and Chuo Mitsui Trust. Another twelve Fallen Angels were acquired after 1996 by non-G500 corporations. The ultimate fate of seven of the 1996 G500 could not be ascertained.

7 The Principles continue, 'Companies may wish to consider whether multiple board memberships by the same person are compatible with effective board performance and disclose the information to shareholders. Some countries have limited the number of board positions that can be held' (OECD 2004: 65–6).

8 Basic correlational analysis supports this interpretation. Across the decade, a linear relationship developed between board size and degree of national interlocking. While in 1996 ($r = -0.012$) and 1998 ($r = -0.043$) there was no correlation, at each subsequent observation the correlation increased until in 2006 it was 0.412. By 2006, there was a tendency for corporations with large directorates to be more interlocked on a national basis. No such tendency of any strength, however, developed regarding transnational interlocking, although the correlation between board size and transnational degree changed sign (from -0.069 in 1996

to 0.164 in 2006). Moreover, cross-lagged correlations over the 287 companies in the G500s of both 1996 and 2006 showed that the difference between board size in 1996 and in 2006 (weakly) predicted national degree in 2006 (r = 0.238) but that national degree in 1996 did not predict 1996–2006 change in board size (r = 0.078). G500 firms whose boards shrank tended to maintain lower degrees of national interlocking in 2006. Note also that degree of national interlocking and degree of transnational interlocking are only weakly correlated with each other. Across the decade, the Pearson correlation between them ranged from 0.210 in 2002 to 0.269 in 1998; in 2006, it was 0.258. Finally, both measures show trait stability. For national degree, biannual correlations ranged from 0.853 (1996–98) to 0.917 (2003–04) and stood at 0.886 most recently; for transnational degree, biannual correlations ranged from 0.850 (1996–98) to 0.882 (1998–2000) and stood at 0.859 most recently.

9 The increasingly cosmopolitan composition of the G500 itself depresses the overall degree of national interlocking. Whereas in 1996 the G500 included firms from 26 countries, by 2006 32 national domiciles were represented, 17 of which hosted 5 or fewer companies.

10 At year-end 2006, 32 G500 firms based on the semi-periphery had no interlocking directors with any other G500 corporations, double the number for 1996. Japan's complement of isolates increased from 24 to 43, to represent 62.3 per cent of its G500 corporations.

11 Pearson r = .431 in 1996, .404 in 2002, .374 in 2006.

12 Krackhardt and Stern's (1988) E-I index is used as the latter indicator. In this context, E-I subtracts the proportion of a firm's interlocks that link to firms domiciled in the same country from the proportion of the firm's interlocks that link to firms domiciled elsewhere. It varies from 1, indicating that all the firm's interlocks are transnational, to –1, indicating that all the firm's interlocks are national. In 1996,

the Pearson correlation between TNI and E-I was .567; in 2006 it was .416.

13 European Top Dogs maintained means of 3.04 and 6.18 national board interlocks in 1996, compared with means respectively of 1.94 and 4.73 among European Fallen Angels.

14 European Top Dogs averaged 4.86 national board interlocks in 2006, compared with a mean of 2.91 among European Rising Stars. North American Top Dogs averaged 4.79 national board interlocks in 2006, compared with a mean of 2.83 among Rising Stars. Asia-Pacific Top Dogs averaged 1.19 national board interlocks in 2006, compared with a mean of 0.47 among Rising Stars.

15 In the triad's Asia-Pacific corner, transnational interlocking was in 2006 entirely restricted to the fifty-four Top Dog corporations, which averaged 0.24 interlocks. In North America, Top Dogs (with a mean of 0.99 transnational interlocks) did not differ substantially from Rising Stars (0.71) in 2006.

16 Indeed, a closer analysis of Rising Stars shows that, as of 2006, the longer the period of time in which a company had been continuously in the G500 (with 5 indicating continuous membership in the G500 since 1998, 4 indicating continuous membership since 2000, etc.), the higher its degree of national (r = 0.295) and transnational (r = 0.236) interlocking. Subgroup analysis shows that this tendency for the more established Rising Stars to be better connected is weaker in North America than in western Europe, where the correlation for transnational interlocking was slightly elevated (0.287). In the core states of the Asia-Pacific region, the correlation for national interlocking was 0.300. In the Asian semi-periphery, the tendency for well-established Rising Stars to interlock, both nationally (r = 0.306) and transnationally (0.309), was slightly accentuated.

17 Coded in four categories, as the three categories of the triad, plus a single category encompassing the entire semi-periphery (n = 58).

18 Survivorship was coded by a contrast between 252 Top Dogs and the rest of the G500.

19 In the case of transnationality, we incorporated for the ANOVA the list of the world's largest transnational financial institutions, in UNCTAD's 2008 *World Investment Report*, which boosts the size of the transnationalized category to 137 corporations and financial institutions. Transnational corporate status was coded as the contract between the 137 major TNCs identified by UNCTAD and all other G500 firms of 2006.

20 These sociograms were produced using a spring-embedded algorithm. The positions of points in the space loosely correspond with the distances between points in the network. In a few cases, we moved firms slightly from their optimal location so that their labels would be visible in the sociograms.

21 As a measure of cohesion, density is highly sensitive to network size. Considering only relations among the fourteen triad countries present in both years, the density actually increases from 0.484 to 0.600.

22 Bermuda has become the tax haven of choice, particularly for several firms with operations primarily in the USA, creating a somewhat dubious set of transnational interlocks.

23 In 1996, 21 of the 116 cities of domicile represented in the G500 were isolated from the dominant component of cities linked via the interlocking directorates of firms they hosted. By 2006, 25 of 136 represented cities were isolates, and 2 (Seoul and Pohang) formed a separate dyad. The changing composition of the 12 most central cities bears comment. In 1996, 7 of the 12 were American, namely New York (52 interlocks to firms based elsewhere), Chicago (31), Detroit (28), Atlanta (22), Dallas and Washington (20 each) and Boston (19). The other five were European: London (37), Paris (24), Frankfurt (22), Düsseldorf and Munich (21 each). By 2006, 6 of the most central cities were American – New York (50),

Chicago (25), Dallas (21), Los Angeles (20), Houston and Atlanta (19 each) – the other six were European – London (38), Paris (35), Munich and Zurich (21 each), Amsterdam and Düsseldorf (19 each). Among these elite centres of corporate command, London and New York retained their positions, Chicago, Detroit, Washington, Boston and Frankfurt lost centrality, and Paris, Zurich, Amsterdam and Los Angeles gained centrality.

5 Transnationalists and national networkers

1 The imagery of the 'inner circle' comes from Useem's (1984) study of the American and British corporate networks in the late 1970s and early 1980s. The inner circle is formed by those whose directorships with multiple large corporations place them near the centre of the corporate network and foster a class-wide rationality, enabling them to play a leading role for the capitalist class as a whole. Robinson (2004: 48) hypothesizes that an increasingly organized, transnational inner circle 'seeks to secure the fundamental class interests of the TCC as a whole'.

2 The number of G500 firms based in Australia, grouped here with Japan as part of the Asia-Pacific 'core', grew slightly from seven to eight.

3 Most spectacularly, and as a mirror image of Japan's decline, the number of G500 firms based in China jumps from 0 to 16. Russia (from 1 to 5), India (from 2 to 5) and Mexico (from 1 to 4) also register major gains, from minuscule bases.

4 It is worth noting, additionally, that among North Atlantic-based firms some significant shifts in national representation occur over the decade, as a function of differential accumulation rates and of relocations of head offices to low-tax zones such as Ireland and Bermuda. Compared to 1996, the 2006 G500 contains fewer firms based in the USA (down from 166 to 154) and Italy (from 15 to 9) and more firms based in Canada (up from 9 to 15), Spain (from 5 to 10) and Ireland (from 0 to 4).

5 This comparison, of course, holds only for the G500 corporations under examination here, whose boards are no doubt more transnationalized than those of smaller companies. Each of the national networks extends well beyond the firms in the G500. This analysis of national networkers captures only the top stratum of each national elite.

6 Network density is simply the proportion of all possible ties that actually exist, which is also the probability that any pair of network members is actually linked (for present purposes, that both persons sit together on a corporate board in common).

7 These percentages refer to the total number of connections that involve transnationalists. In 1996, for instance, of 8,894 total connections in the elite network, 2,602 linked transnationalists either to national networkers (1,602) or to each other (1,000).

8 As noted earlier, within the triad we include the USA, Canada and Bermuda (North America), Japan and Australia (Asia-Pacific; no G500 firms are based in New Zealand) and countries of western Europe extending to the borders of Finland, Germany, Austria and Italy (Europe). Except for three directors of Russian companies in 2006, no members of the global corporate elite directed firms based in eastern Europe.

9 In 1996 there were no directors whose affiliations spanned three or more regions, but by 2006 two such super-cosmopolitans appear. Carlos Ghosn is president of both Renault and Nissan, but also serves as an outside director of US-based Alcoa. For purposes of parsimony and in view of his main affiliations, we have coded him as a Euro-Japanese transnationalist. John Buchanan, former treasurer of BP, sits on the boards of Astrazeneca and Vodafone (both UK-based), BHP Billiton (Australian-based) and D. R. Horton (US-based). For reasons of parsimony and in view of his longer service with BHP, we treat him as a Euro-Australian transnationalist.

10 The number of transnationalists whose ties are contained within North America increases from eight to thirteen; this is due, however, to the emergence of Bermuda, classified as part of North America, as a favoured tax haven for several large American corporations, which relocate their head offices there after 1996, creating, in the process, seven new transnationalists who would otherwise be categorized as national networkers within the USA. The number of transnationalists whose directorships cross the Canada–USA border actually falls from eight to six.

11 Longitudinal analysis reveals that a considerable proportion of 2006's trans-nationalists were national networkers a decade earlier. Among the 86 European transnationalists of 2006, 40.7 per cent were European national networkers in 1996; only 7.1 per cent were already European transnationalists (another 52.3 per cent were not in the 1996 global corporate elite). Among the 80 trans-Atlantic networkers of 2006, 20 per cent were European national networkers in 1996, 25 per cent were North American national networkers, and 8.8 per cent were already North Atlantic linkers (another 43.8 per cent were not in the elite). A good part of the transnational fraction has formed through accrual of transnational affiliations by those who were previously national networkers.

12 These diagrams were created by first implementing a spring-embedding solution (Freeman 2005: 251) for the entire elite network, then temporarily removing the transnationalists in order to reveal national networks. Where necessary, points representing national networkers were slightly repositioned in order to disentangle national networks from each other. Overall, however, points in the two-dimensional space of the sociograms are positioned according to their relative proximity to each other in the global network.

13 In 1996, there was only one transnationalist linking the global North and South. Abdul-Aziz Hani Hussain, a

managing director of Kuwait Petroleum, also had a seat on the board of German-based Hoechst A.G.

14 Similarly, despite endemic weaknesses of Japanese capitalism since the bubble economy burst in January 1990, the eclipse of corporate Japan from the global elite should not be mistaken for a collapse of the Japanese capitalist class per se. As Ahmadjian (2000) has argued, seemingly drastic changes to Japanese corporate governance in the later 1990s did little to disturb basic structures of economic power there (cf. Jacoby 2005).

6 Billionaires and networkers

1 Gilding (1999: 173) points out that the 'rich lists' that annually rank the super-affluent typically underestimate the importance of inherited fortunes, 'at least partly because they are spread across kinship networks. Individuals in these networks fall below the cut-off line for the rich lists, but they are still very wealthy by common standards'. The classic example is the American heirs to the Du Pont fortune, who collectively control 15 per cent of the company shares, but lack cohesion (Broom and Shay 2000).

2 A recent exemplary study of ownership and interlocking in Sweden, where corporate capital has long been organized around strong owner families, evidences a strong association between ownership and director interlocks. This suggests a social process in which 'owners deal with their firms by appointing directors, and if an owner has several firms to handle, a director tied to the owner may get several appointments' (Bohman 2010: 140).

3 The limitations of lists such as Forbes's have been discussed at length by Gilding (1999), who nevertheless makes use of them, and summarized by Potts (2006: 342): 'First, they are biased toward new fortunes in single-businesses and against more diffuse holdings (as for example over an extended family). Second, they tend to underestimate the extent of distributed or concealed wealth.' For a succinct account of the valuation rules Forbes employs in compiling its rich lists, see Canterbury and Nosari (1985: 1076).

4 www.forbes.com/lists/home.jhtml? passListId=10&passYear=1997&passList Type=Person, accessed 11 May 2009.

5 Given patrilineal naming conventions, in some cases surnames change across generations, e.g. the Montreal-based Bombardiers: the daughter married a Beaudoin, who became the succeeding patriarch, although a wing of Bombardiers is still active in the firm that bears the family name.

6 For the sake of comparison, this excludes other family members with G500 directorships but not listed by Forbes.

7 Although our directorship data end in early 2007, the most recent compilations of Forbes billionaires show a further increase to 1,125 in 2007, followed by a sharp decline to 793 by year-end 2008, in the wake of the financial crisis of late 2008.

8 The aggregated fortunes claimed by these billionaire members of the corporate elite amounted to 239.7 billion (representing 51 discrete fortunes of mean size $4.70 billion) in 1996 and 655.7 billion in 2006 (representing 93 discrete fortunes of mean size $7.05 billion), a measure of the enormous inflation of asset prices at the height of an era of financialization.

9 For instance, the late Ken Thomson, Canada's wealthiest capitalist (ranked twentieth in the world by Forbes in 1997), controlled Thomson Corporation in the decade under study, a company whose size did not quite qualify it for the G500.

10 Between 1996 and 2006, the revenue of the 400th-largest industrial grew by 68 per cent to reach $US14,590 million (current dollars). In the same decade the size of the 100th-largest financial institution grew by 93 per cent to reach $US186,975 million.

11 An example is Paul Fribourg, CEO and owner of US-based Continental Grain (1998 revenue estimated at $16 billion by the Wall Street Journal). Instructively, Fribourg does fall within our analysis, but only because he serves as outside director

of Loews and Power Corporation, not owing to his primary corporate affiliation with Continental Grain, whose board members we were unable to identify.

12 South Africa, with two *Forbes* billionaires in each year (the Oppenheimers, owners of De Beers, one of whom is a G500 director), is excluded. The only other African country that was home to any Forbes billionaires is Egypt. Semi-peripheral Middle East (2007 *Forbes* billionaires in parentheses) includes Egypt (4), Lebanon (2), Kuwait (4), UAE (4) and Kazakhstan (7). 'Other core' includes Israel (7), New Zealand (3) and Bermuda (3). Two Canadian families – the Westons and Bronfmans – have been categorized as Canadian, although Forbes shows them as based in the UK and USA respectively in 1997.

13 Among the semi-peripheral states, South Korea stands out as a country whose billionaires tended in 1996 to direct G500 firms, reflecting the tight family control of corporate groups within the so-called 'chaebol'. The Chung (Hyundai), Kim (Daewoo), Koo (LG Group) and Lee (Samsung) families were all represented on G500 boards. As we saw in Chapter 5, however, no South Korean directors had corporate affiliations beyond the national border in 1996.

14 The seven-member component represented the Tisch family's fortune, with four Tisches on the board of Loews and one directing Loews as well as Federated Department Stores.

15 A kinecon group of five links Rupert and Lachlan Murdoch to NewsCorp and to the emergent DirectTV, whose board also includes Haim Saban, a billionaire associate of the Murdochs. A six-member configuration connects two US billionaires – James Crown (who directs and holds a large stake in General Dynamics, and also directs food processor Sara Lee) and Richard Manoogian (heir to the Masco auto parts fortune and director of Ford Motor Company) – through their joint participation on the board of JP Morgan-Chase.

16 E.g., in 1996 the Halleys of Europe,

the Chung-Mong and Koo families of South Korea, the Redstones of the USA, the Toyodas of Japan; in 2006 the Calvo-Sotelo family of Spain, the Mulliez family of France, the Kocs of Turkey. Some of the excluded families could link into the network through directors of their firms who also direct other firms.

17 This sociogram and the next one include the G500 billionaires who serve on multiple G500 boards, their kin who serve on single G500 boards, and all other G500 networkers who sit on any corporate board with any of these billionaires.

7 Constituting corporate Europe

1 Also worthy of note is the exceptional status of Britain, whose special relationship with the USA and scepticism towards the Continent have inhibited engagement with European integration.

2 Even though the European Commission may not be considered a European government, its open methods of coordination seem to be fairly successful (Zeitlin and Pochet 2005).

3 The Greek financial crisis of 2010, however, illustrates the contradictions and *in*completeness of pan-European regulation to date (Scanian 2010).

4 We take as the European zone the twenty-five EU members as of 1 May 2004. We add to these Norway and Switzerland – states whose citizenries rejected EU membership but which have long been integral to Europe as an economic region. Note that the 'other European' category in Figures 7.1 and 7.2 refers almost entirely to the European semi-periphery, including Greece, Portugal, the Czech Republic, Hungary, Slovakia, Lithuania, Latvia, Slovenia, Estonia, Cyprus, Malta and Luxembourg (the last not semi-peripheral, but of negligible size). In 1996, the category also included Poland; by 2006, however, one Polish-based firm had entered the G500, removing Poland from the 'other European' category. Source for population data: United National Department of Economic and Social Affairs, Population Division, 'World population prospects: the

2006 revision population database', esa. un.org/unpp/index.asp?panel=1, accessed 15 July 2008.

5 The over-representation of French and German capital at the ERT is partly a result of the fact that their national networks (especially Germany's) remain well connected through 2006; thus an executive of a given German or French firm who sits on the ERT will very likely be an outside director of other French or German firms. The internal coherence of their respective national networks increases the range of French and German capitalist interests represented on the Round Table.

6 For a discussion of brokerage in community elites see Gould (1989). In 1996 the ERT brokered 2,056 pairs of unconnected firms, of which only 234 involved pairs of companies based in the same country. In 2006, the respective values were 2,210 and 224. In contrast to the ERT, corporate boards tend to broker relations between companies within their home countries.

7 Namely AXA (based in Paris, eleven interlocks), BNP (based in Paris, nine interlocks), KBC (based in Antwerp, seven interlocks), Aegon (based in The Hague, seven interlocks), Banca Commerciale Italiana (based in Milan, five interlocks), Fortis (based in Utrecht, five interlocks) and Paribas (based in Paris, five interlocks).

8 A comparison of most central thirty-five financials and non-financials of 1996 found an even greater concentration of bridging interlocks, at 74 per cent. In 1996, the thirty-five firms most involved in bridging across borders accounted for 57 per cent of all interlocks with the ERT. These comparisons with 1996 underline our previous finding that corporate Europe became somewhat more inclusive in the interim.

9 An additional seven directors in 2006 (and one in 1996) had principal affiliations with European insurance companies, while three directors (two in 1996) were principally affiliated with merchandisers.

10 The five finance capitalists were:

Michael Diekmann (chair of the management board of Allianz and director of BASF, Deutsche Lufthansa and Linde Group), Rijkman Groenink (chair of the management board of ABN-AMRO and director of SHV holdings), Tom McKillop (chair of the Royal Bank of Scotland and director of BP and AstraZeneca), Michel Pébereau (chair of BNP Paribas and director of Lafarge, Saint Gobain and Total), and James Schiro (CEO of Zurich Financial and director of Dutch-based Philips and US-based Pepsico).

11 Among the 28 firms with multiple external linkages, 11 of the 15 scoring highest in E-I are based in Britain (7) or Switzerland (4).

12 Namely, Japan-based Nissan (an affiliate of Renault, interlocked with four European firms) and Sony, Australia-based BHP and China-based China Construction (each interlocked with two). Note that Europe's relative lack of elite ties beyond the North Atlantic is exactly mirrored by the same tendency in the case of the USA. In 1996, European-based corporations had a total of 16 directorship interlocks to firms based outside the North Atlantic (13 of them to Japanese companies, 2 to Australia, 1 to Kuwait); in 2006, the total was 15, 7 linking to Japan, 3 to China, 2 to Brazil and Australia and 1 to Russia. In comparison, in both years US corporations maintained 9 interlocking directorates reaching beyond the North Atlantic. In 1996 these were distributed solely among Japan (4 interlocks) and Australia (5 interlocks). By 2006, Japan claimed only 1 tie, Australia claimed 2, and the remaining 6 terminated in Mexico (2), Singapore (2), China (1) and India (1). Although both corporate Europe and corporate America show a widening of interlocking beyond the triad, neither shows a tendency to proliferate elite ties beyond the North Atlantic.

8 Consolidating the network

1 Namely, the Executive Board for the ICC, the Foundation Board for the WEF, and the board of directors for the

UNGC. At the time of writing, the UNGC claimed '5600 participants, including over 4300 businesses in 120 countries around the world' (United Nations Global Compact 2008). A global policy group not included here but of great importance in the mobilization of neoliberalism is the Mont Pèlerin Society, which has been from its inception in 1947 composed primarily of right-wing intellectuals, not business leaders (see Chapter 9).

2 Note that the third relation constituting the triad – that between the USA and Japan – is missing from our sample. We researched the Japan–US Business Council and the US–Japan Business Council, which are parallel organizations. Although these groups hold an annual joint conference, they do not function as a single transnational policy board. Moreover, in contrast to both TABD and EJBRT, there was no apparent state involvement in the inception of these groups, nor is there an ongoing institutional mechanism through which these groups influence regional state policies.

3 The EU in the case of the ERT, the parties to NAFTA and to the North American Security and Prosperity Partnership in the case of NACC, the US Department of Commerce and the European Commission in the case of TABD, the European Commission and the Japanese Ministry of Economy, Trade and Industry in the case of EJBRT.

4 In addition to its annual meetings preceding the US–EU Summit, the TABD also meets yearly just prior to the World Economic Forum, with the objective of influencing its proceedings.

5 Data for membership of the policy boards were obtained from the organizations themselves, via websites and annual reports. For the Bilderberg Conference, which has no fixed membership, we relied on published lists of those attending the conferences in spring 1997 and spring 2007, available at www.bilderberg. org/1997.htm#USA and www.bilderberg. org/bilderberg2007.pdf.

6 Some of these may well direct non-G500 firms. All of our estimates of structural integration are in this sense conservative. See note 14.

7 In both 1996 and 2006, five national networkers based in the Asia-Pacific core countries participated on the policy boards, but in the interim the contingent of national networkers in this region of the core shrunk from 117 to twenty-one. Another very small category (numbering seven in 2006) – transnationalists who direct firms based in both Europe and Asia – show quite high participation rates in both years.

8 Our use of the term 'inner circle' is inspired by Useem (1984), who includes in the inner circle of the capitalist class all directors of multiple large corporations. Here, our criterion for the inner circle is more stringent. We define the global corporate-policy elite as all those who sit on at least two major boards, whether corporate or policy. For present purposes, the inner circle of this elite includes those who serve on at least two corporate boards *and* two policy boards, comprising the hard core of the network.

9 One inner circle member in 2006 had corporate affiliations in Mexico and the USA; another (Carlos Ghosn, CEO of Renault and president of its affiliate Nissan) had corporate affiliations spanning the triad. See Chapter 5, note 9.

10 As noted in Chapter 4, the numbers of corporations domiciled in each of the four regions shift somewhat over the decade.

11 Whereas unweighted densities give the proportion of pairs of boards that are interlocked, weighted densities take into account how many board members are shared, an important consideration in assessing the degree of social integration within and between different segments of the network.

12 Not surprisingly, the European Round Table of Industrialists makes a major contribution to corporate Europe's prominence, accounting for 1,028 of Europe's 2,617 inter-corporate mediations in 1996 and 1,102 in 2006. This

contribution reflects a reality of socio-political integration within the European business community (see Chapter 7). Even when we leave the ERT out of the analysis, however, corporate Europe still accounts for 29.0 per cent of all inter-corporate relations brokered by the policy-planning boards in 2006.

13 Among the global policy groups not shown in Figure 8.8, the ICC moves to an entirely European set of inter-corporate mediations. The CFRIAB shifts from a Euro-North American profile to one that includes links between the North Atlantic and the core Asia-Pacific as well as links involving the global South. The UNGC brokers relations centred in Europe but including the global South and the North Atlantic.

14 On this issue of structural integration, it is pertinent to note that other links besides those examined here contribute to elite cohesion. Friendships, kinship ties and common club and other memberships all contribute to elite integration. Moreover, directors of corporations not large enough to qualify for the G500, and executives who do not sit on G500 directorates, are not considered here, even though some of them may serve on the policy boards. Our findings provide conservative estimates of elite cohesion.

15 A limitation of this analysis lies in the differing organizational forms of the policy-planning bodies. In some cases, such as the TC, ERT and WBCSD, the policy boards are coextensive with the group itself; in others, (e.g. the WEF and ICC) the organizations greatly exceed the boards we have included in our network analysis. The WEF, for instance, brings together thousands of corporate and other elites annually, with extensive participation from the global South. Our analysis of its Foundation Board underestimates the WEF mediatory and integrative contribution to transnational neoliberalism's historic bloc.

16 In 2006, just two corporate interlockers directing firms domiciled in the semi-periphery participated in the corporate-policy network, namely Ernesto Zedillo and Lorenzo Zambrano, both of Mexico (see Figure 8.3, above). Another seven individuals directed single G500 corporations based outside the Triad while sitting on policy boards.

17 This historic bloc is, of course, more than an elite network of peak organizations. It includes the practices and relations through which transnational corporate interests are articulated to institutions of global governance (such as the World Bank) and to aligned national and local organizations (Robinson 2004: 75–7; Chapter 9, this volume).

9 Hegemony and counter-hegemony

1 As Fraser goes on to explain, justice defined as parity of participation 'requires social arrangements that permit all to participate as peers in social life. Overcoming injustice means dismantling institutionalized obstacles that prevent some people from participating on par with others, as full partners in social interaction' (Fraser 2005: 73). The all-affected principle is what enables development activists, environmentalists, trade unionists, international feminists and indigenous peoples to make claims against the structures that harm them, *'even when the latter cannot be located in the space of places'* (ibid.: 84). This principle holds that 'all those affected by a given social structure or institution have moral standing as subjects in relation to it' (ibid.: 82).

2 As Kelly recounts (2005), the ICC has been particularly proactive in times of crisis – as in the reconstruction following both world wars – helping to shape the global field in the direction of unimpeded market relations. The ICC played a role as the only NGO granted the chance to address sessions at the United Nations Session on Trade and Employment in 1947/48, and thus in the still-birth of the (Keynesian) International Trade Organization.

3 Go to: www.ituc-csi.org/-about-us-.html, accessed 29 December 2009.

4 See www.unglobalcompact.org/

aboutTheGC/The_Global_Compact_Board.html, accessed 15 October 2009.

5 The San Francisco-based International Forum on Globalization (IFG), established in 1994 in the heat of the NAFTA debates, also merits mention here, as a more North American-based group (www.ifg.org), organized along more traditional think-tank lines. Its seventeen-member board includes Walden Bello and John Cavanagh, both TNI Fellows, as well as Canadian activists Tony Clark and Maude Barlow.

6 Details on these are available under 'Projects' at the TNI website, www.tni.org, accessed 15 October 2009.

7 Find 'New Politics' under 'Projects', at www.tni.org, accessed 18 October 2009. Hilary Wainwright, editor of *Red Pepper* and Senior Research Fellow at the Centre for Labour Studies at the University of Manchester, provides a particularly acute interrogation of the new methodology for composing the programme of the fifth World Social Forum. The new methodology was based on 'dissolving a centrally decided programme and involving participating organisations fully in setting the framework of the Forum's activities'. This validated social-movement aspirations to join autonomy with horizontal connectedness while it tested 'the potentiality of the new technologies to facilitate popular participation, share knowledge and develop dense networks of resistance and alternatives' (Wainwright 2005). As a representative of both the TNI and the ESF at the 2004 WSF, Wainwright was tasked with evaluating the new methodology, with an eye to its possible adoption by the ESF. Her detailed report, based on participant observation and extensive interviews with WSF participants, exemplifies the reflexive approach to praxis that characterizes the work of the TNI, especially in its New Politics programme.

8 www.foei.org/en/who-we-are/about, accessed 15 October 2009.

9 The source for this quotation, and for the account in this paragraph, is www.foei.org/en/who-we-are/about/25years.

html, accessed 29 December 2009. Surprisingly little academic analysis of FoEI has been published.

10 The full declaration is available at www.foei.org/en/blog/2009/02/17/climate-justice-assembly-declaration, accessed 15 October 2009.

11 Of 177 member companies listed on its website (accessed 25 February 2006), 74 were based in the European core states, 44 were based in the USA (39) or Canada (5), 16 were based in Japan and 6 were based in Australia/New Zealand. The rest of the world contributed a *total* of 38 corporate members, with 3 based in Africa, 14 in Asia (5 of them in South Korea and 3 in China), 10 based in Latin America (3 in Mexico and 3 in Brazil) and 11 on the European semi-periphery (5 based in Portugal and 3 in Russia).

12 The full list of WBCSD partnerships is available at www.wbcsd.org/templates/TemplateWBCSD2/layout.asp?type=p&MenuId=NDEy&doOpen=1&ClickMenu=LeftMenu, accessed 15 October 2009.

13 A promotional brochure is available at www.wbcsd.org/web/publications/chronos-english.pdf.

14 See various self-characterizations on the WEF website, at www.weforum.org, accessed 15 October 2009.

15 See the Pôrto Alegre Manifesto at opendemocracy.typepad.com/wsf/2005/02/previous_posts_.html, accessed 15 October 2009.

16 From the *WSF Bulletin*, 27 June 2006, available at www.forumsocial mundial.org.br/dinamic.php?pagin=consulta _fsm2007_ing, accessed 15 October 2009.

17 See the Mobilization Calendar at www.forumsocialmundial.org.br/main.php?id_menu=12_1&cd_language=2, accessed 15 October 2009.

18 Callinicos (2006: 241) submits that cosmopolitanism is a stance that can bring together the various strands of global justice politics without sacrificing the specificity of different groups' claims. He borrows the principle from Barry (1999: 36), who defines it as 'a moral stance

consisting of three elements: individualism, equality, and universality. Its unit of
value is individual human beings; it does
not recognize any categories of people as
having less or more moral weight; and it
includes all human beings.' On parity of
participation see note 1 above.

Conclusion

1 As noted in Chapter 4, the number
of US- (or Bermuda-) based G400 firms
engaged in industrial activity fell from 111
to 96. In comparison, for the core European region, the number of firms engaged
in industrial activity grew from 97 to 110.

2 This may be changing, and emerging
developments merit careful attention.
For instance, the major Chinese banks,
which were only recently converted from
government ministries into veritable corporations, are establishing relations with
US and European banks. The purchase
by Bank of America of a 9 per cent stake
in the China Construction Bank, with
the expectation of obtaining one seat on
the latter's board of directors, may be
indicative of things to come (Engardio
2007: 212–13). We noted in Chapter 5
that at year-end 2006, two Europeans and
one American corporate director sat on
the boards of three Chinese banks. No
Chinese capitalist 'returned the favour',
however. As for its domestic corporate
community, the statist character of
Chinese capitalism integrates its elite
in ways that do not require interlocking
directorships.

3 In recent years, western Europe has
been a prime destination for foreign direct
investment, but much of this investment
(71 per cent in 2001) has involved intra-
EU flows (Oxelheim and Ghauri 2004:
7). As Peter Buckley has noted, regional

economic integration is both a means of
attracting TNC investment within the integrating area, 'and of increasing relative
discrimination against firms outside the
area of integration' (2004: 35).

4 The project of European integration
is itself beset by internal tensions rooted
mainly in uneven development, which
have been amplified in the current global
crisis. In December 2009, Ireland, Greece,
Spain and Latvia all faced defaults due
to haemorrhaging debt, and the growing
prospects of one or more of the first three
of them exiting from the euro in order to
regain control of national financial policy
signalled a looming crisis for the Eurozone (Kagarlitsky 2009).

5 In such a protracted, general crisis
'incurable structural contradictions have
revealed themselves'. The 'incessant and
persistent efforts' of the ruling historic
bloc 'to conserve and defend the existing
structure [...] form the terrain of the
"conjunctural", and it is upon this terrain
that the forces of opposition organise'
(Gramsci 1971: 178).

6 As Lumumba Di-Aping, chairman of
the G77 group of 130 developing countries
put it (Batty 2009).

7 This was proposed in November
2009 by Hugo Chávez at a meeting in
Caracas of more than fifty parties and
movement organizations from thirty-one
countries. Formative discussions are
in progress at the time of writing. See
'COMMITMENT OF CARACAS', www.psuv.
org.ve/files/tcdocumentos/commitment.
caracas.pdf, accessed 7 March 2010.
See also 'The Venezuelan call for a new
international organization of the left', *The
Bullet* Socialist Project, E-Bulletin no. 312,
15 February 2010, www.socialistproject.ca/
bullet/312.php.

Bibliography

Aglietta, M. (1979) *A Theory of Capitalist Regulation*, London: New Left Books.

Agnew, J. (2001) 'How many Europes?: the European Union, eastward enlargement and uneven development', *European Urban and Regional Studies*, 8: 29–38.

Aguilera, R. V. (2005) 'Corporate governance and director availability: an institutional comparative perspective', *British Journal of Management*, 16: s39–s53.

Aguilera, R. V. and G. Jackson (2003) 'The cross-national diversity of corporate governance: dimensions and determinants', *Academy of Management Review*, 28: 447–65.

Ahmadjian, C. L. (2000) 'Changing Japanese corporate governance', *The Japanese Economy*, 28(6): 59–84.

Ahmadjian, C. L. and J. Song (2004) *Corporate Governance Reform in Japan and South Korea: Two Paths of Globalization*, New York: Columbia University Business School.

Alderson, A. S. and J. Beckfield (2004) 'Power and position in the world city system', *American Journal of Sociology*, 109: 811–51.

— (2007) 'Globalization and the world city system: preliminary results from a longitudinal data set', in P. Taylor, B. Derudder, P. Saey and F. Witlox (eds), *Cities in Globalization*, London: Routledge, pp. 21–36.

Amin, S. (2000) 'The political economy of the twentieth century', *Monthly Review*, 52(2): 1–17.

— (2005) 'Empire and multitude', *Monthly Review*, 57(6): 1–12.

— (2008) '"Market economy" or oligopoly-finance capitalism', *Monthly Review*, 59(11): 51–61.

Andreff, W. (1984) 'The internationalization of capital and the reordering of world capitalism', *Capital & Class*, 25: 58–60.

Athar, H. (1976) 'Hilferding's finance capital', *Bulletin of the Conference of Socialist Economists*, 5(1): 1–18.

Bairoch, P. (2000) 'The constituent economic principles of globalization in historical perspective', *International Sociology*, 15(2): 197–214.

Balanyá, B., A. Doherty, O. Hoedeman, A. Ma'anit and E. Wesselius (2000) *Europe Inc.*, London: Pluto Press.

Barca, F. and M. Becht (2001) *The Control of Corporate Europe*, Oxford: Oxford University Press.

Barnes, R. C. and E. R. Ritter (2001) 'Networks of corporate interlocking: 1962–1995', *Critical Sociology*, 27(2): 192–220.

Barnet, R. J. and R. E. Mueller (1974) *Global Reach*, New York: Simon & Schuster.

Barry, B. (1999) 'Statism and nationalism: a cosmopolitan critique', in I. Shapiro and L. Brilmayer (eds), *Global Justice: Nomos Volume XLI*, New York: New York University Press, pp. 12–66.

Batty, D. (2009) 'Copenhagen reaction: delegates speak', *Guardian*, 19 December.

Baum, D. J. and N. B. Stiles (1965) *Silent Partners: Institutional Investors and Corporate Control*, Syracuse, NY: Syracuse University Press.

Bearden, J. and B. Mintz (1985) 'Regionality and integration in the American interlock network', in F. N. Stokman, R. Ziegler and J. Scott (eds), *Networks of Corporate Power*, Cambridge: Polity Press, pp. 234–49.

— (1987) 'The structure of class cohesion: the corporate network and its dual', in M. S. Mizruchi and M. Schwartz (eds),

Intercorporate Relations, Cambridge, MA: Cambridge University Press, pp. 187–207.

Beaverstock, J. V., P. Hubbard and J. R. Short (2004) 'Getting away with it? Exposing the geographies of the super-rich', *Geoforum*, 35: 401–7.

Becht, M., P. Bolton and A. Roell (2003) 'Corporate governance and control', in G. M. Constantinides, M. Harris and R. M. Stulz (eds), *Handbook of the Economics of Finance*, vol. 1, Amsterdam: Elsevier, pp. 1–109.

Beckmann, M. (2006) 'Institutional investors and the transformation of the European economy', Presented at 'Finance, industry and power: the capitalist corporation in the 21st century', Department of Political Science, York University, Toronto.

Beder, S. (2006) *Suiting Themselves: How Corporations Drive the Global Agenda*, London: Earthscan.

Bell, D. (1961) *The End of Ideology*, New York: Collier-Macmillan.

Bello, W. (2006) 'The capitalist conjuncture: over-accumulation, financial crises, and the retreat from globalisation', *Third World Quarterly*, 27(8): 1345–67.

— (2008) 'Crisis and the retreat from globalization', in H. Veltmeyer (ed.), *New Perspectives on Globalization and Anti-Globalization*, London: Ashgate Publishing, pp. 89–109.

Berle, A. and G. C. Means (1932) *The Modern Corporation and Private Property*, New York: Macmillan.

Bieling, H. J. (2006a) 'EMU, financial integration and global economic governance', *Review of International Political Economy*, 13(3): 420–48.

— (2006b) 'Neoliberalism and communitarianism: social conditions, discourses and politics', in D. Plehwe, B. Walpen and G. Neunhoffer (eds), *Neoliberal Hegemony: A Global Critique*, London: Routledge, pp. 207–21.

Bohman, L. (2010) *Director Interlocking and Firm Ownership*, Doctoral dissertation, Stockholm Studies in Sociology New Series 41, Stockholm University.

Borgatti, S. P. (2005) 'NetDraw: network visualization', www.analytictech.com/netdraw/netdraw.htm, accessed 30 December 2009.

Borgatti, S. P. and M. G. Everett (1999) 'Models of core/periphery structures', *Social Networks*, 21(4): 375–95.

Borgatti, S. P., M. G. Everett and L. C. Freeman (2002) *Ucinet 6 for Windows: Software for Social Network Analysis*, Harvard, MA: Analytic Technologies.

Bottomore, T. (1991) *Classes in Modern Society*, 2nd edn, London: HarperCollins.

Bottomore, T. B. and R. J. Brym (1989) *The Capitalist Class: An International Study*, New York: New York University Press.

Bourdieu, P. and A. Accardo (1999) *The Weight of the World: Social Suffering in Contemporary Society*, Stanford, CT: Stanford University Press.

Brandeis, L. D. (1913) *Other People's Money*, New York: McClure Publications.

Breton, R. (1964) 'Institutional completeness of ethnic communities and the personal relations of immigrants', *American Journal of Sociology*, 70: 193.

Brewer, A. (1980) *Marxist Theories of Imperialism*, London: Routledge.

Broom, L. and W. Shay (2000) 'Discontinuities in the distribution of great wealth: sectoral forces old and new', Jerome Levy Economics Institute Working Paper, 308.

Brownlee, J. (2005) *Ruling Canada: Corporate Cohesion and Democracy*, Halifax: Fernwood Books.

Bryan, D. (1995) *The Chase across the Globe*, Boulder, CO: Westview Press.

Buckley, P. J. (2004) 'Regional integration and foreign direct investment in a globalised world economy', in L. Oxelheim and P. Ghauri (eds), *European Union and the Race for Foreign Direct Investment in Europe*, Amsterdam: Elsevier, pp. 35–58.

Buckman, G. (2004) *Globalization: Tame It or Scrap It?*, London: Zed Books.

Burbach, R. and W. I. Robinson (1999) 'The fin de siècle debate: globalization as epochal shift', *Science and Society*, 63(1): 10–39.

Burris, V. (2005) 'Interlocking directorates and political cohesion among corporate elites', *American Journal of Sociology*, 111(1): 249–83.

Burt, R. S. (2005) *Brokerage and Closure*, Oxford: Oxford University Press.

Byrd, S. C. (2005) 'The Porto Alegre Consensus: theorizing the Forum movement', *Globalizations*, 2(1): 151–63.

Callinicos, A. (2006) *The Resources of Critique*, Cambridge: Polity Press.

Cammack, P. (2003) 'The governance of global capitalism: a new materialist perspective', *Historical Materialism*, 11(2): 37–59.

Campbell, E. W. (1963) *The 60 Rich Families Who Own Australia*, Sydney: Current Books.

Canak, W. L. (1991) 'Dominant classes, politics and the state in Latin America', *Journal of Interamerican Studies and World Affairs*, 33(1): 149–59.

Canterbury, E. R. and E. J. Nosari (1985) 'The Forbes Four Hundred: the determinants of super-wealth', *Southern Economic Journal*, 51: 1073–83.

Carchedi, G. (1977) *On the Economic Identification of Social Classes*, London: Routledge.

Carroll, W. K. (1982) 'The Canadian corporate elite: financiers or finance capitalists?', *Studies in Political Economy*, 8: 89–114.

— (1986) *Corporate Power and Canadian Capitalism*, Vancouver: University of British Columbia Press.

— (2001) 'Westward Ho? The shifting geography of corporate power in Canada', *Journal of Canadian Studies*, 36(4): 118–42.

— (2002) 'Does disorganized capitalism disorganize corporate networks?', *Canadian Journal of Sociology*, 27(3): 339–71.

— (2004) *Corporate Power in a Globalizing World*, Toronto: Oxford University Press.

— (2006) 'Hegemony, counter-hegemony, anti-hegemony', *Social Studies*, 2(2): 9–43.

— (2007) 'Global cities in the global corporate network', *Environment and Planning, A*, 39: 2297–323.

— (2008a) 'The corporate elite and the transformation of finance capital: a view from Canada', *Sociological Review*, 56(S1): 44–63.

— (2008b) 'Tracking the transnational capitalist class: the view from on high', in Y. Atasoy (ed.), *Hegemonic Transitions, the State and Crisis in Neoliberal Capitalism*, London: Routledge, pp. 43–64.

— (2010) 'Capital relations and directorate interlocking: the global network in 2007', Paper presented at the World Congress of Sociology, Gothenburg, 11–17 July.

Carroll, W. K. and C. Carson (2003) 'The network of global corporations and elite policy groups: a structure for transnational capitalist class formation?', *Global Networks*, 3(1): 29–57.

Carroll, W. K. and M. Fennema (2002) 'Is there a transnational business community?', *International Sociology*, 17: 393–419.

— (2004) 'Problems in the study of the transnational business community', *International Sociology*, 19(3): 369–78.

Carroll, W. K. and J. Klassen (2010) 'Hollowing out corporate Canada? Changes in the corporate network since the 1990s', *Canadian Journal of Sociology*, 35: 1–30.

Carroll, W. K. and S. Lewis (1991) 'Restructuring finance capital: changes in the Canadian corporate network 1976–1986', *Sociology*, 25: 491–510.

Carroll, W. K. and J. P. Sapinski (2011) 'Corporate elites and intercorporate networks', in J. Scott and P. Carrington (eds), *Handbook of Social Network Analysis*, London: Sage.

Carroll, W. K. and M. Shaw (2001) 'Consolidating a neoliberal policy bloc in Canada, 1976 to 1996', *Canadian Public Policy*, 27: 195–216.

Castells, M. (1996) *The Rise of the Network Society*, vol. 1, Oxford: Blackwell.

Chhaochharia, V. and Y. Grinstein (2007)

'The changing structure of US corporate boards: 1997–2003', *Corporate Governance*, 15(6): 1215–23.

Chossudovsky, M. (2003) *The Globalization of Poverty and the New World Order*, 2nd edn, Pincourt, Quebec: Global Research.

Clarke, T. (2007) *International Corporate Governance*, London: Routledge.

Coleman, J. S. (1988) 'Social capital and the creation of human capital', *American Journal of Sociology*, 94: s95–s120.

Compact, U. N. G. (2008) *Participants and Stakeholders*, New York: United Nations.

Conway, J. (2004) 'Citizenship in a time of empire: the World Social Forum as a new public space', *Citizenship Studies*, 8: 367–81.

Cox, R. W. (1987) *Production, Power and World Order*, New York: Columbia University.

Crozier, M., S. P. Huntington and J. Watanuki (1975) *The Crisis of Democracy*, New York: New York University Press.

Cutler, C. (2010) 'The privatization of authority in the global political economy', in G. Teeple and S. McBride (eds), *Global Rule in Crisis*, Toronto: University of Toronto Press.

Dahrendorf, R. (1959) *Class and Class Conflict in Industrial Society*, Stanford, CT: Stanford University Press.

Dahya, J., O. Dimitrov and J. J. McConnell (2007) 'Dominant shareholders, corporate boards, and corporate value: a cross-country analysis', *Journal of Financial Economics*, 87(1): 73–100.

Davis, G. F. (2008) 'A new finance capitalism? Mutual funds and ownership re-concentration in the United States', *European Management Review*, 5: 11–21.

Davis, G. F. and M. S. Mizruchi (1999) 'The money center cannot hold: commercial banks in the U.S. system of corporate governance', *Administrative Science Quarterly*, 44(2): 215–39.

Davis, K. (2004) 'Working at the intersection – a story from Australia', *Development and Practice*, 14(1): 119–26.

De Angelis, M. (2004) 'Opposing fetishism by reclaiming their powers: the Social Forum movement, capitalist markets and the politics of alternatives', *International Social Science Journal*, 56(4): 591–604.

Denord, F. (2002) 'Le prophète, le pèlerine et le missionaire. La circulation internationale du neo-libéralisme et ses acteurs', *Actes de la recherche en sciences sociales*, 145: 9–20.

Derudder, B., P. J. Taylor, F. Witlox and G. Catalano (2003) 'Hierarchical tendencies and regional patterns in the world city network: a global urban analysis of 234 cities', *Regional Studies*, 37: 875–86.

Desai, R. (2007) 'The last empire? From nation-building compulsion to nation-wrecking futility and beyond', *Third World Quarterly*, 28(2): 435–56.

Dicken, P. (2003) *Global Shift*, 4th edn, New York: Guilford Press.

DiDonato, D., D. S. Glasberg, B. Mintz and M. Schwartz (1988) 'Theories of corporate interlocks: a social history', *Research in the Sociology of Organizations*, 6: 135–57.

Dobbin, M. (2009) 'Canada must forge its own economic fate: the SPP is dead', *The Tyee*, Vancouver, 24 September, thetyee.ca/Opinion/2009/09/24/EconomicFate/index.html?commentsfilter=0, accessed 11 December 2009.

Domhoff, G. W. (2006 [1967; 1998]) *Who Rules America?*, New York: McGraw-Hill.

Dore, R. (2002) 'Debate: stock market capitalism vs. welfare capitalism', *New Political Economy*, 7: 115–27.

Doremus, P. N., W. W. Keller et al. (1998) *The Myth of the Global Corporation*, Princeton, NJ: Princeton University Press.

Dye, T. R. (1978) 'Oligarchic tendencies in national policy-making: the role of the private policy-planning organizations', *Journal of Politics*, 40(2): 309–31.

Eising, R. (2007) 'The access of business interests to EU institutions: towards elite pluralism?', *Journal of European Public Policy*, 14: 384–403.

Engardio, P. (ed.) (2007) *Chindia*, New York: McGraw-Hill.

Engels, F. (1977 [1884]) *The Origins of the Family, Private Property and the State*, New York: International Publishers.

Escobar, A. (1996) 'Constructing nature: elements for a post-structuralist political ecology', *Futures*, 28(4): 325–43.

European Financial Services Round Table (2007) 'EFR's vision', Brussels, January.

Farrer, L. (2004) *World Forum Movement: Abandon or Contaminate*, New Delhi: Viveka Foundation.

Femia, J. V. (1981) *Gramsci's Political Thought*, Oxford: Clarendon Press.

Fennema, M. (1982) *International Networks of Banks and Industry*, The Hague: Martinus Nijhoff Publishers.

Fennema, M. and J. Rhijnsburger (2007) *Dr H. M. Hirschfeld en het Nederlands Belang*, Amsterdam: Balans.

Fennema, M. and H. Schijf (1979) 'Analysing interlocking directorates: theory and methods', *Social Networks*, 1: 297–332.

— (1985) 'The transnational network', in F. N. Stokman, R. Ziegler and J. Scott (eds), *Networks of Corporate Power*, Cambridge: Polity Press.

Fennema, M. and K. van der Pijl (1987) 'International bank capital and the new liberalism', in M. Mizruchi and M. Schwartz (eds), *Corporate Relations*, New York: Cambridge University Press.

Fisher, D. R., K. Stanley and G. Neff (2005) 'How do organizations matter? Mobilization and support for participants at five globalization protests', *Social Problems*, 52: 102–21.

Fisk, R. (2009) 'The demise of the dollar', *Independent*, 6 October, www.independent.co.uk/news/business/news/the-demise-of-the-dollar-1798175.html, accessed 11 December 2009.

Ford, L. H. (2003) 'Challenging global environmental governance: social movement agency and global civil society', *Global Environmental Politics*, 3(2): 120–34.

Fox, B. (1989) 'The feminist challenge: a reconsideration of social inequality and economic development', in R. J. Brym (ed.), *From Culture to Power*, Toronto: Oxford University Press, pp. 120–67.

Fraser, N. (2005) 'Reframing justice in a globalizing world', *New Left Review*, 36: 69–88.

Freeman, L. C. (2005) 'Graphic techniques for exploring social network data', in P. J. Carrington, J. Scott and S. Wasserman (eds), *Models and Methods in Social Network Analysis*, Cambridge: Cambridge University Press, pp. 248–69.

Frieden, J. (1980) 'The Trilateral Commission: economics and politics in the 1970s', in H. Sklar (ed.), *The Trilateral Commission and Elite Planning for World Management*, Boston, MA: South End Press.

Friedmann, J. (1986) 'The world city hypothesis', *Development and Change*, 17: 69–147.

Froud, J. and K. Williams (2007) 'Private equity and the culture of value extraction', *New Political Economy*, 12: 405–20.

Gerlach, M. L. (1992) *Alliance Capitalism*, Berkeley: University of California Press.

Giddens, A. (1990) *The Consequences of Modernity*, Cambridge: Polity Press.

— (1998) *The Third Way*, Cambridge: Polity Press.

Gilding, M. (1999) 'Superwealth in Australia: entrepreneurs, accumulation and the capitalist class', *Journal of Sociology*, 35: 170–82.

Gill, S. (1990) *American Hegemony and the Trilateral Commission*, Cambridge: Cambridge University Press.

— (1992) 'Economic globalization and the internationalization of authority: limits and contradictions', *Geoforum*, 23(3): 269–83.

— (1995a) 'Globalisation, market civilization and disciplinary neoliberalism', *Journal of International Studies*, 24(3): 399–423.

— (1995b) 'Theorizing the interregnum: the double movement of global politics in the 1990s', in B. Hettne (ed.), *International Political Economy*, Halifax: Fernwood Books, pp. 65–99.

Gill, S. R. and D. Law (1989) 'Global hegemony and the structural power of capital', *International Studies Quarterly*, 33: 475–99.

Go, J. (2007) 'Waves of empire: US hegemony and imperialistic activity from the shores of Tripoli to Iraq, 1787–2003', *International Sociology*, 22(1): 5–40.

Goldman, M. L. (1998) 'Russian billionaires' club', *International Economy*, 12: 10–15.

Gould, R. V. (1989) 'Power and social structure in community elites', *Social Forces*, 68: 531–52.

Gouldner, A. W. (1957) 'Cosmopolitans and locals: towards an analysis of latent social roles', *Administrative Science Quarterly*, 2: 281–306.

Graham, S. (1999) 'Global grids of glass: on global cities, telecommunications and planetary urban networks', *Urban Studies*, 36: 929–49.

Gramsci, A. (1971) *Selections from the Prison Notebooks of Antonio Gramsci*, New York: International Publishers.

— (1977) *Selections from Political Writings of Antonio Gramsci, 1910–1920*, London: Lawrence and Wishart.

Granovetter, M. S. (1973) 'The strength of weak ties', *American Journal of Sociology*, 78(6): 1360–80.

Graz, J.-C. (2003) 'How powerful are transnational elite clubs: the social myth of the World Economic Forum', *New Political Economy*, 8(3): 321–40.

Graz, J.-C. and A. Nolke (eds) (2008) *Transnational Private Governance and Its Limits*, London: Routledge.

Green, M. (1983) 'The interurban corporate interlocking directorate network of Canada and the United States: a spatial perspective', *Urban Geography*, 4: 338–54.

Green, M. and R. K. Semple (1981) 'The corporate interlocking directorate as an urban spatial information network', *Urban Geography*, 2(2): 148–60.

Hackett, R. A. and W. K. Carroll (2006) *Remaking Media: The Struggle to Democratize Public Communication*, London: Routledge.

Halperin, S. (2007) 'Re-envisioning global development: conceptual and methodological issues', *Globalization*, 44: 543–58.

Harary, F. (1969) *Graph Theory*, Reading, MA: Addison-Wesley.

Hardie, I. and D. Howarth (2009) '*Die Krise* but not *La Crise*? The financial crisis and the transformation of German and French banking systems', *Journal of Common Market Studies*, 47: 1017–39.

Harris, J. (2009) 'Statist globalization in China, Russia and the Gulf States', *Science & Society*, 73(1): 6–33.

Harvey, D. (2005) *The New Imperialism*, New York: Oxford University Press.

— (2006) *The Limits to Capital*, 2nd edn, London: Verso.

Haseler, S. (1999) *The Super-Rich: The Unjust World of Global Capitalism*, London: St Martin's Press.

Heartfield, J. (2007) 'Limits of European economic unification', *Critique*, 35: 37–65.

Heemskerk, E. M. (2007) *Decline of the Corporate Community: Network Dynamics of the Dutch Business Elite*, Amsterdam: Amsterdam University Press.

Heemskerk, E. M. and G. Schnyder (2008) 'Small states, international pressures and interlocking directorates: the cases of Switzerland and the Netherlands', *European Management Review*, 5(1): 41–54.

Heijltjes, M. G., R. Olie and U. Glunk (2003) 'Internationalization of top management teams in Europe', *European Management Journal*, 21: 89–97.

Held, D. and A. Kaya (eds) (2007) *Global Inequality*, Cambridge: Polity Press.

Higley, J. and M. G. Burton (2006) *Elite Foundations of Liberal Democracy*, New York: Rowman & Littlefield.

Hilferding, R. (1981 [1910]) *Finance Capital*, London: Routledge.

Hirst, P. and G. Thompson (1996) *Globalization in Question*, Cambridge: Polity Press.

Hocking, B. and D. Kelly (2002) *Doing the Business? The International Chamber of*

Commerce, the United Nations, and the Global Compact, Tokyo: United Nations University Press.

Holderness, C. G. (2009) 'The myth of diffuse ownership in the United States', *Review of Financial Studies*, 22(4): 1377–408.

Holman, O. and K. van der Pijl (1996) 'The capitalist class in the European Union', in G. Kourvetaris and A. Moschonas (eds), *The Impact of European Integration*, Westport, CT: Greenwood Press.

Höpner, M. and L. Krempel (2004) 'The politics of the German company network', *Competition & Change*, 8(4): 339–56.

Hu, Y.-S. (1992) 'Global or stateless corporations are national firms with international operations', *California Management Review*, 34(2): 107–26.

Hueglin, T. (1999) 'Government, governance, governmentality: understanding the EU as a project of universalism', in B. Kohler-Koch and R. Eising (eds), *The Transformation of Governance in the European Union*, London: Routledge, pp. 249–66.

Huish, R. (2006) 'Logos a thing of the past? Not so fast, World Social Forum!', *Antipode*, 38: 1–6.

Hunt, C. S. and H. E. Aldrich (1998) 'The second ecology: creation and evolution of organizational communities', *Research in Organizational Behaviour*, 20: 267–301.

Hussein, A. (1976) 'Hilferding's finance capital', *Bulletin of the Conference of Socialist Economists*, 5(1): 1–18.

Hyman, R. (2005) 'Shifting dynamics in international trade unionism: agitation, organisation, bureaucracy, diplomacy', *Labour History*, 46(2): 135–54.

Hymer, S. (1979) *The Multinational Corporations: A Radical Approach*, Cambridge: Cambridge University Press.

Ikeda, S. (2004) 'Japan and the changing regime of accumulation: a world-system study of Japan's trajectory from miracle to debacle', *Journal of World-Systems Research*, 10(2): 363–94.

Jacoby, S. M. (2005) *The Embedded Corporation*, Princeton, NJ: Princeton University Press.

Jakobsen, K. (2001) 'Rethinking the International Confederation of Free Trade Unions and its inter-American regional organization', *Antipode*, 33(3): 363–83.

Jeidels, O. (1905) 'Das Verhältnis der deutschen Grossbanken zur Industrie mit besonder Berücksichtigung der Eisenindustrie' [Relation of German big banks to industry with special reference to the iron industry], *Staats- und sozialwissenschaftliche Forschungen*, 24(2): 1–271.

Jessop, B. (2000) 'Good governance and the urban question: on managing the contradictions of neo-liberalism', Department of Sociology, Lancaster University, www.lancs.ac.uk/fass/sociology/papers/jessop-good-governance-and-the-urban-question.pdf, accessed 30 December 2009.

— (2002) *The Future of the Capitalist State*, Cambridge: Polity Press.

Johnston, E. (1944) *America Unlimited*, Garden City, NY: Doubleday.

Kagarlitsky, B. (2009) 'Default in Europe', *Transnational Institute*, 16 December, www.tni.org/article/default-europe, accessed 21 December 2009.

Kalb, D. (2005) 'From flows to violence: politics and knowledge in the debates on globalization and empire', *Anthropological Theory*, 5: 176–204.

Kautsky, K. (1970) 'Ultra-imperialism', *New Left Review*, 59: 41–46.

Keane, J. (2003) *Global Civil Society?*, New York: Cambridge University Press.

Keck, M. E. and K. Sikkink (1998) *Activists beyond Borders*, Ithaca, NY: Cornell University Press.

Kellogg, P. (2007) 'Regional integration in Latin America: dawn of an alternative to neo-liberalism?', *New Political Science*, 29: 187–210.

Kelly, D. (2005) 'The International Chamber of Commerce', *New Political Economy*, 10(2): 259–71.

Kennedy, M. C. (1998) 'The new global network of corporate power and the decline of national self-determination', *Contemporary Crises*, 12: 245–76.

Kennett, P. (2004) *Governance, Globalization and Public Policy*, Cheltenham: Edward Elgar.

Kentor, J. and Y. S. Jang (2004) 'Yes, there is a (growing) transnational business community: a study of global interlocking directorates 1983–98', *International Sociology*, 19(3): 355–68.

Keraghel, C., J. Sen and B. Klandermans (2004) 'Explorations in open space: the World Social Forum and the culture of politics. The social construction of protest and multiorganizational fields', *International Social Science Journal*, 56(4): 483–93.

Klepper, M. and R. Gunther (1996) *The Wealthy 100*, Secausus, NJ: Citadel Press.

Koenig, T. and R. Gogel (1981) 'Interlocking corporate directorships as a social network', *American Journal of Economics and Sociology*, 40(1): 37–50.

Kono, C. et al. (1998) 'Lost in space: the geography of corporate interlocking directorates', *American Journal of Sociology*, 103(4): 863–911.

Kotz, D. M. (1978) *Bank Control of Large Corporations in the United States*, Berkeley: University of California Press.

Kovel, J. (2006) *The Enemy of Nature*, 2nd edn, New York: Zed Books.

Krackhardt, D. and R. N. Stern (1988) 'Informal networks and organizational crises: an experimental simulation', *Social Psychology Quarterly*, 51: 123–40.

Krätke, S. (2003) 'Global media cities in a world-wide urban network', *European Planning Studies*, 11: 605–28.

Krippner, G. R. (2005) 'The financialization of the American economy', *Socio-Economic Review*, 3: 173–208.

Kroll, L. and M. Miller (2010) 'The world's billionaires', *Forbes*, 10 March 2010, www.forbes.com/2010/03/10/worlds-richest-people-slim-gates-buffett-billionaires-2010_land.html, accessed 19 March 2010.

La Porta, R., F. Lopez-de-Silanes and A. Shleifer (1999) 'Corporate ownership around the world', *Journal of Finance*, 54(2): 471–517.

Lacey, A. (2005) 'Spaces of justice: the social divine of global anti-capital activists' sites of resistance', *Canadian Review of Sociology and Anthropology*, 42: 403–20.

Lacher, H. (2005) 'International transformation and the persistence of territoriality: toward a new political geography of capitalism', *Review of International Political Economy*, 12(1): 26–52.

Langille, D. (1987) 'The Business Council on National Issues and the Canadian state', *Studies in Political Economy*, (24): 41–85.

Lapavitsas, C. (2009) 'Financialised capitalism: crisis and financial expropriation', *Historical Materialism*, 17: 114–48.

Lee, K. (2009) 'Towards a reformulation of core/periphery relationship: a critical reappraisal of the trimodality of the capitalist world-economy in the early 21st century', *Perspectives on Global Development and Technology*, 8: 263–94.

Leger, K. (1997) 'Power in Europe', *Financial Post*, 12–14 July, pp. 6–7.

Lenard, D. M. (2006) 'Arcelor Mittal: the dawn of a steel giant', *Asian Times*, 27 June, www.atimes.com/atimes/Asian_Economy/HF27Dk01.html, accessed 30 December 2009.

Leys, C. (2001) *Market-driven Politics*, London: Verso.

Lipschutz, R. D. (1996) *Reconstructing World Politics*, New York: St Martin's Press.

Livesey, S. M. (2002) 'Global warming wars: rhetorical and discourse analytic approaches to ExxonMobil's corporate public discourse', *Journal of Business Communication*, 39(1): 117–46.

Lundberg, F. (1937) *America's Sixty Families*, New York: Citadel Press.

Maclean, M., C. Harvey and J. Press (2006) *Business Elites and Corporate Governance in France and the UK*, Basingstoke: Palgrave Macmillan.

Mahon, R. (1977) 'Canadian public policy: the unequal structure of representation', in L. Panitch (ed.), *The Canadian State*, Toronto: University of Toronto Press.

Maman, D. (1997) 'The power lies in the structure: economic policy forum networks in Israel', *British Journal of Sociology*, 48.

Mandel, E. (1970) *Europe versus America?*, London: NLB.

Mann, M. (2002) 'Globalization is (among other things) transnational, international and American', *Science & Society*, 65(4): 464–8.

Marcuse, P. (2002) 'Depoliticizing globalization: from neo-Marxism to the network society of Manuel Castells', in J. Eade and C. Mele (eds), *Understanding the City*, Oxford: Blackwell, pp. 131–58.

Marx, K. (1967) *Capital*, vol. 1, New York: International Publishers.

Marx, K. and F. Engels (1968 [1848]) 'Manifesto of the Communist Party', in K. Marx and F. Engels (eds), *Selected Works*, New York: International Publishers, pp. 35–63.

Mazlish, B. and E. R. Morss (2005) 'A global elite?', in A. D. Chandler Jr and B. Mazlish (eds), *Leviathans: Multinational Corporations and the New Global History*, Cambridge: Cambridge University Press, pp. 167–86.

McBride, S. (2006) *Paradigm Shift*, Halifax: Fernwood Publishing.

McNally, D. (2009) 'From financial crisis to world-slump: accumulation, financialisation, and the global slowdown', *Historical Materialism*, 17: 35–83.

Menshikov, S. (1969) *Millionaires and Managers*, Moscow: Progress Publishers.

Mills, C. W. (1956) *The Power Elite*, New York: Oxford University Press.

Mintz, B. and M. Schwartz (1985) *The Power Structure of American Business*, Chicago, IL: University of Chicago Press.

Mizruchi, M. S. (1996) 'What do interlocks do? An analysis, critique, and assessment of research on interlocking directorates', *Annual Review of Sociology*, 22: 271–99.

Mokken, R. J. and F. N. Stokman (1978) 'Traces of power IV: the 1972 intercorporate network in the Netherlands', Joint Sessions of Workshops of the European Consortium for Political Research, Grenoble.

Montgomerie, J. (2008) 'Bridging the critical divide: global finance, financialisation and contemporary capitalism', *Contemporary Politics*, 14: 233–52.

Moore, J. W. (2002) 'Capital, territory, and hegemony over the longue durée', *Science & Society*, 65(4): 476–84.

Moreno, J. L. (1934) *Who Shall Survive?*, Beacon, NY: Beacon House.

Mügge, D. (2008) *Widen the Market, Narrow the Competition. The Emergence of Supranational Governance in EU Capital Markets*, Doctoral dissertation, Amsterdam School for Social Science Research, University of Amsterdam.

Munck, R. (2002) *Globalisation and Labour*, New York: Zed Books.

Neufeld, M. (2001) 'Theorizing globalisation: towards the politics of resistance – a neo-Gramscian response to Mathias Albert', *Global Society*, 15(1): 93–106.

Niosi, J. (1978) *The Economy of Canada*, Montreal: Black Rose Books.

Nollert, M. (2005) 'Transnational corporate ties: a synopsis of theories and empirical findings', *Journal of World Systems Research*, 11(2): 289–314.

Nooteboom, B. (1999) 'Voice-exit-based forms of corporate control: Anglo-American, European, and Japanese', *Journal of Economic Issues*, 33(4): 845–61.

Nowell, G. P. (2009) 'Hilferding's finance capital versus Wal-Mart world: disaggregating the dollar's hegemony', *Perspectives on Global Development and Technology*, 8: 315–46.

OECD (Organisation for Economic Co-operation and Development) (2004) *OECD Principles of Corporate Governance*, Paris: OECD.

Offe, K. and H. Wiesenthal (1980) 'Two logics of collective action: theoretical notes on social class and organizational form', *Political Power and Social Theory*, I: 67–115.

Olesen, T. (2004) 'The struggle inside democracy: modernity, social movements and global solidarity', *Distinktion*, 8: 19–35.

— (2005a) *International Zapatismo*, London: Barnes & Noble.

— (2005b) 'Transnational publics: new spaces of social movement activism and the problem of global long-sightedness', *Current Sociology*, 53: 419–40.

Ornstein, M. D. (1984) 'Interlocking directorates in Canada: intercorporate or class alliance?', *Administrative Science Quarterly*, 29: 210–31.

Overbeek, H. (1980) 'Finance capital and crisis in Britain', *Capital & Crisis*, 11: 99–120.

— (2000) 'Transnational historical materialism: theories of transnational class formation and world order', in R. Palan (ed.), *Global Political Economy: Contemporary Theories*, London: Routledge, pp. 168–83.

Overbeek, H. and K. van der Pijl (1993) 'Restructuring capital and restructuring hegemony: neo-liberalism and the unmaking of the post-war order', in H. Overbeek and K. van der Pijl (eds), *Restructuring Hegemony in the Global Political Economy*, London: Routledge, pp. 1–27.

Oxelheim, L. and P. Ghauri (2004) 'The race for FDI in the European Union', in L. Oxelheim and P. Ghauri (eds), *European Union and the Race for Foreign Direct Investment in Europe*, Amsterdam: Elsevier, pp. 3–34.

Palloix, C. (1975) *L'Internationalisation du capital. Eléments critiques*, Paris: Maspero.

Paretsky, N. (2004) *Policy-planning Organizations and Capitalist Support for Industrial Policy, 1970–1984*, Unpublished PhD dissertation, University of Missouri, Columbia.

Patel, R. and P. McMichael (2004) 'Third Worldism and the lineages of global fascism: the regrouping of the global South in the neoliberal era', *Third World Quarterly*, 25(1): 231–54.

Peet, R. (2007) *Geography of Power: Making Global Economic Policy*, London: Zed Books.

Perlo, V. (1958) 'People's capitalism and stock ownership', *American Economic Review*, 48: 333–47.

Peschek, J. G. (1987) *Policy-planning Organizations: Elite Agenda and America's Rightward Turn*, Philadelphia, PA: Temple University Press.

Pierri, R. (2009) 'Climate change: Chávez, Morales lash out at wealthy North', Inter Press Service, 16 December, ipsnews.net/news.asp?idnews=49716, accessed 21 December 2009.

Pieterse, J. N. (2004) *Globalization or Empire?*, London: Routledge.

Pigman, G. A. (2007) *The World Economic Forum: A Multi-stakeholder Approach to Global Governance*, London: Routledge.

Plehwe, D. and B. Walpen (2006) 'Between network and complex organization: the making of neoliberal knowledge and hegemony', in D. Plehwe, B. Walpen and G. Neunhoffer (eds), *Neoliberal Hegemony: A Global Critique*, London: Routledge, pp. 27–50.

Polanyi, K. (1944) *The Great Transformation*, Boston, MA: Beacon Press.

Potts, J. (2006) 'How creative are the super-rich?', *Agenda*, 13: 339–50.

Pred, A. (1977) *City Systems in Advanced Economies*, London: Hutchinson.

Ratcliff, R. E. (1980) 'Banks and corporate lending: an analysis of the impact of the internal structure of the capitalist class on the lending behaviour of banks', *American Sociological Review*, 45: 553–70.

Reyes, O. (2009) 'Taking care of business', *New Internationalist*, 428, December, pp. 16–18.

Rhodes, M. and B. van Apeldoorn (1998) 'Capital unbound? The transformation of European corporate governance', *Journal of European Public Policy*, 5(3): 406–27.

Richardson, R. J. (1982) '"Merchants against industry": an empirical study of the Canadian debate', *Canadian Journal of Sociology*, 7(3): 279–95.

Robinson, W. I. (2003) 'The debate on globalization: the transnational capitalist class and the transnational state', in W. Dunaway (ed.), *New Theoretical Directions for the 21st Century World-System*, Greenwood Press.

— (2004) *A Theory of Gobal Capitalism.* Baltimore, MD: Johns Hopkins University Press.

— (2005) 'Global capitalism: the new transnationalism and the folly of conventional thinking', *Science & Society*, 69(3): 316–28.

— (2007) 'Beyond the theory of imperialism: global capitalism and the capitalist class', *Societies without Borders*, 2: 5–26.

Robinson, W. I. and J. Harris (2000) 'Towards a global ruling class? Globalization and the transnational capitalist class', *Science & Society*, 64(1): 11–54.

Ronit, K. (2001) 'Institutions of private authority in global governance: linking territorial forms of self-regulation', *Administration and Society*, 33(5): 555–78.

Rothkopf, D. (2008) *Superclass: The Global Power Elite and the World They are Making*, New York: Farrar, Straus and Giroux.

Rowe, J. K. (2005) *Corporate Social Responsibility as Business Strategy*, London: Routledge.

Rugman, A. M. and A. Verbeke (2007) 'Liabilities of regional foreignness and the use of firm-level versus country-level data: a response to Dunning *et al*', *Journal of International Business Studies*, 38: 200–205.

Ruigrok, W. and R. van Tulder (1995) *The Logic of International Restructuring*, New York: Routledge.

Rupert, M. (2002) *Ideologies of Globalization*, London: Routledge.

— (2005) 'Reflections on some lessons from a decade of globalisation studies', *New Political Economy*, 10: 457–78.

Saint-Simon, H. and A. Thierry (1975 [1814]) *The Reorganization of European Society*, New York: Holmes and Meier Publishers.

Samuel, H. (2008) 'Nicolas Sarkozy calls for overhaul of capitalism', *Daily Telegraph*, 24 October, www.telegraph.co.uk/news/worldnews/europe/france/3082611/Nicolas-Sarkozy-calls-for-overhaul-of-capitalism.html, accessed 30 December 2009.

Santos, B. de S. (2006) *The Rise of the Global Left: The World Social Forum and Beyond*, London: Zed Books.

Sassen, S. (2001) *The Global City: New York, London, Tokyo*, 2nd edn, Princeton, NJ: Princeton University Press.

— (2002) *Global Networks, Linked Cities*, New York: Routledge.

— (2007) 'Introduction: deciphering the global', in S. Sassen (ed.), *Deciphering the Global: Its Scales, Spaces and Subjects*, New York: Routledge.

Scanian, O. (2010) 'Europe faces stark choice between dissolution and cohesion after Greek crisis', *Open Democracy*, 21 May, http://www.opendemocracy.net/oliver-scanlan/europe-faces-stark-choice-between-dissolution-and-cohesion-after-greek-crisis, accessed 29 May 2010.

Scott, J. (1991) 'Networks of corporate power: a comparative assessment', *Annual Review of Sociology*, 17: 181–203.

— (1997) *Corporate Business and Capitalist Class*, New York: Oxford University Press.

— (2003) 'Transformations in the British economic elite', *Comparative Sociology*, 2(1): 155–73.

— (2008) 'Modes of power and the reconceptualization of elites', in M. Savage and K. Williams (eds), *Remembering Elites*, Oxford: Blackwell, pp. 27–43.

Scott, J. and P. J. Carrington (eds) (2011) *Handbook of Social Network Analysis*, London: Sage.

Sen, J. (2004) 'Forum as logo, the Forum as religion: scepticism of the intellect, optimism of the will', in J. Sen, A. Anand, A. Escobar and P. Waterman (eds), *World Social Forum: Challenging Empires*, New Delhi: Viveka Foundation, pp. 210–27.

Shaw, M. (2000) *Theory of the Global State*,

Cambridge: Cambridge University Press.

Sims, G. T. (2007) 'Siemens chief latest to be ousted amid scandals', *International Herald Tribune*, 21 October, www.iht.com/articles/2007/04/25/business/siemens.php, accessed 30 December 2009.

Sklair, L. (2001) *The Transnational Capitalist Class*, Oxford: Blackwell.

Sklair, L. and P. T. Robbins (2002) 'Global capitalism and major corporations from the Third World', *Third World Quarterly*, 23(1): 81–100.

Smith, D. A. and M. Timberlake (1995) 'World cities: a political economy/global network approach', *Research in Urban Sociology*, 3: 181–207.

— (2002) 'Hierarchies of dominance among world cities: a network approach', in S. Sassen (ed.), *Global Networks, Linked Cities*, New York: Routledge, pp. 117–41.

Smith, J. (2001) 'Globalizing resistance: the Battle of Seattle and the future of social movements', *Mobilization*, 6: 1–19.

— (2002) 'Bridging global divides? Strategic framing and solidarity in transnational social movement organizations', *International Sociology*, 17: 505–28.

Smith, J. and D. Wiest (2005) 'The uneven geography of global civil society: national and global influences on transnational association', *Social Forces*, 84: 621–52.

Soederberg, S. (2006) *Global Governance in Question*, Winnipeg: Arbeiter Ring Publishing.

— (2007) 'Taming corporations or buttressing market-led development? A critical assessment of the Global Compact', *Globalizations*, 4(4): 500–513.

— (2010) *Corporate Power and Ownership in Contemporary Capitalism*, London: Routledge.

Sonquist, J. A. and T. Koenig (1975) 'Interlocking directorates in the top U.S. corporations: a graph theory approach', *Insurgent Sociologist*, 5(3): 196–229.

Soref, M. (1980) 'The finance capitalists', in M. Zeitlin (ed.), *Classes, Class Conflicts and the State*, Cambridge, MA: Winthrop Publishers.

Soref, M. and M. Zeitlin (1987) 'Finance capital and the internal structure of the capitalist class in the United States', in M. S. Mizruchi and M. Schwartz (eds), *Intercorporate Relations*, Cambridge: Cambridge University Press.

Sprague, J. (2009) 'Transnational capitalist class in the global financial crisis: a discussion with Leslie Sklair', *Globalizations*, 6(4): 499–507.

Sprenger, C. J. A. and F. N. Stokman (1989) *GRADAP: Graph Definition and Analysis Program*, Groningen: iec ProGAMMA.

Stanford, J. (1999) *Paper Boom*, Toronto: Lorimer.

Staples, C. L. (2006) 'Board interlocks and the study of the transnational capitalist class', *Journal of World-Systems Research*, 12(2): 309–19.

— (2007) 'Board globalisation in the world's largest TNCs 1993–2005', *Corporate Governance*, 15: 311–21.

Stein, B. (2006) 'In class warfare, guess which class is winning', *New York Times*, 26 November, www.nytimes.com/2006/11/26/business/yourmoney/26every.html, accessed 16 December 2009.

Steven, R. (1994) 'New world order: a new imperialism', *Journal of Contemporary Asia*, 24: 271–96.

Stiglitz, J. (1998) 'More instruments and broader goals: moving toward the post-Washington consensus', 1998 WIDER Annual Lecture, 7 January.

Stokes, D. (2005) 'The heart of empire? Theorising US empire in an era of transnational capitalism', *Third World Quarterly*, 26(2): 217–36.

Stokman, F. N. and F. W. Wasseur (1985) 'National networks in 1976: a structural comparison', in F. N. Stokman, R. Ziegler and J. Scott (eds), *Networks of Corporate Power*, Cambridge: Polity Press.

Stokman, F. N., R. Ziegler and J. Scott (1985) *Networks of Corporate Power*, Cambridge: Polity Press.

Stone, D. (2001) 'Think tanks, global lesson-drawing and networking social policy ideas', *Global Social Policy*, 1(3): 338–60.

Sweezy, P. M. (1953) 'The illusion of the managerial revolution', in P. M. Sweezy (ed.), *The Present as History*, New York: Monthly Review Press, pp. 39–66.

Swift, J. (1999) *Civil Society in Question*, Toronto: Between the Lines.

Tabb, W. K. (2009) 'Globalization today: at the borders of class and state theory', *Science & Society*, 73(1): 34–53.

Taylor, P. J. (2004) *World City Networks*, London: Routledge.

Taylor, P. J., G. Catalano and D. R. F. Walker (2002) 'Exploratory analysis of the world city network', *Urban Studies*, 39: 2377–94.

Taylor, S. (2008) 'Sarkozy calls for "new form of capitalism"', EuropeanVoice. com, 24 October, www.europeanvoice. com/article/2008/10/sarkozy-calls-for-new-form-of-capitalism-/62677.aspx, accessed 24 October 2008.

Teeple, G. (2000) *Globalization and the Decline of Social Reform*, 2nd edn, Aurora, Ontario: Garamond Press.

Teivainen, T. (2004) 'The World Social Forum: arena or actor?', in J. Sen, A. Anand, A. Escobar and P. Waterman (eds), *World Social Forum: Challenging Empires*, New Delhi: Viveka Foundation, pp. 122–9.

Therborn, G. (2000) 'Globalization', *International Sociology*, 15(2): 151–79.

Thompson, E. P. (1991 [1963]) *The Making of the English Working Class*, London: Penguin.

Thompson, G. (1977) 'The relationship between the financial and industrial sector in the United Kingdom economy', *Economy and Society*, 6: 235–83.

Tilly, C. (1978) *From Mobilization to Revolution*, Reading, MA: Addison-Wesley.

Tomasic, R. (1991) *The Fiduciary Duties of Directors in Listed Public Companies*, Canberra: Centre for National Corporate Law Research.

Torgler, B. and M. Piatti (2009) 'Extraordinary wealth, globalization, and corruption', Working paper, Centre for Research in Economics, Management and the Arts, Basle.

Transnational Institute (1974) *World Hunger, Causes and Remedies*, Amsterdam: Transnational Institute.

UNCTAD (United Nations Conference on Trade and Development) (2008) *World Investment Report*, New York: United Nations.

United Nations Global Compact (2008) *Participants and Stakeholders*, New York: United Nations, www. unglobalcompact.org/ParticipantsAnd-Stakeholders/index.html, accessed 23 September 2008.

Urry, J. (1981) *Anatomy of Capitalist Societies*, London: Macmillan.

Useem, M. (1984) *The Inner Circle: Large Corporations and the Rise of Business Political Activity in the U.S. and U.K.*, New York: Oxford University Press.

— (1996) *Investor Capitalism*, New York: Basic Books.

Van Apeldoorn, B. (1999) *Transnational Capitalism and the Struggle over European Order*, Florence: Department of Political Science, European University Institute.

— (2000) 'Transnational class agency and European governance: the case of the European Round Table of Industrialists', *New Political Economy*, 5(2): 167–81.

— (2002) *Transnational Capitalism and the Struggle over European Order*, London: Routledge.

Van der Pijl, K. (1984) *The Making of an Atlantic Ruling Class*, London: Verso.

— (1998) *Transnational Classes and International Relations*, London: Routledge.

— (2005) 'A theory of global capitalism, feature review', *New Political Economy*, 10(2): 273–7.

— (2006) *Global Rivalries: From the Cold War to Iraq*, London: Pluto Press.

Van Veen, K. (2010) 'National and international interlocking directorates within Europe: corporate networks within and among fifteen European countries', *Economy and Society*, forthcoming.

Vitols, S. (2005) 'Changes in Germany's bank-based financial system: implications for corporate governance', *Corporate Governance: An International Review*, 13(3): 386–96.

Von Hayek, F. A. (1949) *The Intellectuals and Socialism*, vol. X, Chicago, IL: University of Chicago Press.

— (1976) *The Mirage of Social Justice*, Chicago, IL: University of Chicago Press.

Wainwright, H. (2005) *Report on the Methodology of the WSF and Its Possible Relevance on the 2006 ESF*, Transnational Institute, www.tni.org/socforum/index.htm, accessed 30 December 2009.

Walker, R. B. J. (1993) *Inside/Outside: International Relations as Political Theory*, Cambridge/New York: Cambridge University Press.

Wallerstein, I. (1974) *The Modern World System: Capitalist Agriculture and the Origins of the European World-Economy in the Sixteenth Century*, New York/London: Academic Press.

— (1980) *The Modern World System II: Mercantilism and the Consolidation of the European World-Economy, 1600–1750*, New York/London: Academic Press.

Watanabe, T., J. Lesourne and R. S. McNamara (1983) 'Facilitating development in a changing Third World: trade, finance, aid', Task Force Report 27, Trilateral Commission, New York.

Waterman, P. (2001) 'Trade union internationalism in the age of Seattle', *Antipode*, 33(3): 312–36.

— (2004) 'The global justice and solidarity movement and the World Social Forum: a backgrounder', in J. Sen, A. Anand, A. Escobar and P. Waterman (eds), *World Social Forum: Challenging Empires*, New Delhi: Viveka Foundation, pp. 55–66.

— (2005) 'Labour and new social movements in a globalizing world system: the future of the past', *Labour History*, 46(2): 195–207.

Watkins, G. P. (1907) *The Growth of Large Fortunes*, New York: A. M. Kelly.

WBCSD (World Business Council for Sustainable Development) (1997) *World Business Council for Sustainable Development Annual Review*, Geneva.

— (2005) Eco-Efficiency Learning Module, www.wbcsd.org/DocRoot/UROf8cWqw37ZpR3wrDm6/ee_module.pdf, accessed 30 December 2009.

Weller, C. E. and L. Singleton (2006) 'Peddling reform: the role of think tanks in shaping the neoliberal policy agenda for the World Bank and International Monetary Fund', in D. Plehwe, B. Walpen and G. Neunhoffer (eds), *Neoliberal Hegemony: A Global Critique*, London: Routledge, pp. 70–86.

Wellman, B. (1988) 'Structural analysis: from method and metaphor to theory and substance', in B. Wellman and S. D. Berkowitz (eds), *Social Structures: A Network Approach*, Cambridge: Cambridge University Press.

Went, R. (2002) 'Globalization: towards a transnational state? A skeptical note', *Science & Society*, 65(4): 484–91.

Westney, D. E. (1996) 'The Japanese business system: key features and prospects for change', *Journal of Asian Business*, 12(1): 21–50.

Whitaker, C. (2004) 'The WSF as open space', in J. Sen, A. Anand, A. Escobar and P. Waterman (eds), *World Social Forum: Challenging Empires*, New Delhi: Viveka Foundation, pp. 111–21.

Whitley, R. (1999) *Divergent Capitalisms*, New York: Oxford University Press.

Wilford, H. (2003) 'CIA plot, socialist conspiracy, or new world order? The origins of the Bilderberg Group, 1952–5', *Diplomacy and Statecraft*, 14(3): 70–82.

Williamson, J. (1990) *What Washington Means by Policy Reform*, Washington, DC: Institute for International Economics.

Windolf, P. (2001) 'Markets and networks: corporate networks in six countries', Presented at 'Corporate governance in a globalizing world', NIAS, Wassenaar, 23–25 April.

— (2002) *Corporate Networks in Europe and the United States*, New York: Oxford University Press.

Wolfe, A. (1980) 'Capitalism shows its face: giving up on democracy', in H. Sklar (ed.), *The Trilateral Commission and Elite Planning for World Management*, Boston, MA: South End Press.

World Economic Forum (1995) *World Economic Forum Annual Report*, Conches-Geneva: World Economic Forum.

Young, M. N., A. K. Buchholtz and D. Ahlstrom (2003) 'How can board members be empowered if they are spread too thin?', *SAM Advanced Management Journal*, 68(4): 4–11.

Zeitlin, J. and P. Pochet (2005) *The Open Method of Co-ordination in Action: The European Employment and Social Inclusion Strategies*, Brussels: Peter Lang.

Zeitlin, M. and R. E. Ratcliff (1988) *Landlords & Capitalists*, Princeton, NJ: Princeton University Press.

Zeitlin, M., L. A. Ewan and R. E. Ratcliff (1974) '"New princes" for old? The large corporation and the capitalist class in Chile', *American Journal of Sociology*, 80(1): 87–123.

Zeretsky, E. (1976) *Capitalism, the Family and Personal Life*, New York: Harper & Row.

Index

networks, 146; in global corporate elite, 135; mobility of, 140
Sustainable Societies Programme, 215
Sutherland, Peter, 189
Switzerland, 174

Tabb, William, 5, 231
Tada, Hiroshi, 128
Taiwan, 88
Taylor, Peter, 58–60
telecommunication industry, 25
tertiary sector, growth of, 83
Texaco, 32
Thatcher, Margaret, 38, 209, 212
Therborn, G., 19
Thierry, Augustin, 155
Third Way, 39
Thornton, John, 128, 149
Tokyo, 58, 62, 71, 73, 75, 80, 89, 193
Toyoda, Shoichiro, 143
Toyoda family, 143
TransAtlantic Business Dialogue (TABD), 183, 187, 193, 196
transnational accumulation, and global networking, 83–108
transnational capital circuits, density of, 109
transnational capitalist class (TCC), 1, 18, 45, 109–31, 173, 227, 230, 234, 235; centred on North Atlantic area, 34; debate about, 2; formation of, 3, 5, 36, 37, 38, 42, 55, 98, 110, 113, 115, 132, 201, 232, 235 (complexity of, 231; qualified version of thesis, 228); four fractions of, 2; regionalization of, 233; unity and difference within, 229–33; use of term, 19–20
transnational corporate community, 17–35, 54
transnational corporate-policy network, 36–56; consolidation of, 179–202
transnational corporations (TNC), 1, 80, 130, 204
Transnational Institute (TI), 212
transnational policy boards *see* policy groups
transnational segment of global corporate elite, 110, 111–16, 185
transnationalists, 129; as articulation points, 114
transnationality, tabulation of, 91

Triad (Japan/Australia, Western Europe, USA/Canada), 84, 85, 92, 105, 112, 115, 139, 181, 197, 216
triadization, 229
Trilateral Commission (TC), 36, 38, 42–3, 45, 48, 54, 56, 142, 143, 145, 151, 157, 180, 181, 182, 187, 189, 193, 196, 197, 200, 201, 212, 227; *The Crisis of Democracy*, 43, 205
Trujillo, Solomon D., 128
Turkey, 139, 140

UCINET software package, 12
ultra-imperialism, 232
uneven development, in Europe, geography of, 178
Unilever, 18, 67, 193
United Kingdom (UK), 28, 49, 63, 96, 106, 107, 113, 123, 161, 162, 174, 193; finance sector in, 87; transnational interlocking in, 97
United Nations (UN), 182, 209, 218
UN Conference on Environment and Development (UNCED), 44
UN Conference on Trade and Development (UNCTAD), 44, 91; trans-nationality index (TNI), 98–9, 101, 220
UN Economic and Social Council (UNESCO), 205
UN Environmental Programme (UNEP), 44
UN Global Compact (UNGC), 180, 182, 189, 193, 210, 211, 235
United States of America (USA), 21, 24, 33, 65, 71, 77, 87, 89, 92, 95, 104, 113, 117, 123, 127, 155, 159, 160, 173, 193, 201, 202, 231, 232; billionaires in, 138, 140; debt relations with world, 3; hegemony of, decline in, 83, 89, 130, 224, 230; interlocking less common in, 77–8; networking in, decline of, 202; Open Door policy, 207, 210; shareholders in, 135; super-rich in, 133

Vallance, Lord, 147
valorization, cycles of, 101–2
van der Pijl, Kees, 4, 5, 36, 233; *The Making of an Atlantic Ruling Class*, 10 *see also* Atlantic ruling class
voice-based corporate governance, 23; decline of, 32
Volkswagen, 32